P9-DHE-886

*Margaret Atwood*

*Ad Feminam: Women and Literature*
*Edited by Sandra M. Gilbert*

*Christina Rossetti*
*The Poetry of Endurance*
*By Dolores Rosenblum*

*Lunacy of Light*
*Emily Dickinson and the Experience of Metaphor*
*By Wendy Barker*

*The Literary Existence of Germaine de Staël*
*By Charlotte Hogsett*

# *Margaret Atwood*
## *Vision and Forms*

*Edited by Kathryn VanSpanckeren and Jan Garden Castro*

*With an Autobiographical Foreword by Margaret Atwood*

*Southern Illinois University Press*
*Carbondale and Edwardsville*

*Printed in the United States of America*

*Edited by Curtis L. Clark*
*Designed by Joyce Kachergis*
*Production supervised by Linda Jorgensen-Buhman*

90 89 88 4 3 2

Publication of this volume has been made possible in part by funds provided by the Canadian Embassy, Washington, D.C.

Margaret Atwood's foreword originally appeared under the title "Great Unexpectations," in *Ms.,* July-August 1987. Copyright Margaret Atwood.

A longer version of Lorna Irvine's "The Here and Now of *Bodily Harm*" originally appeared under the title "Atwood's Parable of Flesh" in the author's *Sub/Version* (Toronto: ECW Press, 1986). Reprinted by permission of ECW Press.

Jan Garden Castro's interview with Margaret Atwood is used by permission of American Audio Prose Library. Copyright 1983 American Audio Prose Library. All rights reserved.

**Library of Congress Cataloging-in-Publication Data**

Margaret Atwood : vision and forms.

(Ad feminam)
Bibliography: p.
Includes index.
1. Atwood, Margaret Eleanor, 1939– —Criticism and interpretation. I. VanSpanckeren, Kathryn. II. Castro, Jan Garden. III. Series.
PR9199.3.A8Z76 1988 818'.5409 88–6452
ISBN 0–8093–1408–8

The paper used in this publication meets the minimum requirements of American National Standard for Information Sciences—Permanence of Paper for Printed Library Materials, ANSI Z39.48-1984. ∞™

*To Paul B. Breslow and Jomo J. Castro*

# *Contents*


Ad Feminam: Women and Literature *xi*
*Sandra M. Gilbert*

Great Unexpectations *xiii*
*An Autobiographical Foreword*
*Margaret Atwood*

Acknowledgments *xvii*

Introduction *xix*
*Kathryn VanSpanckeren*

A Margaret Atwood Chronology *xxix*

1 *Canlit/Victimlit* 1
Survival *and* Second Words
*June Schlueter*

2 *The Two Faces of the Mirror* 12
*in* The Edible Woman *and* Lady Oracle
*Pamela S. Bromberg*

3 *Pilgrimage Inward* 24
*Quest and Fairy Tale Motifs in* Surfacing
*Elizabeth R. Baer*

4 *In Search of Demeter* 35
*The Lost, Silent Mother in* Surfacing
*Sherrill E. Grace*

5 *The Transforming Eye* 48
Lady Oracle *and Gothic Tradition*
*Ann McMillan*

6 Life Before Man — 65
*"Can Anything Be Saved?"*
*Gayle Greene*

7 *The Here and Now of* Bodily Harm — 85
*Lorna Irvine*

8 *Nature and Nurture in Dystopia* — 101
The Handmaid's Tale
*Roberta Rubenstein*

9 *Future Tense* — 113
*Making History in* The Handmaid's Tale
*Arnold E. Davidson*

10 *Weaving Her Version* — 122
*The Homeric Model and Gender Politics in* Selected Poems
*David Buchbinder*

11 *Politics, Structure, and Poetic Development in Atwood's Canadian-American Sequences* — 142
*From an Apprentice Pair to "The Circle Game" to "Two-Headed Poems"*
*Judith McCombs*

12 *Real and Imaginary Animals in the Poetry of Margaret Atwood* — 163
*Kathleen Vogt*

13 *Shamanism in the Works of Margaret Atwood* — 183
*Kathryn VanSpanckeren*

14 *Sexual Politics in Margaret Atwood's Visual Art* — 205
*(With an Eight-Page Color Supplement)*
*Sharon R. Wilson*

15 *An Interview with Margaret Atwood* — 215
20 *April* 1983
*Jan Garden Castro*

16 *A Conversation* — 233
*Margaret Atwood and Students*
*Moderated by Francis X. Gillen*

Works Cited 247

Notes on Contributors 257

Index 261

# *Ad Feminam: Women and Literature*

Ad Hominem: to the man; appealing to personal interests, prejudices, or emotions rather than to reason; ***an argument ad hominem.***
—*American Heritage Dictionary*

Until quite recently, much literary criticism, like most humanistic studies, has been in some sense constituted out of arguments *ad hominem.* Not only have examinations of literary history tended to address themselves "to the man"—that is, to the identity of what was presumed to be the *man* of letters who created our culture's monuments of unaging intellect—but many aesthetic analyses and evaluations have consciously or unconsciously appealed to the "personal interests, prejudices, or emotions" of male critics and readers. As the title of this series is meant to indicate, the intellectual project called "feminist criticism" has sought to counter the limitations of *ad hominem* thinking about literature by asking a series of questions addressed *ad feminam*: "to the woman"—to the woman as both writer and reader of texts.

First, and most crucially, feminist critics ask What is the relationship between gender and genre, between sexuality and textuality? But in meditating on these issues they raise a number of more specific questions. Does a woman of letters have a literature —a language, a history, a tradition—of her own? Have conventional methods of canon-formation tended to exclude or marginalize female achievements? More generally, do men and women have different modes of literary representation, different definitions of literary production? Do such differences mean that distinctive male- (or female-) authored images of women (or men), as well as distinctly male and female genres, are part of our intellectual heritage? Perhaps most important, are literary differences between men and women essential or accidental, biologically determined or culturally constructed?

Feminist critics have addressed themselves to these problems with increasing sophistication during the last two decades, as they sought to revise, or at times replace, *ad hominem* arguments with *ad feminam* speculations. Whether explicating individual texts, studying the *oeuvre* of a single author, examining the permutations of a major theme, or charting the contours of a tradition, these theorists and scholars have consistently sought to define literary manifestations of difference and to understand the dynamics that have shaped the accomplishment of literary women.

As a consequence of such work, feminist critics, often employing new modes of analysis, have begun to uncover a neglected female tradition along with a heretofore hidden history of the literary dialogue between men and women. This series is dedicated to publishing books that will use innovative as well as traditional interpretive methods in order to help readers of both sexes achieve a better understanding of that hidden history, a clearer consciousness of that neglected but powerful tradition. Reason tells us, after all, that if, transcending prejudice and special pleading, we speak to, and focus on, the woman as well as the man—if we think *ad feminam* as well as *ad hominem*—we will have a better chance of understanding what constitutes the human.

Sandra M. Gilbert

# *Great Unexpectations*
## *An Autobiographical Foreword*
*Margaret Atwood*

In 1960 I was nineteen years old. I was in third-year college in Toronto, Ontario, which was not then known as People City or The Paris of the Northeast; but as Hogtown, which was not an inaccurate description. I had never eaten an avocado or been on an airplane or encountered a croissant or been south of Vermont. Panty hose had not yet hit the market; neither had the Pill. We were still doing garter belts and repression. Abortion was not a word you said out loud, and lesbians might as well have been mythological hybrids, like Sphinxes; in any case I was quite certain I had never met one. I wanted to be—no, worse—was determined to be, was convinced I was—a writer. I was scared to death.

I was scared to death for a couple of reasons. For one thing, I was Canadian, and the prospects for being a Canadian and a writer, both at the same time, in 1960, were dim. The only writers I had encountered in high school had been dead and English, and in university we barely studied American writers, much less Canadian ones. Canadian writers, it was assumed—by my professors, my contemporaries, and myself—were a freak of nature, like duck-billed platypuses. Logically they ought not to exist, and when they did so anyway, they were just pathetic imitations of the real thing. This estimate was borne out by statistics: for those few who managed, despite the reluctance of publishers, to struggle into print (five novels in English in 1960), two hundred copies of a book of poetry was considered average to good, and a thousand made a novel a Canadian best seller. I would have to emigrate, I concluded gloomily. I faced a future of scrubbing restaurant floors in England—where we colonials could go, then, much more easily than we could to the United States—writing masterpieces in a freezing cold garret at night, and getting T.B., like Keats. Such was my operatic view of my own future.

But it was more complicated than that, because, in addition to being a Canadian, I was also a woman. In some ways this was an advantage. Being a male writer in Canada branded you a sissy, but writing was not quite so unthinkable for a woman, ranking as it did with flower painting and making roses out of wool. As one friend of my mother's put it, trying to take a cheerful view of my eccentricity, "Well, that's nice dear, because you can do it at home, can't you?" She was right, as it turned out, but at that moment she aroused nothing but loathing in my adolescent soul. Home, hell. It was garret or nothing. What did she think I was, inauthentic? However, most people were so appalled by my determination to be a writer that no one even thought of saying I couldn't because I was a girl. That sort of thing was not said to me until later, by male writers, by which time it was too late.

Strangely, no one was pushing early marriage, not in my case. Canada, being a cultural backwater, had not been swept by the wave of Freudianism that had washed over the United States in the fifties—Canadian women were not yet expected to be fecund and passive in order to fulfill themselves—and there were still some bluestockings around in the educational system, women who warned us not to get silly about boys too soon and throw away our chances. What my elders had in mind for me was more along academic lines. Something, that is to say, with a salary.

But, since gender is prior to nationality, the advantages of being a Canadian woman writer were canceled out by the disadvantages of being a woman writer. I'd read the biographies, which were not encouraging. Jane Austen never married Mr. Darcy. Emily Brontë died young, Charlotte in childbirth. George Eliot never had children and was ostracized for living with a married man. Emily Dickinson flitted; Christina Rossetti looked at life through the wormholes in a shroud. Some had managed to combine writing with what I considered to be a normal life—Mrs. Gaskell, Harriet Beecher Stowe—but everyone knew they were second rate. My choices were between excellence and doom on the one hand, and mediocrity and cosiness on the other. I gritted my teeth, set my face to the wind, gave up double dating, and wore horn-rims and a scowl so I would not be mistaken for a puffball.

It was in this frame of mind that I read Robert Graves's *The White Goddess,* which further terrified me. Graves did not dismiss women. In fact he placed them right at the center of his poetic theory; but they were to be inspirations rather than creators, and a funny sort of inspiration at that. They were to be incarnations of the White Goddess herself, alternately loving and destructive, and men who got involved with them ran the risk of disembowelment or worse. A woman just might—might, mind you—have a chance of becoming a decent poet, but only if she too took on the attributes of the White Goddess and spent her time seducing men and then doing them in. All this sounded a little strenuous, and appeared to rule out domestic bliss. It wasn't my idea of how men and women should get on together—raking up leaves in the backyard, like my mom and dad—but who was I to contradict the experts? There was no one else in view giving me any advice on how to be a writer, though female. Graves was it.

That would be my life, then. To the garret and the T.B. I added the elements of enigma and solitude. I would dress in black. I would learn to smoke cigarettes, although they gave me headaches and made me cough, and drink something romantic and unusually bad for you, such as absinthe. I would live by myself, in a suitably painted attic (black) and have lovers whom I would discard in appropriate ways, though I drew the line at bloodshed. (I was, after all, a nice Canadian girl.) I would never have children. This last bothered me a lot, as before this I had always intended to have some, and it seemed unfair, but White Goddesses did not have time for children, being too taken up with cannibalistic sex, and Art came first. I would never, never own an automatic washer-dryer. Sartre, Samuel Beckett, Kafka, and Ionesco, I was sure, did not have major appliances, and these were the writers I most admired. I had no concrete ideas about how the laundry would get done, but it would only be my own laundry, I thought mournfully—no fuzzy sleepers, no tiny T-shirts—and such details could be worked out later.

I tried out the garrets, which were less glamorous than expected; so was England, and so were the cigarettes, which lasted a mere six months. There wasn't any absinthe to be had, so I tried bad wine, which made me sick. It began to occur to me that maybe

Robert Graves didn't have the last word on women writers, and anyway I wanted to be a novelist as well as a poet, so perhaps that would let me off the homicide. Even though Sylvia Plath and Anne Sexton had been setting new, high standards in self-destructiveness for female poets, and people had begun asking me not whether but when I was going to commit suicide (the only authentic woman poet is a dead woman poet?), I was wondering whether it was really all that necessary for a woman writer to be doomed, any more than it was necessary for a male writer to be a drunk. Wasn't all of this just some sort of postromantic collective delusion? If Shakespeare could have kids and avoid suicide, then so could I, dammit. When Betty Friedan and Simone de Beauvoir came my way, like shorebirds heralding land, I read them with much interest. They got a lot right, for me, but there was one thing they got wrong. They were assuring me that I didn't have to get married and have children. But what I wanted was someone to tell me I could.

And so I did. The marriage and the children came in two lots—marriage with one, child with another—but they did come. This is the part that will sound smug, I suppose, but I also suppose it's not that much smugger than my black-sweatered, garter-belted, black-stockinged, existential pronouncements at the age of nineteen. I now live a life that is pretty close to the leaves-in-the-backyard model I thought would have been out of bounds forever. Instead of rotting my brains with absinthe, I bake (dare I admit it?) chocolate chip cookies, and I find that doing the laundry with the aid of my washer-dryer is one of the more relaxing parts of my week. I worry about things like remembering Parents' Day at my daughter's school and running out of cat food, though I can only afford these emotional luxuries with the aid of some business assistants and a large man who likes kids and cats and food, and has an ego so solid it isn't threatened by mine. This state of affairs was not achieved without struggle, some of it internal—did an addiction to knitting brand me as an inauthentic writer?—but it was reached. The White Goddess still turns up in my life, but mainly as a fantasy projection on the part of certain male book reviewers, who seem to like the idea of my teeth sinking into some cringing male neck. I think of this as fifties nostalgia.

As for writing, yes. You *can* do it at home.

# *Acknowledgments*

Appreciation is expressed to the Canadian government for providing, through its embassy in Washington, D.C., the Faculty Research Award that made the completion of this volume possible. We also thank Margaret Atwood for graciously granting permission to quote from her published and archival material and to reproduce her watercolors. For use of Atwood's archival material, including her watercolors, we acknowledge the permission of the Thomas Fisher Rare Book Library at the University of Toronto. The art photographs are by Thomas Moore Photography, Inc., Toronto. Appreciation, finally, is expressed to the American Audio Prose Library (P.O. Box 842, Columbia, Missouri, 65205) where audio tapes of Jan Garden Castro's interview with Margaret Atwood are available.

Special thanks are due to Marlyn Pethe and Mickey Wells, reference librarians at the Merl Kelce Library at the University of Tampa; to Dorothy Iorio, formerly of that library; to Ruth Cash, Secretary of the Humanities Division; and to Curtis L. Clark, Editor, Southern Illinois University Press.

# *Introduction*

Margaret Atwood, acknowledged as a foremost Canadian author, is rapidly achieving world-class stature. At age forty-seven, she has published thirty books, including six novels, twelve volumes of poetry, two books of short stories, a collection of literary essays, and a book of criticism. In 1986 she coedited *The Oxford Book of Canadian Short Stories,* published American editions of books in three genres—*Bluebeard's Egg* (short stories), *The Handmaid's Tale* (novel), and *Interlunar* (poetry)—and appeared at writers' conferences, universities, and other cultural programs.

Atwood's writings have elicited enthusiastic responses. The Modern Language Association has held four special sessions on her work (in 1977, 1984, 1985, and 1986), and she was a featured reader at the 1975 and 1984 MLA national conventions. An International Margaret Atwood Society has sprung up; in Canada she is so well known that she has had to go in disguise. By 1982 her works had been translated into fourteen languages. In 1986 over 122 articles, reviews, and letters about her books were published in America alone. John Updike (in the *New Yorker*), Paul Gray (in *Time*), Doris Grumbach (in the *Chicago Tribune*), Mary McCarthy (in the *New York Times Book Review*), and over sixty others who reviewed *The Handmaid's Tale* showed that writers of critical acumen and great reputation are taking Atwood seriously.

Why has Atwood become so widely discussed? What are the reasons for her increasing popularity? For one thing, she transcends categories and polemics: She is a witty author who writes about serious subjects. She is a feminist who likes men and who can create believable men on her pages. She mines popular culture but parodies it, appealing to the reader who likes old-fashioned romance while entertaining the critic who spies allusions inside every character and act. She attracts American readers—in part because she knows the United States well and takes its measure as only an informed outsider can—while she is not afraid to criticize the States for ecological carelessness, excessive materialism, and violence. (One senses that the mirror she holds up is meant to show the way to correction, not serve as an accusation.)

Atwood is increasingly involved in national and international cultural issues, as a founding member of Canada's Writers' Union and an active member of Amnesty International and P.E.N. Her involvement is part of her appeal. Atwood has become that rare figure—an artist who is also a cultural diplomat, a woman whose energy, commitment, and vision spill over into public life.

No account of Atwood's work is complete without mention of her striking expertise in a wide variety of genres. One is hard pressed to think of other writers equally gifted as novelists and poets (though Hardy and D. H. Lawrence come to mind). Sylvia Plath, Marge Piercy, Erica Jong, and Alice Walker, among contemporary women, write in both forms, and it is in the company of such feminists, often concerned with environmental and social issues, that Atwood seems most at home.

Some have said that the challenge, in writing about Atwood, is just to keep up with her as she continues publishing books of high quality with alarming rapidity. More important, though, is the need to understand and to respond to the issues she raises. To do her writing justice means going deeply into her major works while keeping her enormous range in mind.

Our book was undertaken with the sense that a new, comprehensive critical collection encompassing Atwood's recent work was needed. We thought it significant to include both U.S. and Canadian critics and to address enduring concerns in her work: among them, feminism, ecology, the Gothic novel, the theories of Frye and Jaynes, and politics, especially the relationship between Canada and the United States and between French and English cultures in Canada. We wanted to explore the references to Canadian authors and literary events unknown or less than familiar to readers in the States and to offer added attention to Atwood's poetry, which is particularly valued in Canada, where poetry finds a broader audience than in the United States.

We were particularly interested in Atwood's feminism. Many

of the following essays dwell on women's issues and employ feminist literary approaches to trace Atwood's refashioning of traditional genres. Some essays demonstrate how, as Atwood's characters confront gender issues with varying degrees of self-awareness and success, the reader is forced to become involved.

On a related plane, another concern of Atwood's is the myth and reality of the United States, where, for Atwood, people have lost touch with themselves under the pressure of high technology, mass culture, and consumerism. Atwood's view presents an important challenge for American critics; our collection begins and ends with Atwood's views of the United States.

Another special interest that inspired this collection was Atwood's pervasive awareness of nature. Two essays—one on Atwood's animals, another on shamanism in her work—investigate Atwood's ecological and spiritual orientation to nature. Her use of myth and folklore, as an oral expression of a pretechnological and communal life rooted in nature, is the focus of two more of our essays.

As a prolific and versatile writer—she has authored two children's books (*Up in the Tree* and *Anna's Pet*) and works for radio—Atwood also provides source materials that offer insights into creativity and the development of the creative process. Atwood has donated some of her early unpublished work to the University of Toronto archives. Two of our essays use archival materials and Atwood's own commentaries to explore the author's creative development; one traces her changing literary treatment of American and Canada, and one explores her haunting watercolors, reproduced in book form for the first time.

Like current literary scholarship in general, the critical approaches in our collection are eclectic. While most of our writers use fairly traditional critical methods involving textual analysis, studies of influence, genre analysis, and literary history, we also include two semiotic interpretations and two original pieces by Atwood—an interview and a conversation. These mingled viewpoints offer readers a range of insightful approaches to Atwood's complex art.

*Survival,* the first widely read expression of a distinctively Canadian literary identity, catapulted Atwood to fame and controversy as a critic, and the publication of *Second Words* in 1982 confirmed her position as one of Canada's leading literary spokespersons. Feminists in particular—both in and out of Canada—have welcomed Atwood's *Survival* because it clearly identifies the victim role and outlines concretely how female and Canadian cultural identities have been repressed over the years. June Schlueter's essay "Canlit/Victimlit: *Survival* and *Second Words*" analyzes the treatment of Canada (equated with the female, the exploited victim, and nature) and the United States (equated with the male, the exploiter, and the victimizer) in Atwood's criticism, noting that these are not only actual countries but also states of mind, ways of being and seeing. Sexual and regional contradistinctions also, according to Atwood, have global repercussions. Since Tocqueville, Freneau, and Martineau, Americans have gained in self-awareness from informed foreign responses to the United States. Through Schlueter's thought-provoking essay we see Atwood continuing this tradition.

Following Schlueter's examination of Atwood as critic, our book turns to the novels, each of which is covered individually and in detail. "The Two Faces of the Mirror in *The Edible Woman* and *Lady Oracle,*" by Pamela S. Bromberg, explores how the female protagonists of each of the two novels under discussion become trapped in relationships that mirror nineteenth-century romance plots. Marian MacAlpin's *anorexia nervosa,* and her fear of impending marriage suggest a linkage between consumerism and gender politics in *The Edible Woman.* Bromberg analyzes Atwood's distortions of nineteenth-century perceptions and of narrative methods in Milton's *Paradise Lost* and Eliot's *Adam Bede.* In *Lady Oracle,* Joan doubles and redoubles her inner and outer selves as Atwood's plots and narratives examine otherness and separateness in many forms.

The third essay, "Pilgrimage Inward: Quest and Fairy Tale Motifs in *Surfacing,*" by Elizabeth R. Baer, continues the discussion of issues Bromberg raises by showing *Surfacing* as a feminist and nature-based search for self. Baer convincingly presents *Surfacing* as the loup-garou folk story the unnamed protagonist wants to include in the collection of Quebec folk tales she is illustrating. Based on a transformation of the Grimm tale "Fitcher's Feathered Bird" (further discussed by Sharon Wilson in a later essay), the story revolves around a werewolf who turns from male to female and from deadly to positive. The animal nature the werewolf represents is welcomed, not exorcised; only the return to a wild animal state allows the protagonist to meet the spirits of her dead parents and incorporate their power.

Atwood's *Surfacing* is clearly one of her finest novels; hence we have devoted two essays to it. Sherrill E. Grace's essay "In Search of Demeter: The Lost, Silent Mother in *Surfacing*" demonstrates that the novel can be read as a quest within a quest. Ostensibly the novel describes the search for a father, but inscribed within this search is a hidden retelling of the ancient myth of Demeter and Persephone that was celebrated in the Eleusinian mystery cult of the Great Mother. To decode the novel in this way is, for Grace, to recover a central female discourse long suppressed by male history.

If *Surfacing* can be read as a suppressed werewolf folktale or myth, Atwood's next novel explicitly deals with the supernatural. Ann McMillan's wide-ranging essay "The Transforming Eye: *Lady Oracle* and Gothic Tradition" clearly sets Atwood's "anti-Gothic" into the Gothic tradition crucial to Atwood's work as a whole. Beginning with a discussion of Horace Walpole, McMillan distinguishes between the Gothic fantasy of escapist wish fulfillment in popular novels and the darker Gothic naturalism of Mary Shelley's *Maria.* The essay suggests that *Lady Oracle,* like Austen's *Northanger Abbey,* falls into a third and mediating "mixed Gothic" tradition. In "mixed Gothic," the female protagonist's "transforming eye" does not convert the dangerous, attractive male from threat to savior as in Gothic fantasy. Instead, her eye turns inward, allowing her to see—and save—herself through an increase in self-awareness. McMillan's overview of the central issues in major historical Gothic texts gives a context for understanding Atwood's brilliant reshaping of genre and her continuing exploration of the psychology and literature of women.

*Life Before Man,* Atwood's most realistic novel, continues her concern with how humans can break through predetermined, negative patterns. The issue is not the Gothic quest for love so much as it is the search for identity as a process of healing. Many forms of pain—deaths, divorce, abandonment, discrimination, madness—threaten the novel's female characters, particularly Elizabeth. Posing the central question of how people can change for the better when they are psychologically burdened by the past,

Gayle Greene, in "*Life Before Man:* 'Can Anything Be Saved?'" explores the healing power of recognition and acceptance that can transcend time. Especially important, as Greene demonstrates, is women's recognition of the power of the mother figure, and the depth of her pain.

*Bodily Harm,* the novel that follows, continues the psychological investigations of *Life Before Man,* yet there is a striking contrast—Atwood's mood, tone, and style are more dramatic and dynamic as the new protagonist, Rennie, faces life and death crises. Lorna Irvine's "The Here and Now of *Bodily Harm*" pursues Atwood's provocative suggestion that this novel, at first glance a straightforward adventure romance, actually takes place in a Caribbean prison, where flashback pasts and imagined future intersect. Within the jail of "here, now," the novel expands, as Irvine shows, to include the past of Rennie, of her mother and grandmother, of Lora, and of others. Irvine elegantly reveals the subtext of inscription, in which the female body is a blank page penetrated and inscribed by the male pen. Rennie's female wound—her partial mastectomy—like the male intruder in her apartment and her incarceration, is a violation of her personal space akin to rape. As a writer, Rennie introjects violation by cutting herself off from writing about important issues and limiting herself to trendy journalism. Rennie's final achievement lies in the repossession of her body and her own female power to inscribe the truth upon the blank page of the world.

"Nature and Nurture in Dystopia: *The Handmaid's Tale,*" by Roberta Rubenstein, is the first of two essays devoted to Atwood's controversial vision of the fascist Republic of Gilead—the northeastern United States after a nuclear war in the late twentieth century. Rubenstein clearly shows how in this novel "female anxieties associated with fertility, procreation, and maternity are projected as cultural catastrophe." In Gilead the "natural" world—including sex and procreation—has become denatured, contaminated, and artificial. Rubenstein sensitively traces the myriad ways in which the inhuman politics of Gilead mirror and enforce the slavery of its women.

Arnold E. Davidson's "Future Tense: Making History in *The Handmaid's Tale,*" on the other hand, inverts the novel by seeing it through the lens of its short final section of "Historical Notes." These notes consist of the proceedings from an academic meeting devoted to analyses of the foregoing narrative, which we learn is the story of the handmaid Offred fortuitously preserved on audiotape. As a pedantic academic of the future discusses Offred's tale, he inadvertently reveals his masculinist assumptions: Davidson warns that a sexist legacy is not easily overcome.

Atwood's books of poetry are too numerous to treat in detail. We begin with an essay on Atwood's poetics and conclude with explorations of developing issues in her poems. In "Weaving Her Version: The Homeric Model and Gender Politics in *Selected Poems,*" David Buchbinder gives a close semiotic reading that posits an inner integrity to the volume as a whole. Employing polysystems theory, his interpretation of *Selected Poems* reveals Atwood's subtle but pervasive use of Homeric women: the victimizer Siren, the victim Circe, and the victor Penelope. The essay includes a challenging consideration of the placement of the reader in relation to the text. Writing from Perth, Australia, Buchbinder offers a reading that overlooks U.S.-Canadian issues in order to focus on Atwood's relation to the greater Western tradition.

Judith McCombs's extensively researched essay "Politics, Structure, and Poetic Development in Atwood's Canadian-American Sequences: From the Apprentice Years to 'The Circle Game to' 'Two-Headed Poems'" reveals the creative process at work as Atwood develops and matures as a poet. In Atwood's juvenalia, deposited in the Atwood archive at the University of Toronto, we see her first using then abandoning long Whitmanesque lines borrowed from Ginsberg's *Howl* in favor of short, vertical poems. Examinations of English- and French-Canadian relations and critiques of the United States run throughout Atwood's works: McCombs closely follows Atwood's changing treatment of these themes from her earliest, unpublished work to the demanding volume *Two-Headed Poems.* In the process, McCombs reveals the complex meanings and elegant structures of Atwood's Canadian-American sequences.

Readers have often remarked on Atwood's pervasive primitivism and the movement in her work from the "static, the mythological, or the sculptural" to the "kinetic, the actual, or the temporal," to borrow Frank Davey's terminology from his essay "Atwood's Gorgon Touch." Kathleen Vogt's "Real and Imaginary Animals in the Poetry of Margaret Atwood" sensitively explores the intersection between primitivism and presentation (whether "mythic" or "actual"). Establishing the dominance of animal imagery in Atwood's poetry, Vogt distinguishes between animals used as mythic counters to make statements about people and integral animals appearing as actual live creatures in Atwood's work. The "best" animal images, Vogt contends, combine the two modes and "remind us of the integrity of both animals and humans and the necessary interconnectedness of the two." She concludes by suggesting that Atwood's most moving and fully realized animals issue from a participatory female awareness of the natural world instinct with its own freedom, wholeness, and value.

My own "Shamanism in the Works of Margaret Atwood" complements the essays by Baer and Vogt, which stress Atwood's vision of nature. In this essay, I attempt to locate Atwood's works as a whole in a primal, shamanic mode that employs specific shamanic images, such as reflecting surfaces and skeletons, an "alphabet" of natural imagery, and the theme of transformation through symbolic death. The essay suggests that Atwood's work bears close affinities with contemporary ethnopoetic writings and that the shamanic mode is inherently akin to a female, nature-oriented vision.

A special feature of this volume is its eight-page color supplement reproducing Atwood's rich and disturbing original watercolors. Previously unpublished in book form, many of these paintings evoke themes that dominate her literary works. Sharon R. Wilson's stimulating essay "Sexual Politics in Margaret Atwood's Visual Art" carefully discusses each painting, drawing on conversations with Atwood to illuminate the paintings and their place in Atwood's poems and fictions.

It is fitting, in a book on a contemporary, to give the author herself the last word. In Jan Garden Castro's freewheeling interview, the conversation covers writing and feminism, ambiguous endings and the setting of *Bodily Harm,* the stories behind the revolutions on Grenada and Petit Martinique, petroglyphs, and the aesthetics of swift denouement. Atwood's increasing engagement in feminist and political issues and organizations such as Amnesty International show in her habit of turning conversation to the political and in her witty comments on nationalism and imperialism. Atwood discusses a number of specific points (such as her use of oppositional paradigms in *Surfacing*), and her comments on her part in Canadian literary life—her work with Anansi Press and the Writers' Union of Canada—round out our picture of Atwood as a many-sided literary person.

Atwood's recent remarks to candid questions asked by a group of college undergraduates from the States show her in her sometime role as teacher and mentor. She stresses the need for these students—and for the United States as a world power—to enlarge their acquaintance with international affairs and assume the responsibility that comes with power. In "A Conversation: Margaret Atwood and Students," Atwood clarifies her belief that most writers in the States today have cut themselves off from politics, seeing the political as inherently antiliterary and limiting. Atwood argues that writers have a responsibility to acknowledge social and political issues through their writing. For her, literature, like life, is inherently political. Atwood's recommendations of other Canadian authors and list of favorite authors (her favorite American is Faulkner) should interest students and teachers alike. It is for them, and the concerned reader, that these essays were collected.

Kathryn VanSpanckeren

# *A Margaret Atwood Chronology*

*Born:* 18 November 1939, Ottawa, Ontario

*Places of Residence:* Ottawa, Ontario, 1939–1945
Sault Ste. Marie, Ontario, 1945
Toronto, 1946–1961
Boston, 1961–1963
Toronto, 1963–1964
Vancouver, 1964–1965
Boston, 1965–1967
Montreal, 1967–1968
Edmonton, 1968–1970
England, France, Italy, 1970–1971
Toronto, 1971–1973
Alliston, Ontario, 1973–1980
Toronto, 1980–1983
England, Germany, 1983–1984
Tuscaloosa, Alabama, 1985
New York, 1986
Australia, 1987

*Education:* Victoria College, University of Toronto, B.A., 1961
Radcliffe College, A.M., 1962
Harvard University, 1962–1963, 1965–1967

*Employment:* Lecturer in English, University of British Columbia, Vancouver, 1964–1965
Instructor in English, Sir George Williams University, Montreal, 1967–1968

Instructor in English, University of Alberta, Edmonton, 1969–1970
Assistant Professor of English, York University, Toronto, 1971–1972
Writer-in-Residence, University of Toronto, 1972–1973
Writer-in-Residence, University of Alabama, Tuscaloosa, 1985
Berg Chair, New York University, 1986
Writer-in-Residence, Macquarie University, New South Wales, Australia, 1987

In addition, Ms. Atwood has worked as a cashier, a summer camp tripper, a waitress, a writer for a market-research firm, and a film-script writer.

*Awards:* E. J. Pratt Medal, 1961
President's Medal, University of Western Ontario, 1965
Governor General's Award, 1966
Centennial Commission Poetry Competition, First, 1967
Union Poetry Prize, *Poetry* (Chicago), 1969
The Bess Hoskins Prize, *Poetry* (Chicago), 1974
The City of Toronto Book Award, 1977
The Canadian Bookseller's Association Award, 1977
Periodical Distributors of Canada, Short Fiction Award, 1977
St. Lawrence Award for Fiction, 1978
Radcliffe Graduate Medal, 1980
Molson Award, 1981
Guggenheim Fellowship, 1981
Companion of the Order of Canada, 1981
Welsh Arts Council International Writer's Prize, 1982
Periodical Distributors of Canada and the Foundation for the Advancement of Canadian Letters Book of the Year Award, 1983
Ida Nudel Humanitarian Award
Toronto Arts Award, 1986

Governor General's Award, 1986
Los Angeles Times Fiction Award, 1986
Booker Price Shortlist, 1987
Arthur C. Clarke Award for Best Science Fiction, 1987
Council for Advancement and Support of Education, Silver Medal, Best Articles of the Year, 1987
Humanist of the Year Award, 1987
Fellow of the Royal Society of Canada, 1987

*Honorary Degrees:* D. Litt., Trent University, Peterborough, Ontario, 1973
LL.D., Queen's University, Kingston, Ontario, 1974
D. Litt., Concordia College, Edmonton, 1980
Smith College, Northampton, Massachusetts, 1982
University of Toronto, 1983
University of Waterloo, Waterloo, Ontario, 1985
University of Guelph, Guelph, Ontario, 1985
Mount Holyoke College, South Hadley, Massachusetts, 1985
Victoria College, University of Toronto, 1987

*Margaret Atwood*

# 1 *Canlit/Victimlit*
## Survival *and* Second Words
*June Schlueter*

In Margaret Atwood's second novel, *Surfacing,*[1] the image of Canada as colony, physically exploited and psychologically oppressed by the United States, is manifest. As the unnamed protagonist journeys to the home of her missing father, she and her three companions drive past the evidence of American influence: bulldozed trees, power lines running into the forest, a rocket base—"the disease is spreading up from the south" (p. 7). Against the background of Anna's mindless singing of American songs, David brazenly asserts, "If we could only kick out the fascist pig Yanks and the capitalists this would be a neat country" (p. 43).

David's politics are blunt but ironic, coming from a citified man who is himself ambitious, with little interest in stopping progress and none in curbing aggression in either national or sexual politics. His anti-Yank comment, however, does reflect the attitude of the protagonist, who measures every violation of nature she encounters in terms of the Americans. When she and her companions discover a dead heron, hanging upside down like an abandoned lynch victim, she sees the bird as a testimony to the Americans' wanton destruction. And when she discovers its killers are not Americans after all, but Canadians, she concludes that "it doesn't matter what country they're from . . . [t]hey're still Americans, they're what's in store for us, what we are turning into" (p. 48).

This vision of Canada's colonial mentality finds repeated expression in the novel, as the protagonist, plagued by a suppressed memory of an abortion, connects the destruction of the Canadian wilderness with her own experience, until the Americans become objects of personal hostility and Canada a surrogate for herself. But even as the protagonist personalizes Canada's position, it becomes clear that her view is not idiosyncratic. It is, rather, emblematic of a collective national mentality that, Atwood contends, pervades and defines "Canlit." Like the protagonist of *Surfacing*—who, finally, emerges from the collapse of her civilized self and refuses to be victim—Canada is vulnerable, consumable, and oppressed.

The same year Atwood published *Surfacing*, she also published *Survival: A Thematic Guide to Canadian Literature*. Recognizing that the study of Canadian literature was still in its infancy, even in Canada, Atwood hoped to speak about Canada "as a state of mind, as the space you inhabit not just with your body but with your head" (p. 18). Her approach would be to identify a number of key patterns in Canadian literature, providing, in effect, a "map of the territory" (p. 18). But the cartographer/critic who constructs this survival manual proposes a map of Canada with boundaries shaped not by bold, dark, impenetrable lines but by tentative, pencil-drawn dotted lines that physically—and psychologically—admit intruders. For Atwood, the hypothesis that Canada is a "victim," or an "oppressed minority," or "exploited"—in short, a "colony" (p. 35)—needs no testing; it immediately becomes a model constructed from her experiences with Canadian literature, which have convinced her that seeing itself as victim is a national habit of mind.

In Atwood's analysis of nature, animals, native Canadians, and early settlers; of family and cultural symbols; and of writers frustrated in their attempts to record the Canadian experience, "victim" becomes the operative term. The kind of victim presented in any particular piece of Canadian poetry or prose may be understood by reference to a four-category paradigm of "Basic Victim Positions":

1. To deny the fact that you are a victim.
2. To acknowledge the fact that you are a victim, but to explain this as an act of Fate, the Will of God, the dictates of Biology (in the case of women, for instance), the necessity decreed by History, or Economics, or the Unconscious, or any other large general powerful idea.
3. To acknowledge the fact that you are a victim but to refuse to accept the assumption that the role is inevitable.
4. To be a creative non-victim. (pp. 37–38)

Though unquestionably a negative look at Canada's collective sense of self as reflected in its literature, *Survival* provided an interpretive lens through which Canadians might see and share and react.

In the months that followed the publication of *Survival,* Canadians did, indeed, react: they bought the book in such quantities that it quickly became the most widely read work of literary criticism in Canada. As James Steele points out in "The Literary Criticism of Margaret Atwood," *Survival* "introduced many Canadians to their own literature for the first time" (p. 74). But those knowledgeable about Canlit responded not with applause for the clarity of Atwood's vision but with defenses: hers was a myopic view, seen through a distorted lens. Steele was himself among the dissenters; victim hunting, he claimed, was productive with those authors Atwood had chosen to feature, but it was an empty game with just as many others. Frank Davey, in "Atwood Walking Backwards," also found fault with Atwood, especially for ignoring "the very large and significant celebratory tradition in Canadian poetry," represented by such writers as W. W. E. Ross, Dorothy Livesay, Irving Layton, Victor Coleman, bpNichol, and Gwendolyn MacEwen (p. 83). And Patricia Morley, in "Survival, Affirmation, and Joy," noticed that though she read the same prose Atwood did—F. P. Grove's "Snow," Ernest Buckler's *The Mountain and the Valley,* Gabrielle Roy's *Where Nests the Water Hen,* Wallace Stegner's "Carrion Spring," Adele Wiseman's *Each Man's Son,* Margaret Laurence's *The Stone Angel,* and Roch Carrier's *Is It the Sun, Philibert?* for example—she saw affirmation where Atwood saw negation (pp. 21–30).

The historical-materialist position, expressed by Paul Cappon in "Towards a Sociology of English Canadian Literature," rejected Atwood's approach as "liberal idealism":

> Atwood plays the common liberal trick of *psychologizing* social phenomena—in this case American imperialism. American dominance for her becomes something purely cultural and abstract. For her, *individuals* react to it by being victimized, but the more enlightened ones can resist it *individually* and become "creative non-victims." . . . Atwood's solutions to an American dominance which is in fact *material* (economic), not abstract, are those of individualism and elitism, characteristics which conform to the dominant ideology. (*Our House,* p. 50)

Steele agreed that Atwood's criticism "reveals more about the poetic world-vision of Margaret Atwood than about the structural principles of Canadian literature" (pp. 80–81).

Atwood, however, insists she is describing a cultural phenomenon: "Canadians themselves feel threatened and nearly extinct as a nation, and suffer also from life-denying experience as individuals—the culture threatens the "animal" within them—and . . . their identification with animals is the expression of a deep-seated cultural fear (*Survival,* p. 79). Atwood even suggests in *Survival* that the "*real* condition" of Canadians may not be "exploited victims" so much as it is the "*need* to be exploited victims" (p. 84).

A number of Canadian writers and academics complained that Atwood's argument in *Survival* had the force of prescription, urging Canadians into a vision of self that was neither palatable nor true. Chief among the dissenters was Robin Mathews, who noted that the pessimistic literature that Atwood describes—the literature of a people who are "torn, caged, colonized, despairing, undone" (p. 115)—has a vital and substantial counterpart in Canadian struggle literature, which is *not* a literature of surrender. Citing George Grant as representative of the kinds of authors Atwood chooses to include in her analysis, Mathews condemns Grant's presentation of "a monolithic and Establishment view of Canadian experience which makes us all guilty of the sins of the Bank of Montreal, the Family Compact, the multi-national corporations and their docile, fawning servants" (p. 113). As a consequence of this "refusal to discriminate among the forces of community, and exploitation, between the people and capitalism in Canada, George Grant rests self-condemned, guilty, an alien in his own land and history, unable . . . to become a spiritual inhabitant of his own nation." Like many of the other writers Atwood selects, Grant finds "as a solution to the death of a conservative ideal a psychological state which can only be described as liberal individualist anarchism" (p. 113).

Atwood's response, "Mathews and Misrepresentation," objected to Mathews's assumptions about her political principles, implying that he himself was imposing his own (Marxist) views on Canadian literature. His contention concerning a significant strain of struggle literature she dismissed as wishful thinking. To his admonishment for omitting those writers "who have dealt deeply with out colonial condition, writers that are at home in the recognition of oppression and the struggle against it" (p. 117), Atwood retorted that when she made a special effort to discover such literature she found very little. Moreover, Atwood clearly does not agree with Mathews's belief that in order to effect change a society needs to have positive role models. Though she would wish for such models, she believes that, in order to effect change, "you need to have a fairly general consciousness of what is wrong. . . ." In other words, society must first admit "that it *should* be changed": "to fight the Monster, you have to know that there is a Monster . . ." (*Second Words,* p. 146). Atwood repeated her belief that the mainstream of Canadian literature has been describing that Monster—"in all its forms, including those in our heads—accurately" (p. 148) and that in doing so it has been urging and encouraging survival.

Atwood's refutation was reprinted in *Second Words,* a collection of reviews and other critical writing which she grouped into three chronological segments: 1960–1971, 1972–1976, and 1977–1982. In the introduction to the volume, Atwood explains that she called the book *Second Words* for two reasons: "The first is that I am not primarily a critic but a poet and novelist, and therefore my critical activities, such as they are, necessarily come second for me. . . . The other reason is based on precedence: that is, a writer has to write something before a critic can criticize it" (p. 11). She also comments on the division into three parts, noting that in the first part she develops "some of the ideas set forth in *Survival*" and that the second "runs from 1972 (or the publication of *Survival*) to 1976," thus covering a period when she "was being attacked a lot," when much of what she wrote was "in response to some of these attacks." She notes as well that this second period "corresponds to the peak of cultural nationalism and the popularization of feminism" (p. 14). The third grouping, which has no material connection with *Survival,* begins with the publication of *Lady Oracle* in 1976 and runs through the appearance of *Second Words* in 1982. In that period, she remarks, her writing becomes increasingly involved with human rights and with a "larger, non-exclusive picture" (p. 282); still, a number of essays in this third section return us to the thesis of *Survival* either in provincial or global form.

Much of Atwood's early criticism is college writing, done for *Acta Victoriana,* the literary magazine of Victoria College, University of Toronto. In the 1960s, Canadian literature was just beginning to burgeon, and Atwood was reviewing many of the writers—Margaret Avison, James Reaney, D. G. Jones, Eli Mandel, Al Purdy, Gwendolyn MacEwen—who would later appear in *Survival.* In 1962, she published a review of J. P. Matthews's *Tradition in Exile: A Comparative Study of Social Influences on the Development of Australian and Canadian Poetry in the Nineteenth Century,* a critical book that evaluates Canadian and Australian poetry in relation to colonial attitudes. As Atwood describes Matthews's claim, Canadian colonialism "ignores the indigenous and strives to emulate the mother country"; Australian colonialism "reacts against its parent and turns in upon itself" (p. 30). The corresponding forms of poetry are the academic and the popular, with the Canadian tradition favoring the academic. Curiously, the woman who, ten years later, was to propose her paradigm of Canlit as victim literature is puzzled by Matthews's apparent preference for the popular as a national literature and offended by the image of the nineteenth-century Canadian as "a nail-gnawing . . . intellectual, smothered in Englishness, bleating and effete," to be measured against "the Bushman, virile, lawless, unwashed and above all virile, composing four-line ballad verses with irrepressible gusto . . ." (p. 31).

Two other essays in this early group are of special interest in Atwood's developing vision on Canlit: "Eleven Years of *Alphabet*" and "Nationalism, Limbo, and the Canadian Club," both from 1971. She begins the *Alphabet* essay, written on the occasion of that little magazine's last issue, with a quotation from an editorial by James Reaney, which had appeared in an earlier *Alphabet:* "Now the young intellectual living in this country, having gone perhaps to a Wordsworth high school and a T. S. Eliot college, quite often ends up thinking he lives in a waste of surplus USA technology, a muskeg of indifference spotted with colonies of inherited, somehow stale, tradition. What our poets should be doing is to show us how to *identify* our society out of this depressing situation" (p. 90). In this essay, Atwood offers a "hypothetical generalization" about the Canadian habit of mind. Unlike English thinking, which is empirical, and American thinking, which is abstract and analytical, Canadian thinking, she suggests, is synthetic. The Canadian tendency, reflected in such critical works as Northrop Frye's *Anatomy of Criticism* and Marshall McLuhan's

*The Gutenberg Galaxy,* is to propose large, accommodating systems in order to synthesize all parts of experience. This need to discover the whole connects with Reaney's comment about the literary need "to *identify* our society out of this depressing situation," with the experience of the protagonist in *Surfacing,* and with the implicit plea of *Survival.* It also connects with the sad story of cultural neglect Atwood tells in "Nationalism, Limbo, and the Canadian Club."

As a child in the Canadian public-school system, Atwood sang "Rule Britannia," drew pictures of the Union Jack, learned the names of the kings of England and of that country's explorers. At home, she read Batman, Captain Marvel, and other comic books from America. In high school, she studied the world wars and assorted European and American history. The one year her teachers "got around to Canada," they "touched on such engrossing subjects as Wheat, The Beaver and Transportation Routes" (p. 85). At home, she read *Life* magazine, where she learned about American drum majorettes and spaniels and Eugene McCarthy. In college, there was no room in the English literature course for Canlit, but in college she discovered a library of Canadian little magazines.

Elsewhere, recalling her experience as a graduate student at Harvard University, where she went originally so she could study under Jerome H. Buckley, a leading Victorian scholar (and a Canadian), she commented that "Americans found a revelation of one's Canadian-ness . . . about as interesting as the announcement that one had had mashed potatoes for lunch." As Atwood explains to Joyce Carol Oates, "The beginning of Canadian cultural nationalism was not 'Am I really that oppressed?' but 'Am I really that boring?' " (p. 10) Americans "had been taught that they were the centre of the universe, a huge, healthy apple pie, with other countries and cultures sprinkled round the outside, like raisins." Canadians "had been taught that we were one of the raisins . . ." (*Second Words,* pp. 87–88).

Atwood concludes her essay with a story about the Canadian Club at the Harvard Business School. At one of its parties, which featured Canadian Club and Canada Dry, mixed with talk of Canadian nationalism and American opportunity, an inebriated club member played a recording of "The Star Spangled Banner" at high volume. Others, who had all evening been talking about not wanting to go back to Canada but wanting to make their fortunes in the United States, objected and removed the record, only to have the drunk man replace it. When, finally, one of them shouted, "Cut that out, you bloody Yank," the wounded—and angry—man replied, "I'm not a Yank, I'm a Canadian!" then put the record back on again. Atwood's sober conclusion—a prolegomenon to *Survival*—is that "it was our own choices, our own judgements, that were defeating us" (p. 89).

Atwood continues to write about Canadian literature in the second group of essays. In "Travels Back" (1973), she speaks of her poetry readings in Canadian schools where kids didn't study Canlit and of her evangelistic refrain: "Refusing to acknowledge where you come from . . . is an act of amputation. . . . By discovering your place you discover yourself" (p. 113). In "Canadian Monsters" (1977), she looks at the supernatural in Canadian fiction, suggesting that the metamorphosis of the natural monster into the humanmade monster reflects "the changes in Canadian society and outlook over the last sixty years . . ." (p. 252). And in "What's So Funny? Notes on Canadian Humour" (1974), she examines examples of Canadian parody, satire, and humor, locating the Canadian funny bone not in the insistence that "I am a gentleman" (as in England) or "I am not a dupe" (as in America) but in the insistence that "I am not provincial." She notes, however, "as provinciality is seen as something irrevocably connected with being Canadian, the audience can renounce its provinciality only by disavowing its Canadianism as well" (p. 188). Recalling the habit of mind in *Survival,* Atwood concludes:

> The concealed self-deprecation, even self-hatred, involved in such disavowal, the eagerness to embrace the values of classes and cultures held superior, the wish to conciliate the members of those other groups by deriding one's own—these are usually attitudes displayed by people from oppressed classes or ethnic groups who have managed to make their way out of the group, alienating themselves in the process. "Yes, *they* are awful," such jokes seem to be saying, "But look, I am laughing at them. I am no longer one of them." (p. 188)

Clearly Atwood's assessment of Canlit after the publication of *Survival* did not change: Canlit does not reflect the more general postwar despair, nor is victimization as she describes it—the individual as social representative—a universal theme. Moreover, had she the opportunity to elaborate her thesis through a second edition of *Survival,* she would, she insists, include sections on

"Humour, War, Magic, Struggle (if [she could] find enough material), and something about the shapes of critical theories . . ." (p. 131).

But there is another concern developing in the essays included in this group, readily surmised by a glance at the writers whose work she reviews. Essays on Adrienne Rich, Audrey Thomas, Erica Jong, Kate Millett, Marie-Claire Blais, and Marge Piercy accompany "On Being a 'Woman Writer' " (1976) and "The Curse of Eve—Or, What I Learned in School" (1978). It is telling that when Atwood moves to a consideration of feminism in literature and to the female writer, she moves beyond Canada's boundaries, proposing a model of gender victimization that, while not exclusive to Canada, corresponds to the Canadian paradigm *Survival* describes. In the Mathews refutation, she offers ("just for fun") specific female responses for the Basic Victim Positions:

1. Ignore her victimization, and sing songs like "I Enjoy Being a Girl."
2. Think it's the fault of Biology, or something, or you can't do anything about it; write literature on How Awful It Is, which may be a very useful activity up to a point.
3. Recognize the source of oppression; express anger; suggest ways for change. . . . (p. 145)

Because a woman in Canada cannot "write as a *fully* liberated individual-as-woman-in-society" (p. 145), Atwood omits Position 4, the creative nonvictim.

In "The Curse of Eve," Atwood speaks of the fictional women she has encountered in fairy tales, novels, plays, and poems, composing a mammoth catalog of stereotypes common to the Western literary tradition, all of them acquired from "the media, books, films, radios, television and newspapers, from home and school, and from the culture at large, the body of received opinion." Cynically, she adds "personal experience"—sometimes—"which contradicts all of these" (p. 219).

Atwood does not linger over the female victim in *Survival,* finding enough evidence of victimization in Indians, Eskimos, animals, settlers, immigrants, futile heroes, and paralyzed artists. But she does devote one chapter to "Ice Women vs Earth Mothers." Using Robert Graves's model, proposed in *The White Goddess,* of woman as "maiden" (Diana), as "goddess of love, sex and fertility" (Venus), and as the forbidding "goddess of the underworld" (Hecate), Atwood notices that, in Canadian literature, Dianas die young, Venuses seldom appear, and Hecates, especially as frozen old women, abound (p. 199). She is particularly struck by the absence of Venuses, noting that there is a tendency in Canadian literature to divide the two traditional functions of Venus, "sexual love and babies": "to have the sexual love department presided over by whores, or by easy and therefore despised women, and to reserve the babies for Diana figures, nonentities or even Hecates" (p. 206). The Nature-as-Woman metaphor, common to the literature of other nations as well, is special in Canadian literature in that the recurring fictional character is "not just an Ice-Virgin-Hecate figure, but a Hecate with Venus and Diana trapped inside" (p. 210).

In the final section of *Second Words,* Atwood's criticism acquires greater range, as she moves into regular reviewing of books by men and by non-Canadians: Timothy Findley, John Thompson, W. D. Valgardson, E. L. Doctorow, Nadine Gordimer, Ann Beattie, and Anne Sexton, for example. But a number of essays suggest that her extended range both endorses and broadens her *Survival* thesis. In "Diary Down Under" (1978), she records her impressions of Australia, a country that seems to her to be even more oppressed than Canada, and she measures Australia's idea of Canada against her own. In particular, her account of Fay Zwicky's address at the writers' conference she attended reflects her continuing—and humorously self-effacing—preoccupation with the Canada of *Survival:*

> Fay Zwicky from Western Australia speaks last. She begins by referring to D. H. Lawrence's *Kangaroo,* in which he said that Australians had great dead empty hearts, like the continent, despite their outward boisterous amiability. She then wonders when Australia is going to write *Moby Dick,* laments its provincialism, asks when it's going to stop nosing around for its identity and get down to it, and affirms its potential. This is all painfully familiar. Canada is lucky D. H. Lawrence never wrote a book called *Beaver.* If he had, he'd doubtless have commented on that rodent's fabled habit of biting off its own testicles, thus defining us forever. (p. 304)

Similarly, she begins her review of *Midnight Birds: Stories of Contemporary [American] Black Women Writers* (1981) by registering the fact that, though she was asked to assess this collection of fiction, she was neither American nor black: "I am in fact Canadian, a citizen of a country which was until recently dominated by one imperial power and is now dominated by another. Could it be that the editors of *The Harvard Educational Review* perceived that I have something in common with the writers in this collection?" (p. 358). The refrain reappears in "Canadian-American Relations: Surviving the Eighties" (1981), which might just as well have been written a decade earlier, for it reiterates the concerns of *Survival* and *Surfacing,* insisting that Canada is still the edible country. But Atwood concludes her essay by contending that the most important field of study has become "the study of human aggression." Updating "No taxation without representation," she proposes a contemporary equivalent: "No annihilation without representation" (p. 391).

Since Atwood's "second words" speak so pointedly to her role as Canadian, as woman, and, most importantly, as critic and writer of Canlit, I shall end with them as they appear in the introduction to the third segment of that critical volume:

> I have always seen Canadian nationalism and the concern for women's rights as part of a larger, non-exclusive picture. We sometimes forget, in our obsession with colonialism and imperialism, that Canada itself has been guilty of these stances towards others, both inside the country and outside it; and our concern about sexism, men's mistreatment of women, can blind us to the fact that men can be just as disgusting, and statistically more so, towards other men, and that women as members of certain national groups, although relatively powerless members, are not exempt from the temptation to profit at the expense of others. Looking back over this period, I see that I was writing and talking a little less about the Canadian scene and a little more about the global one. (p. 282)

### *Note*

1. Page references in the text are to the following editions: *Surfacing* (New York: Simon and Schuster, 1972); *Survival: A Thematic Guide to Canadian Literature* (Toronto: Anansi, 1972).

# 2 *The Two Faces of the Mirror in* The Edible Woman *and* Lady Oracle

*Pamela S. Bromberg*

In her poetry and novels[1] Margaret Atwood exposes one of many contradictions in the Western cultural construct of femininity. In the English literary tradition, women are often criticized and punished for the sin of narcissism, for loving their own images and selves above all (especially masculine) others. Yet it is precisely women's images, that is, their beauty, that society most prizes and rewards in the marriage market. Few, if any, successful—courted and married—eighteenth- and nineteenth-century heroines lack beauty. But that beauty must be validated in the eyes of the masculine beholder. The power of beauty is then necessarily derivative and secondary. The woman who looks in the mirror and finds herself beautiful (without merely seconding or mimicking the specular judgment of patriarchal society) is dangerous, because she has appropriated the masculine scopic power of approval. She must then be corrected or punished.

Milton's portrayal of the narcissistic Eve in *Paradise Lost* furnishes a paradigm of this process and its contradictions. A representative nineteenth-century English novel, George Eliot's *Adam Bede* also uses the test of the mirror to define its two diametrically opposed female protagonists. The beautiful Hetty Sorrel enjoys the admiring gazes of the local men and looks approvingly in the mirror; she plans to make her fortune with her face. Dinah Morris, the methodist preacher, gazes not in the mirror of narrow egoism, but looks out the window of her own soul toward compassionate understanding of others. And yet, in addition to rewarding Dinah's selflessness with her (relatively) happy ending, Eliot cannot resist making her beautiful too, albeit in a quieter, less obvious, and more spiritually acceptable way. George Eliot's two women in *Adam Bede* are as imprisoned by specularity and the dominant patriarchal culture (both in their plots and in her judgments of their desire) as Milton's Eve.

In Margaret Atwood's two early novels *The Edible Woman* (1969) and *Lady Oracle* (1976), mirrors symbolize not the moral and psychological limitations of their female protagonists, but rather the crippling emphasis that society places on the female image as a consumer item. Atwood shows that the mirror, long a literary symbol of female narcissism and childish self-absorption, more truly reflects a culture where women are objectified and packaged for the marriage market. Literature itself, especially the popular romance (originating in the nineteenth-century novel), is one of society's primary tools for indoctrinating women into the religion of beauty and promising them the happy ending of marriage if only they learn to market themselves properly.

Or, to use a different terminology, let me cite a recent essay by Margaret Homans that explores "The Rhetorics of Sexuality" in lyric poetry by women. Homans connects the rhetoric of the nineteenth-century "lyric of romantic desire" with the sexual politics of the culture it reflects, arguing that "the cultural construction of gender" shapes both the forms and rhetoric of all literature (p. 569). Working from Luce Irigaray's analysis of "the interdependence of language and sexuality," Homans explains that "specular metaphors" are "the expression of conventions of male sexuality that operate continuously in our culture. . . . Like the quest plot they replicate, specular metaphors speak for that sexuality whose story is constructed as a story of looking. A culture that privileges the phallus . . . also privileges sight . . ." (p. 572). Female sexuality, on the other hand, privileges touch. In a passage cited by Homans, Irigaray writes that "the predominance of the visual . . . is particularly foreign to female eroticism. Woman takes pleasure more from touching than from looking, and her entry into a dominant scopic economy signifies, again, her consignment to passivity: she is to be the beautiful object of contemplation" (*This Sex,* pp. 25–26). Homans applies Irigaray's theory to Roman Jacobson's linguistic distinctions between metaphor and metonymy, arguing that female textuality privileges the latter, a verbal equivalent to touching rather than looking (p. 580).

Both *The Edible Woman* and *Lady Oracle* exemplify Irigaray's ideas; their plots subvert patriarchal literary conventions and their language deconstructs traditional specular metaphors. Each novel, furthermore, identifies touch with the female protagonist's potential for wholeness and escape from the "dominant scopic economy." Atwood also recognizes the dominance of the male gaze over the female appearance (image) in the romantic quest plot. She suggests that female narcissism proceeds from the internalization of the male gaze and imprisonment of the self in objectifying roles dictated by the dominant, patriarchal culture. Women look so often in the mirror because their primary market value in the marriage exchange depends upon the allure of their images. Women, in this culture, *are* their images.

*The Edible Woman* reverses the marriage plot of nineteenth-century fiction. Marian MacAlpin, the protagonist, begins as a conventional heroine. She is young, unmarried, working for a marketing company called Seymour Surveys. This is a job, not a career; signing up for the company pension plan produces a mild panic in her as she imagines a future spinster self defined by a lifetime's service to the company. Marian is saved from that unwelcome destiny when her boyfriend, Peter Wollander, proposes at the end of the novel's first section.

Peter, a young lawyer, is prosperous, well-dressed, "good-looking." His distinction is his normalcy. Peter is not a monster of male-chauvinism; he is, in Marian's words, "ordinariness raised to perfection, like the youngish well-groomed faces of cigarette ads" (p. 62). Peter and Marian date casually, "taking each other at [their] face values" (p. 62). In a wonderfully comic sequence, Marian becomes panicked, then angry, as she realizes he is depending on her as an accessory to his corporate image, "a stage-prop . . . a two-dimensional outline" (p. 72), instead of a person in her own right. When she tries to escape from his subordination of her to his own needs, first by running away and then by hiding under a bed, Peter, predictably stimulated by the chase and capture, proposes. What for a nineteenth-century heroine would be triumph is the beginning of Marian's entrapment in the mirror of masculine approval and marriage: "As we stared at each other in that brief light I could see myself, small and oval, mirrored in his eyes" (p. 84). As the rests of the novel reveals, to be mirrored in Peter's eyes is to become Peter's image of her and society's image of a wife.

By taking her at "face value" Peter uses her as a mirror. In her poem "Tricks with Mirrors," Atwood writes, "Mirrors are the perfect lover," perfect because they give back the self rather than the challenges and reality of the other. But to become a mirror for the other requires the subjugation, or "restraint," of ego: "breath withheld, no anger / or joy disturbing the surface / of the ice" (*Selected Poems,* p. 183). Marian willingly engages in that self-suppression. The morning after Peter's proposal she hears a new voice in herself, "soft flannelly" (p. 92), hardly recognizable, that cedes all power of choice and desire to her new fiancé.

Atwood's parodic subversion of the marriage plot becomes obvious in the novel's long second section, as Marian step by step loses her identity as an independent, active self and drifts passively toward her fatal metamorphosis into Peter's wife. The first section is narrated in the first person—Marian begins the novel as a subject self—but in the second section her story is told in the third person. Marian is now defined as other and object. Expressed by her loss of narrative authority, Marian's escalating loss of self is accompanied by an increasing loss of appetite. Throughout part 1 she is hungry and eating. But in part 2 she begins to identify herself with the objects she has previously ingested and consumed. As she turns from subject to object, consumer to consumed, she loses her capacity to eat, to take the world into her self. This anorexia also reflects the division of her body (the primary subject self) from her image (the self as seen).

This is the division effected by mirrors. The novel's counterplot is told through specular metaphors. The language of vision—mirrors, reflection, surfaces, outsides, and images—permeates the text. Throughout the first section of the novel, Atwood introduces mirrors as realistic details, establishing the vocabulary of image and self-image. In the second section, as Marian becomes progressively divided and objectified, she views progressively more distorted, alienated images of herself in a series of reflecting surfaces. In one scene she and Peter are having dinner in an expensive restaurant. The chapter opens: "Marian gazed down at the small silvery image reflected in the bowl of the spoon: herself upside down, with a huge torso narrowing to a pinhead at the handle end. She tilted the spoon and her forehead swelled, then receded. She felt serene" (p. 150). The image of a pinhead expresses Marian's altering sense of self. Since her engagement Marian has fallen into the habit of letting Peter choose her food for her: "Peter could make up their minds right away." Her lack of desire and inability to choose are symptomatic of her dwindling subjectivity. When she looks at Peter in the restaurant she sees him through the eyes of the world, not her own, thinking with pleasure that "anyone seeing him would find him exceptionally handsome" (p. 150). He, meanwhile, is watching her (p. 153), as he has ever since the engagement, in repeated acts of scopic possession.

The distorted image Marian sees in the spoon echoes her earlier perception of her pregnant friend Clara, whom she perceives as "a swollen mass of flesh with a tiny pinhead, . . . a queen-ant, . . . a semi-person—or sometimes, she thought, several people, a cluster of hidden personalities that she didn't know at all" (pp. 117–18). Clara, who in high school "was everyone's ideal of translucent perfume-advertisement femininity" (p. 35), represents Marian's fate as a married woman. The spoon-mirror of marriage to Peter will turn her also into a pinhead with a huge torso, will objectify her soon-to-be-swollen body into the same terrifying nonhuman forms that Clara's has assumed.

The transformation of self to other and accompanying division of body from mind do not require pregnancy's actual invasion of self by other. Marian has been just as effectively split by the male gaze and her new definition as wife-to-be. As the marriage date draws near, Marian's image takes on increasing power and her subjective self nearly disappears. The plot reaches its crisis when Peter gives a final party to introduce Marian to his friends. In preparation for the party, Marian has her hair done and buys a new red dress at Peter's urging. She is totally objectified at the hairdresser's. Her head is "like a cake: something to be carefully iced and ornamented" (p. 214). She observes the "operation," "fascinated by the draped figure imprisoned in the filigreed, gold oval of the mirror. . . ." Her body feels "curiously paralysed" (p. 215).

Later, as she bathes, she sees her naked body reflected back in the globes at the base of the faucets and spout on the bathtub: "She moved, and all three of the images moved also. They were not quite identical." Her self has fragmented and divided away from her. She looks at the water and at "the body that was sitting in it, somehow no longer quite her own. All at once she was afraid that she was dissolving, coming apart layer by layer like a piece of cardboard in a gutter puddle" (p. 224). This specular dissolution parallels Marian's panic over becoming her image under the "uncomprehending eyes" of Peter's friends: "she was afraid of losing her shape, spreading out, not being able to contain herself any longer, beginning (that would be worst of all) to talk a lot, to tell everybody, to cry" (p. 225). In the third-person narrative of the second section Marian has lost her voice. Now she fears simultaneously the total loss of her shape (her subject identity) *and* the opposing assertion of subject (real) self that would take place if she began to talk, to tell, to cry, to abandon the "restraint it / takes" to be a mirror. Faced with these paradoxically contrary fears, Marian finally recognizes that she is unhappy. Her self-division is imaged in two old dolls "sitting there inertly on either side of the mirror, just watching her" (p. 225). The dolls represent her dawning awareness that she has become divided into two selves, the image seen by others and the other deeper self that feels and sees inside. But even this knowledge is objectified, transferred from her self to the two dolls: "By the strength of their separate visions they were trying to pull her apart" (p. 226).

This is a decisive moment, for by acknowledging her feelings Marian is struggling against the division between self as subject and object. She asserts herself, takes action and invites *her* friends to the party. She arrives sporting all the accoutrements her impending role requires: regulation hairdo, sexy red dress and girdle underneath, a total makeup job courtesy of her roommate, Ainsley. Peter approves: " 'Darling, you look absolutely marvellous' " (p. 235), implying that she should look like that all the time. When Marian looks at herself in Peter's mirror she feels fractured and alienated: "What was it that lay beneath the surface these pieces were floating on, holding them all together?" (p. 235). Marian's insistence on inviting her friends, her first willed assertion of self in relation to Peter since the engagement, saves her. When her mysterious acquaintance Duncan arrives he refuses to join the party, pulls her out the door, examines her and finally says, "You didn't tell me it was a masquerade" (p. 245). Marian escapes before Peter can take her picture. The photographic image would forever capture the alien image of this masquerade as reality, trapping her in the nineteenth-century marriage plot with its "happy" ending. The camera is a specular gun: "Once he pulled the trigger she would be stopped, fixed indissolubly in that gesture, that single stance, unable to move or change" (p. 252).

*The Edible Woman* ends comically though, when Marian does not get married, does not happily find her identity in Peter's mirror. She recognizes that marrying Peter would destroy her by assimilating her; knowledge that her body or subconscious has registered all along by refusing to eat. Marian breaks the spell by creating a doll-like cake, the edible woman of the novel's title. She is afraid to confront Peter with language; she wants to avoid words (p. 274). The edible woman caricatures Marian's increasingly objectified identity as a "living doll." In constructing the sugary idol Marian carefully chooses sponge cake, an apt representation of her former pliancy. Atwood again uses the language of ornamentation and operation employed earlier in the hairdresser's passage to describe Marian's culinary creation. Here, however, Marian has become the sculptor rather than the lifeless statue erected in the name of beauty.

When Peter arrives, angry at her disappearance from the party, Marian makes no rhetorical statement in her defense. Instead she offers him the sugary image as her substitute, suggesting, "This is what you really wanted all along, isn't it?" (p. 279). By making the symbolic literal she deconstructs Peter's image of her, along with the language of specularity. As soon as Peter refuses the subversive discourse of the cake, Marian (magically) regains her lost appetite—that is, her lost self; she feels "extremely hungry" and eats the cake (p. 279). Marian destroys her identity as image and other by incorporating it; Ainsley's shocked comment, "Marian! . . . You're rejecting your femininity!" accurately defines the politics of Marian's act. By consuming the woman/cake, the mirror image of herself (the image desired by Peter, hired by Seymour Surveys, manipulated by Ainsley), she is quite literally joining her subject and object selves, healing the mirror's split. Metaphor becomes metonymy. She has become active again, an agent, a subject, a consumer, rather than a consumable object of exchange traded on the marriage market.

Atwood counterpoints the aborted marriage plot with the narrative of Marian's relationship with Duncan. This cadaverous graduate student of English functions as Peter's contrary and plays an increasingly important role in Marian's story as she moves toward marriage. Atwood also uses Duncan and his two roommates to satirize literary discourse and thus reinforce the novel's more subtle intertextual debate with literary conventions of form and rhetoric. After leaving Peter's party to find Duncan, Marian finally has sex with him, an act which helps to release her from impending captivity as Peter's wife. Her behavior liberates her from the nineteenth-century heroine's plot by inverting it. But even before this ultimate transgression, for Marian to see Duncan without Peter's knowledge is an act of self-assertion and betrayal of him and of her financée role. Keeping a part of herself private and secret from Peter, she remains partially unseen and uncontrolled.

Who Duncan is—a matter for critical speculation[2]—matters less than the fact that he exists at all as rival, alternate, opposition to Peter. He enables Marian to be a self in relation to Peter. She has no image to maintain for Duncan and therefore tells him the truth about her increasing inability to eat. Unlike Peter, Duncan does not need Marian for a self-image. He is far too narcissistic, too ravenously hungry and absorbed in his own self, to care what anyone thinks of him, or to care much about her.

Significantly, Marian responds to and is aware of Duncan in primarily tactile ways, as opposed to the visual perception that governs her relationship with Peter. According to Irigaray's argument, Marian experiences her own sexuality with Duncan, rather than becoming the passive object of Peter's gaze. Marian generally wants to touch Duncan, and Atwood repeatedly describes in detail how he feels to her when she embraces him. This instance from chapter 19 is representative: "He was wearing a shaggy sweater. She stroked it with one of her hands as though it was a furry skin. Beneath it she could feel his spare body, the gaunt slope of a starved animal in time of famine. He nuzzled his wet face under her scarf and hair and coat collar, against her neck" (p. 176). Although her relationship with Peter is sexual, she perceives him in the purely visual, even abstract, terms with which he defines her.

Duncan, on the other hand, has broken the mirror in his own apartment (p. 142). He doesn't reflect back to Marian the socially successful, "normal" image of herself that Peter does. Peter, a "good catch," confers upon her the identity of a worthy, desirable, normal woman. When she looks in Duncan's mirror, however, she cannot see herself, only the wooden frame and a few jagged pieces of glass. Atwood writes in the poem "Tricks with Mirrors": "Think about the frame . . . / it exists, it does not reflect you, / it does not recede and recede, it has limits / and reflections of its own" (*Selected Poems,* p. 183). Duncan does not view Marian as his reflection; he does not want her to complete or "rescue" him and refuses to rescue her (p. 254). He will not conform to expectations created by the nineteenth-century plot of romantic desire. Marian's relationship with Duncan acknowledges otherness and separateness. He tells her she's just an escape: "You know, I don't even *like* you very much" (p. 188). Yet, paradoxically, their distance makes possible genuine contact.

In part 3, Marian regains her first-person narrative voice and looks for another job. She is eating again, and as Duncan observes, looking "jaunty and full of good things" (p. 286). But the novel's closing image is unsettling. Duncan finishes her cake, and since Marian has not been able to put her understanding into words, the reader is left to wonder whether he will then devour her. It is not clear that Marian has learned the secrets of Atwood's "Tricks with Mirrors." She is more self-assertive and healthy, but for how long?

In *Lady Oracle,* published seven years after *The Edible Woman,* Atwood again uses mirror symbolism to explore the issues of image and reality, the self as seen by others and the self as known from within. In this, her third novel, however, Atwood extends the concepts of doubling, of inner and outer selves, of surfaces and depths, appearances and reality, with the symbolism of mirrors, reflections, clothing, makeup, and photographs, and also as major elements in the plot and narrative structure.

In *Lady Oracle,* Joan Foster shares Marian's division of self, but she possesses conscious knowledge of past, present, and multiple selves. Marian shows different sides of herself to Peter and Duncan, but Joan invents new identities, even new pasts, for a variety of different men. After a childhood of maternal rejection, she is actively in search of a self she can love. She realizes late in the novel that she has used men as her mother had tried to use her, as Peter had unknowingly used Marian: "I felt I'd never really loved anyone, not Paul, not Chuck the Royal Porcupine, not even Arthur. I'd polished them with my love and expected them to shine, brightly enough to return my own reflection, enhanced and sparkling" (pp. 314–15). Joan's attempt at mirror-magic fails because she retains the secret identities of her past as the fat Joan Delacourt, and of her present alter-ego, Louisa K. Delacourt, successful writer of Costume Gothics. She would like to believe in the fairy-tale marriage plot of the popular romances she writes, but she is prevented from taking up her happy status in the mirror of feminine social success by the inconsistent realities of her fat, unhappy childhood and her lovers and husband, none of whom is a prince in disguise.

The creation of yet another identity, the wildly successful pop poet Lady Oracle, forces a crisis. Joan's fame dislodges the secrets of her past and present identities, and her multiple selves collide. In the novel's complex ending, she begins to integrate her selves through her writing, abandoning the romantic heroine and plot for a story much closer to her own.

Joan is divided initially by her mother's rejection of her. A bitter, closet alcoholic trapped into marriage by an undesired pregnancy, Mrs. Delacourt names the child after Joan Crawford, hoping that Joan will redeem her mother's failure by becoming beautiful. Mrs. Delacourt tries to use Joan as her life's project: "Our relationship was professionalized early. She was to be the manager, the creator, the agent; I was to be the product" (p. 70). But Joan turns out to be fat, the "embodiment" of her mother's "own failure and depression, a huge edgeless cloud of inchoate matter which refused to be shaped into anything for which she could get a prize" (p. 71). Joan's obesity is in fact a weapon; she refuses to become her mother's desired reflection, to be objectified by the mirror of female beauty: "I wouldn't ever let her make me over in her image, thin and beautiful" (p. 94).

Joan's resistance empowers her to see beneath the surface of her mother's conventionality to her masked anger and unhappiness. In a key dream Joan watches her mother reflected in the triple mirror of her vanity table as a three-headed monster. Mrs. Delacourt works strenuously at keeping up appearances, succeeding with her house and her face, though failing with Joan. But the mother revealed to Joan in her dream is filled with self-loathing, and she hates Joan for being the uncontrollable image of her own failure. After her death, Joan understands that, her mother "was not what she seemed," that she herself "was a throwback, the walking contradiction of her [mother's] pretensions to status and elegance" (p. 202). The triple mirror is the altar of Mrs. Delacourt's failed rituals of specular transformation. She sits there, sadly succeeding in remaking herself into society's image of feminine beauty. But Joan concretely manifests the inner failure of her mother's anger, self-hatred, and maternal rejection.

As in *The Edible Woman,* Atwood balances the central plot of Joan's specular imprisonment with a countermovement toward wholeness that is mediated through touch. Like Marian's relationship with Duncan, Joan's relationship with Aunt Lou is also primarily tactile: "hers was the only lap I remember sitting on" (p. 86). Joan's mother avoids contact with Joan (except when she attacks her daughter in murderous anger at the end of part 2): "I could always recall what my mother looked like but not what she felt like." On the other hand, the "soft, billowy, woolly, befurred" Aunt Lou, who loves Joan rather than her potentially beautiful image, frees her from the prison of obesity, chosen by Joan as a rebellious distortion of the prison of beauty (p. 95).

In her adult life Joan searches for mirror images of a lovable, "successful" self in romantic relationships with men and in the marriage plots of the heroines she fantasizes for her secret career as a writer of Gothic romances. But the new identities she creates for herself are all formed out of the unfilled need for her mother's loving approval of her image. Thus, although she has left home and lost weight, Joan continues to be imprisoned by her mother's legacy of specular identity. She imagines herself as the woman her mother would have wanted her to be, until finally in the novel's brilliant ending, Joan recognizes that her mother had been Joan's "reflection" too long: "She'd never really let go of me because I had never let her go. It had been she standing behind me in the mirror . . ." (p. 363).

Letting go of her mother may enable Joan to accept her real self, past, present, and future. The plot of the Gothic romance she is now trying to complete refuses to follow the conventions; she begins instead to find words and images that represent her own fractured self, to incorporate her past and present identities. The book, however, ends ambiguously. Joan gives up writing romances and finally tells the true story of her life (with only a few lies) to a reporter. She is considering writing science fiction instead, though, and she looks like she may be in danger of making the reporter into yet another mirror for a not entirely true version of herself.

Both novels end ambiguously because their female protagonists have not yet become armed with conscious, rhetorical analyses of the mirror's divisive power over them. Each has resisted entrapment and objectification in the nineteenth-century plot of romantic desire. But Marian ends up feeding Duncan with the head of her cake, and Joan delays her return to the reality of her past to stay a little longer with her latest romantic hero. While the protagonists, however, remain only conditionally freed from the romantic quest plot and the "dominant scopic economy," both novels succeed powerfully in exposing the rhetoric and politics of women's entrapment in the mirror of gender.

## *Notes*

1. Page references in the text are to the following editions: *The Edible Woman* (New York: Warner Books, 1983); *Lady Oracle* (New York: Avon, 1976); *Selected Poems* (New York: Simon and Schuster, 1976).

2. McLay argues that Duncan "symbolizes total withdrawal into the self" (p. 131), thus serving as the antithesis to Peter, who represents society. Grace suggests that "Duncan is most successful as a symbol of Marian's inner life or subconscious" (*Violent Duality,* p. 93). The novel supports both views, though neither fully explains Duncan's role or behavior. Lecker emphasizes Duncan's duplicity.

# 3 *Pilgrimage Inward*
## *Quest and Fairy Tale Motifs in* Surfacing

*Elizabeth R. Baer*

Margaret Atwood's fascination with folk and fairy tales is by now well-established, although not widely recognized by critics. "I would say that *Grimm's Fairy Tales* was the most influential book I ever read," Atwood has told one interviewer (Sandler, p. 14).[1] Atwood herself explains this attraction in terms of two aspects of fairy tales: the motif of transformation and positive images of women. "You could . . . link it with my childhood reading; most fairy tales and religious stories involve miraculous change of shape. Grimm's tales, Greek and Celtic legends have them. North American Indian legends have people who are animals in one incarnation, or who can take the shape of a bird at will" (Sandler, p. 14). In an interview with Joyce Carol Oates, furthermore, Atwood mentions two Grimm's tales, both about transformation, as her favorites: "The Juniper Tree" and "Fitcher's Feathered Bird." In addition, Atwood admires the image of women in many fairy tales: "The unexpurgated *Grimm's Fairy Tales* contain a number of fairy tales in which women are not only the central characters, but win by using their intelligence. Some people feel fairy tales are bad for women. This is true if the only ones they are referring to are those tarted-up French versions of 'Cinderella' and 'Bluebeard,' in which the female protagonist gets rescued by her brother. But in many of them, women rather than men have the magic powers" (Hammond, p. 28).[2] Both metamorphosis and this second source of fascination to Atwood—female protagonists with intelligence and magic powers—are at the core of Atwood's novel *Surfacing.*

The narrator of *Surfacing* is working on a series of illustrations for an edition of *Quebec Folk Tales* while on her pilgrimage. She feels a certain frustration at the limits placed upon her by her boss, a man with the suggestive name of Mr. Percival.[3] For financial and aesthetic reasons, Mr. Percival will not allow the heroine to use red or frightening images in her illustrations: "We had an argument about that: he said one of my drawings was too frightening and I said children like being frightened. 'It isn't the children who buy the book,' he said, 'it's their parents' " (p. 39).

In addition to these dissatisfactions, the narrator feels that the anthology is incomplete: "There should be a 'loup-garou' story in *Quebec Folk Tales,* perhaps there was and Mr. Percival took it out; it was too rough for him. But in some of the stories, they do it the other way around: the animals are human inside and they take their fur skins off as easily as getting undressed" (p. 63). According to the *Standard Dictionary of Folklore, loup-garou* is:

> The French word for werewolf; one who transforms himself into a wolf at night and runs the countryside devouring animals and people. In French Canada, a man (always a man) becomes a loup-garou because of some curse or a punishment from heaven. One man, for instance, found that he was a loup-garou because he had not been to mass (or confession) for ten years. The loup-garou is not always a wolf; he may be almost any other animal: a white horse, a dog, pig, even a tree, or an inanimate object. The loup-garou de cimitiere digs up and eats dead bodies. Those who take the shapes of other animals devour both animals and people; some, however, do little damage except to frighten passers-by and await their deliverance. Deliverance from the state of loup-garou comes by religious exorcism, by a blow on the head, or by the shedding of his blood while in the metamorphosed state. (Leach, p. 647)

What I would like to suggest is that *Surfacing* is the loup-garou story the narrator feels is missing from her anthology.

A close comparison of the elements of the *Dictionary of Folklore*'s definition with *Surfacing* is provocative. The loup-garou story chronicles a transformation (one of the sources of Atwood's fascination with fairy tales), and transformation is the object of the narrator's quest in *Surfacing.* The loup-garou story is also indigenous to French Canada, where Atwood spent some of her childhood.[4] The traditional loup-garou story, however, features a male protagonist. Here "Margaret the Magician" (as she has been termed by one critic) performs a metamorphosis of her own by grafting the strong female character from the Grimm tradition onto the loup-garou story. This sex reversal, then, is the first of many inversions Atwood uses in adopting the loup-garou motif to her own purposes.

The transformation into a werewolf occurs because of a transgression or "sin" of some kind; the narrator of *Surfacing* recounts a conversation she had with her brother regarding this belief:

> [My brother] said, "They believe if you don't go to Mass you'll turn into a wolf."
> "Will you?" I said.
> "We don't go," he said, "and we haven't." (p. 63)

The narrator's "sin," of course, is her abortion, which represents the loss of the animal in her. Her lover rationalizes the abortion by telling her "it wasn't a person, only an animal" (p. 165). The abortion has thus been a sort of exorcism, and the narrator now needs to reclaim her animal nature.

The loup-garou can be a wolf, or any other animal, even a tree. Early in the novel, the narrator speculates: "Maybe that's why they didn't waste any sweat searching for my father, they were afraid to, they thought he'd turned into a wolf; he'd be a prime candidate since he never went to Mass at all" (p. 63). And, in a metaphorical sense, she's right. Near the end of the novel, she has visions in which she sees her father as a wolf and her mother as a bird; she herself undergoes change near the end of her quest into several animal states. Again, Atwood has used a reversal of the tradition, suggesting that this primal state is a kind of apotheosis, not a badge of shame.

Eating or devouring is part of the curse of the loup-garou; great attention is paid in the novel to eating, to taboos about food, and to devouring as a metaphor for the guilt of the Americans and the narrator.[5] We are told in detail what the four eat at the cabin, how they gather food in the garden, how they fish and pick blueberries. At first, the narrator feels justified in killing animals for eating; later this sickens her. She is horrified by wanton killing of animals, such as the heron. As the narrator is slowly transforming into an animal, she increasingly senses a mysterious power, associated with nature, that dictates her actions, especially her eating. First the food in the cabin, in cans and jars, is forbidden her by the power (p. 206), then the vegetables growing in the garden are forbidden, and she is allowed only food growing wild such as raspberries and roots: "Now I understand the rule. They can't be anywhere that's marked out, enclosed: even if I opened the doors and fences they could not pass in, to houses and cages, they can move only in the spaces between them, they are against borders. To talk with them I must approach the condition they themselves have entered; in spite of my hunger, I must resist the fence, I'm too close not to turn back" (p. 209). Again, Atwood uses a reversal: in the metamorphosed state, her narrator is forbidden from eating, rather than compelled to do so.

Obviously, I am not claiming that the narrator of *Surfacing* is a werewolf. Atwood's use of the motif is more subtle than that. And she has made some significant shifts in her adoption of the loup-garou story. In essence, she sees the transformation into the animal state as positive rather than negative, and she conveys this by the series of inversions that I have just described. Let us now take a look at the two Grimm's fairy tales mentioned above, "The Juniper Tree" and "Fitcher's Feathered Bird," to determine their influence on, and transformation within, *Surfacing.*

A close reading of these two tales reveals that both are tales of transformation. The central character of the former is male, and of the latter, female. In both stories, characters are dismembered (beheaded in "Tree" and hacked limb from limb in "Bird"). Also in each story, the central character uses cunning, magic, and metamorphosis into a bird in order to triumph over the evil character, who is consumed by flames at the conclusion of the tale. The dismembered characters in both stories are magically restored to wholeness.

Although Atwood calls "The Juniper Tree" her favorite, it is "Fitcher's Feathered Bird," with its central female protagonist, that bears closer comparison with *Surfacing.* The similarities between the two are startlingly provocative. A variant of the Bluebeard tale, "Fitcher's Feathered Bird" is the story of a sorcerer who spirits one of three sisters away to his house in the forest and gives her a key and an egg. Telling her she may open any chamber in the house but one, he leaves; she, of course, opens the forbidden chamber. She finds there a bloody basin, filled with the limbs and heads and torsoes of his former guests. In astonishment, she drops the egg, thereby staining it with blood; when the sorcerer returns, he thus knows she has trespassed, and he hacks her apart and adds her to the basin. A similar fate awaits the second sister. When the third sister is left alone, however, she puts away the egg before unlocking the room, thereby tricking the sorcerer. She magically restores the dismembered sisters, sends them home, dons the disguise of a bird, traps the sorcerer in his house, and burns him to death.

Like *Surfacing,* this is the story of a quest, of a journey into the woods, of a young woman who is split apart and then made whole, of transformation into an animal state (here the loup-garou motif) in order to achieve vision and triumph. If, as is common practice in reading fairy tales,[6] we see the various men in the narrator's life as aspects of the sorcerer, the similarities come clear. At the beginning of the Grimm story, the sorcerer comes to the door, looking like a beggar, and asks for food. When the eldest girl gives him a piece of bread, he touches her and she is unable to keep herself from jumping into his basket (Grimm, p. 216). So, too, the narrator of *Surfacing* has gone twice into the woods at the behest of her father, first as a child, when "he picked the most remote lake he could find" (p. 66), and second as an adult, to find her father when he disappears.

If the sorcerer as kidnapper is represented in *Surfacing* as the narrator's father, then the sorcerer as murderer is both her father and her "lover." Her father's rationalism is one of the forces most powerful in splitting the narrator, dismembering her; likewise, the lover's insistence that she have an abortion has also divided her. The very language she uses to describe the event reveals this: "A section of my own life, sliced off from me like a Siamese twin, my own flesh cancelled" (p. 54).

Similarly, if we look at *Surfacing*'s narrator as a version of the three sisters in the original tale, we can more clearly see her at various stages. Initially, her relationships with men have disastrous effects, and she is left emotionally paralyzed. But she is not destined to remain so. Ultimately, her intelligence, her ability to learn by experience and survive, which surfaces in the wilderness, will save her. Just so in "Fitcher's Feathered Bird": "Now the sorcerer went and fetched the third girl, but she was clever and cunning" (Grimm, p. 218). This third sister reveals her cunning by safely putting the egg away before entering the forbidden chamber. Then, "Ah, what did she see! There in the basin lay her dear sister, miserably murdered and hacked to pieces. But she set to work and gathered all the parts and laid them in the right order, head, body, arms, and legs. And when there was nothing missing, the limbs began to stir and joined together and the two girls opened their eyes and were alive again" (Grimm, p. 218). So, too, does Atwood's heroine put the missing pieces of herself back together and effect a transformation. When she and Joe make love, she conceives a child to replace the one "sliced off." She describes it: "I can feel my lost child surfacing within me, forgiving me, rising from the lake where it has been prisoned for so long, its eyes and teeth phosphorescent; the two halves clasp, interlocking like fingers, it buds, it sends out fronds" (p. 187).

Attention to the role of the fetus/abortion in *Surfacing* brings us, of course, to the significance of the egg and the key in "Fitcher's Feathered Bird." It is fairly obvious that the key is a masculine symbol and the egg a feminine one. Beyond that, Jung tells us that the egg is frequently a symbol of the self in dreams (Fordham, p. 65). The egg in "Fitcher's Feathered Bird" certainly can be identified with both the narrator of *Surfacing* and the fetus. The bloodstains on the first two eggs, which give away the secret of entry to the forbidden chamber, can represent complicity, the death of the abortion. The third sister wisely puts the egg away; the narrator of *Surfacing* resolves to protect her second fetus.

So, dismemberment and subsequent reunification is one transformation motif Atwood appropriated from fairy tales; let us now look at the second set of transformations in "Fitcher's Feathered Bird" and *Surfacing*. Critics must not stop at the narrator's pregnancy and cluck about how difficult her life will be when she has that child back in the city, but must examine the even more significant transformation, unification, that occurs when the narrator is alone on the island. In "Fitcher's Feathered Bird," the third sister uses two disguises to trick the sorcerer into his own death. Once the sister produces the spotless egg, the sorcerer says, " 'You have stood the test and shall be my bride.' " (Grimm, p. 218). First, she bedecks a skull with jewels and flowers and puts it in the attic window to represent herself as a bride. Then she crawls into a barrel of honey, rolls herself in feathers, and goes out to greet the arriving wedding guests. The clever sister divides herself in half, one half an image of convention, of acceptability in society, which is also an image of death (like mad women in much literature, as

Gilbert and Gubar have shown, in the attic), the other half an animal, a loup-garou, a bird, a disguise that gives her the freedom to confront her demon and destroy it.

Atwood has divided her novel into three sections, roughly equivalent to the three parts of any journey/quest: separation, descent/initiation, return. Section 2 of the novel ends appropriately with the narrator's descent into water and the discovery of her father's body. Having dived below the surface of her image, back into—as one critic has put it—"the undifferentiated wholeness of archaic consciousness" (Piercy, p. 41), the narrator becomes whole again. She vows to bear a child, who will represent the released guilt of the past and the potentiality of the future. Having made that vow, she proceeds to the next steps in liberating and naming herself, in finding her identity. She makes love with Joe, replacing in herself the life which the abortion had destroyed. She dumps "Random Samples" into the lake, freeing "the invisible captured images to swim away like tadpoles" (p. 195). She stays behind when Anna, Joe, and David leave the island, gradually attuning herself to "the power" of irrational, instinctual animal life.

In chapters 22 to 25, the novel reaches a stunningly poetic climax. The narrator divorces herself step by step from the trappings of civilization: "I know I must stop being in the mirror. I look for the last time at my distorted glass face: eyes light blue in dark-red skin, hair standing tangled out from my head, reflection intruding between my eyes and vision. Not to see myself, but to see. I reverse the mirror so it's toward the wall, it no longer traps me. Anna's soul closed in the gold compact, that and not the camera is what I should have broken" (p. 203). Without the mirror, her split self cannot exist. The heroine continues with her destruction: the canned food, her clothing, all enclosures are rejected. She burns her artwork (symbol of a falsely docile self) and her wedding ring (symbol of her fake wifehood). She thus divests herself of other doubles. She tears apart the cabin: "Everything from history must be eliminated" (p. 207). She must pierce the layers of artificiality to get back to the source, the source of her feelings, her instincts, her humanity. To get in touch with her body again, she becomes virtually an animal.

Here, the influence of "Fitcher's Feathered Bird" and the loup-garou motif upon *Surfacing* is strongest. The narrator leaves the cabin, taking a blanket with her, saying, "I will need it until the fur grows" (p. 206). She submerges herself in the lake, a ritual of purification: "When I am clean, I come up out of the lake, leaving my false body floated on the surface, a cloth decoy" (p. 206). She is reenacting and reversing the folk tales where an animal unzips its skin and becomes human; she instead takes off her human skin (clothing) to become animal, a werewolf transformation. She continues to think of herself as an animal:

> I leave my dung, droppings, on the ground and kick earth over. All animals with dens do that.
>
> I hollow a lair near the woodpile. . . . I sleep in relays like a cat. (p. 207)

The fetus, too, she imagines as an animal, but this time it is a positive conceptualization: "I put it there, I invoked it, the fur god with tail and horns, already forming" (p. 210) and not the negative one that allowed her to abort her first pregnancy.

In her final apotheosis, the narrator merges completely with nature, the irrational, the instinctive:

> I lean against a tree, I am a tree leaning
>
> I am not an animal or a tree, I am the thing in which the trees and animals move and grow, I am a place. (p. 210)

As a result of this apotheosis, she sees visions of her dead parents. Indeed, these visions are the apex of her quest. These epiphanies allow her to acknowledge the duality of her existence and to move from before to after, to accept her parents' deaths, to put away her image of herself as a child, and to reenter the world as an adult.

Her vision of her mother comes first: "Then I see her. She is standing in front of the cabin, her hand stretched out. . . . She doesn't move, she is feeding the jays: one perches on her wrist, another on her shoulder" (p. 211). The narrator has always connected her mother with this pose and with calmly shooing a bear away; in other words, she has seen her in communion with nature. Earlier in the novel, she had tried to evoke an image of her mother: "I tried to think about my mother, but she was blanked out; the only thing that remained was a story she once told about how, when she was little, she and her sister had made wings for themselves out of an old umbrella; they'd jumped off the barn roof, attempting to fly, and she broke both her ankles. She would laugh about it, but the story seemed to me then chilly and sad, the failure unbearable" (p. 142). Now her mother will succeed in making the transformation: "The jays cry again, they fly up from her, the shadows of their wings ripple over the ground and she's gone. I go up to where she was. . . . I squint up at them, trying to see her, trying to see which one she is" (p. 211).

Ellen Moers, who has written extensive commentary on the frequency and function of bird imagery in women's literature, believes that the "central sense" of such imagery in women's literature "is not flying as a way for a woman to become a man, but as a way for the imprisoned girl-child to become a free adult" (p. 382). And in the fairy tale "Fitcher's Feathered Bird," it is the bird disguise that allows the third sister to become a free adult. Thus, in *Surfacing* the narrator's mother is a kind of phoenix. The narrator had tried to paint an illustration for *Quebec Folk Tales* of a princess "gazing up at a bird rising from a nest of flames, wings outspread like a heraldic emblem" (p. 60), but she couldn't get the image of the princess right, just as she couldn't get her own image right. During her vision of her dead mother, it's as if she had just stepped into that picture and, looking up at the jays, acknowledges her mother's and her own transformation.

If the narrator has suffered as a result of embracing her father's rationalism, she has also suffered as a result of rejecting her mother's "irrationalism." So her quest is for her father, but even more it is for a reconciliation with her mother. The search for the mother looms largely in many of the paradigms of the female quest that I have examined, including those of Margaret Scarborough and Rachel Blau DuPlessis. The reunion of mother and child, immortalized in the Demeter and Persephone myth, is the ultimate goal. Only by integrating the gifts of both parents can the heroine balance her life.

As *Surfacing*'s narrator sees her mother, so must she see her father. Her vision of him comes next:

> From the lake a fish jumps
>
> An idea of a fish jumps
>
> A fish jumps, carved wooden fish with dots painted on the sides, no, antlered fish thing drawn in red on cliffstone, protecting spirit. It hangs in the air, suspended, flesh turned to icon, he has changed again, returned to the water. How many shapes can he take. (pp. 216–17)

As he changes shape, her father becomes the very drawing he was researching as he died. He will represent a "protecting spirit" to his daughter, not the terrifying figure of the usual loup-garou. Thus, Atwood again inverts the Quebec werewolf motif, stressing the positive rather than the negative in the animal metamorphosis.

Finally, the narrator dreams about her parents, "the way they were when they were alive and becoming older," and when she wakes in the morning, she knows "they have gone finally, back to the earth, the air, the water, wherever they were when [she] summoned them." (p. 219). She reaffirms life: her life, the life inside her. She survives. She has seen the ghosts of her parents and has accepted a gift, a heritage from each of them. From her father, she gets a map, a map to a genuine sacred place where each person confronts her/his personal truth. This is the gift of knowledge, from the head, how to see. From her mother, she receives knowledge from the heart, how to feel: a picture she has drawn herself of a pregnant woman, a sun, and a moon. Accepting these gifts allows her to join her masculine and feminine halves and become whole.

The integration, the "centering," that the heroine of *Surfacing* experiences comes as a result of the realizations she makes while in the animal state. Her growing awareness, in fact, of the connection between herself and animals (the fish, the heron) throughout the novel signals her ability to get in touch with that side of herself and become whole again. The most radical change Atwood makes in the loup-garou motif, then, from the patriarchal version, is to emphasize how absolutely essential it is for human beings to stay in contact with the animal side of their nature. That is what the narrator had lost; the split between nature and culture, the irrational and rational, intuition and logic, women and men, emotion and intellect, has crippled her. The feminist inversion, then, of the loup-garou story is to have a ritual, not to "exorcise" the werewolf, but to "inorcise" it, to claim the value of what has previously been seen as the negative side of all those dichotomies just listed and, further, to assert that full humanity must be both.

## *Notes*

1. More recently, Atwood reconfirmed the influence of the Brothers Grimm on her work in a lecture entitled "One Writer's Use of Grimm," delivered on 20 November 1985 under the sponsorship of the Delaware Humanities Forum. Citing magic, metamorphosis, and active heroines as the appeals of the tales, she went on to draw parallels between specific

tales and "The Animals in That Country," *Surfacing,* "A Red Shirt," "Variation on the Word 'Sleep,'" "Bread," "The Robber Bridegroom," and *Bluebeard's Egg.*

2. I assume that Atwood is here referring to the fairy tale collections of Charles Perrault.

3. Percival, it will be remembered, was the ignorant, bumbling newcomer to King Arthur's court, whose quest for the grail is eventually rewarded with a glimpse of it. Atwood suggests that Mr. Percival, like the narrator, is a neophyte on the quest. Page references in the text are to Margaret Atwood, *Surfacing* (New York: Simon and Schuster, 1973).

4. "I was born in the Ottawa General Hospital . . . in 1939. Six months later I was backpacked into the Quebec bush," Atwood told Joyce Carol Oates in a *New York Times* interview.

5. Eating plays an even more central role in Atwood's other novels, including *The Edible Woman, Lady Oracle,* and *The Handmaid's Tale.*

6. See especially Bruno Bettelheim, *The Uses of Enchantment;* Gilbert and Gubar, *The Madwoman in the Attic;* and Roger Sale, *Fairy Tales and Afterward.*

# 4 *In Search of Demeter*
## *The Lost, Silent Mother in* Surfacing

*Sherrill E. Grace*

Let the woman learn in silence with all subjection. But I suffer not a woman to teach, nor to usurp authority over man, but to be in silence.
St. Paul.
1 Timothy 4:11–12

A voice is a gift; it should be cherished and used, to utter fully human speech if possible. Powerlessness and silence go together.
Atwood
"A Disneyland of the Soul"

Recently feminists have claimed that feminist criticism represents, on the one hand, the "discovery/recovery of a voice" and that, on the other, women's writing is a "double-voiced discourse" because it incorporates *both* the cultural heritage of the "dominant," male group and the "muted," female group (Fetterley, xxxiii; Showalter, p. 31). While these two views differ insofar as the first posits the existence of a distinctive, *because exclusively*, female voice and the second locates the distinctively female in a characteristic merging of two voices or cultural experiences, they agree on this important point: the task of the feminist writer and critic is to find and release something lost, ignored, denied, devalued, and repressed, not only to women themselves, of course, but to the whole of patriarchal society. Freud was right, it seems, though not in the way he thought; women suffer from an acute sense of loss of that full, acknowledged humanity identified by the dominant group with maleness, male speech, male *his*tory. In addition to being lost, this thing, object, source of female identity and power is silent and silenced; therefore, the problem of discovery, recovery, and articulation is indeed difficult.

In *Surfacing,* however, the problem has been faced and, to a degree, solved. Loss and silence could fairly be said to be the keynotes of Atwood's novel—indeed, Atwood has probed and anatomized both conditions from a female speaker's or character's point of view throughout her work. She is a poet haunted by loss and silence and by the urgent need to speak. In fact, it is possible to read *Surfacing* as a retelling, hence a revoicing, of the ancient Greek myth that many claim to be the quintessential female story—the story of Demeter and Persephone, which inscribes the cult of the Great Mother and the sacred rites at Eleusis.[1] Briefly, what I want to suggest is that *Surfacing* is a "double-voiced discourse" incorporating a "muted" story of Persephone's successful search for Demeter within a "dominant" story of an equally successful wilderness quest for a father.

In so doing, I am applying Elaine Showalter's dominant/muted model for feminist criticism (from "Feminist Criticism in the Wilderness") to *Surfacing* because I prefer its broader cultural perspective to exclusively linguistic, psychological, or biological models and because it enables me to isolate what Showalter herself calls "double-voiced discourse"—a quality of language and narrative closely related to Bakhtin's notion of "dialogism" and, as such, a central concern and characteristic, I believe, of Canadian writing. Although I cannot entirely agree with Rachel Blau DuPlessis (in *Writing Beyond the Ending*) that *Surfacing* is a *Künstlerroman,* her general concept that to be female is to negotiate "difference and sameness, marginality and inclusion in a constant dialogue" (p. 43) applies very well to this novel. Not only does Atwood negotiate "sameness and difference" in a "revisionary mythopoesis" (as DuPlessis would put it), she also allows the "muted story of Demeter and Persephone to speak *together with* the "dominant" voice of the father; she illustrates how the wilderness—that preserve of the the male imagination—and the "wild space" of female invisibility and silence can be made to overlap when that "space" is articulated, given form.[2]

The story of Demeter was silenced for centuries and all but extinguished from human memory by successive waves of masculine repression and gynophobia (see Friedrich; Rich; and Stiller). Such treatment attests to the power felt to be vested in Demeter and voiced in her rage at the rape of Persephone. Silence, silencing, and loss are intimately associated with the myth, both in its fundamental meaning and as it has been received by modern women: either the myth is not known at all, or if it is, it has not been given much importance in Western culture because, as one male interpreter suggests, Persephone wanted to be raped and carried away from her mother and there is nothing, therefore, to fuss about (cited by Friedrich, p. 178). In any case, mothers and daughters have come to be seen as suspect, either because they are depicted as extensions of one another in their desire to prey upon men (in Joyce's "The Boarding House" and "A Mother," for example), or because they are cast as "natural" enemies in the eternal battle for the male (Fetterley, p. 10). What has been lost in these distortions or dismissals of the myth are the interrelated aspects of Demeter's power, the extent of her love, and the necessity of her existence, not only for Persephone's well-being, but for the survival of all life: "As the myth of the Koré tells us, upon the mother-daughter cathexis depends the renewal of the world" (Stiller, p. 31).

According to the second Homeric Hymn (c. 650 B.C.), as translated by Paul Friedrich in *The Meaning of Aphrodite*, Persephone, the daughter by Zeus of Demeter, awesome goddess of vegetation, was "gathering flowers" in a meadow with some female friends one day. When she picked a beautiful narcissus, which had been planted there on purpose by Zeus and Hades, her "husband" to be, the god of the underworld appeared and carried her, loudly protesting, off to the underworld in his chariot. Demeter heard Persephone's cries and went in search of her only to find that no god or goddess would explain what had happened. Finally, Hecate took pity on Demeter and told her the truth, but Demeter would not be comforted and vowed to stop all growth and to destroy humankind unless her daughter were returned to her. Zeus finally relented and ordered his brother Hades to return Persephone to her mother. Because Hades wanted to keep his new wife, he put some pomegranate seeds in her mouth, thereby ensuring that she would return to him for one third of the year. Driven by Hermes in his chariot, Persephone was then returned to Demeter, and their reunion is described in ecstatic terms: "Seeing them, [Demeter] darted forward like a maenad down a mountain shadowy with forest. [ . . . ] Persephone, on her part, when she saw the beautiful eyes of her mother, left the chariot and lept down to run forward. She fell on [Demeter's] neck, embracing her" (quoted in Friedrich, p. 177–78). The two women exchange their stories at considerable length, and Demeter learns of the fatal pomegranate, but the story ends on a positive note:

> Thus the whole day, in harmony of feeling, they greatly cheered each other's hearts and breasts, embracing each other. The spirit stopped its grieving. They gave and received joy from each other. And bright coifed Hecate came near them. And many times she embraced the daughter of holy Demeter. And from that time Hecate was minister and comrade to Persephone. (quoted in Friedrich, p. 178)

Many points could be made about the myth of Demeter and Persephone, but I would like to review a few that seem of particular relevance to *Surfacing*. Demeter has "awesome" power, the power over life and death in fact. But although she is active, angry, and revengeful, she must act indirectly to regain her child. Persephone's rebirth, and the renewal of life, depend upon her return to her mother: only Demeter can bestow this gift because, from Persephone's point of view, she has been violently separated from the source of her life and identity. Central to their reunion is the restoration of their *speech* and their joy and mutual comfort in open communication. In addition, the myth explores not only the struggle between the forces of life and death, but also the bitter hostility and power politics of males and females—Demeter, Persephone, and Hecate are allied against Zeus, Hades, and, by association, Helios (Poseidon also attacks Demeter while she is looking for Persephone). The battle between the sexes ends in a compromise of sorts with the women winning back two-thirds of their precious time together—and Demeter and Persephone have a helper and friend in Hecate—while males are seen as enemies or, at best, peripheral beings (as are, for example, Helios and Hermes).

As we turn from the myth to the novel, several questions arise: For example, why does the daughter search for the mother in *Surfacing*? What or who is to blame for their separation? To what degree and purpose are they united? And why, although loss is central to the myth, does silence become so important in this reworking of the mythic material (as it does in others—see, for example, Joy Kogawa's 1981 novel *Obasan*)? Although silence was required of all initiates into the Eleusian mysteries, in the Homeric Hymn Demeter herself is not silenced and Persephone speaks at length after their reunion. Finally, why stress this aspect of *Surfacing* above many other possibilities? I do so because I see it as important to the voice and structure of the narrative, as crucial to our understanding of the nature and outcome of the quest undertaken, and as absolutely central to our appreciation of the feminist issues raised by Atwood. By joining in this search for Demeter, it is possible to gain further insight into an extremely fine novel and then to speculate about the wider issues it raises. Certainly, the search allows us to recognize the power of the "muted" story, hence the "double-voicing" strategy, of the text.

*Surfacing* has been widely discussed and sometimes criticized as a "stagy" adaptation of the male quest into the wilderness, as too negative in its treatment of men and Americans, and as a feminist "sell-out" affirming a dangerous, patriarchal conflation of woman with nature and implying that a baby is the answer to a woman's problems. As a rule, however, Canadian feminists (unlike many of their American and French counterparts) have fewer misgivings about either woman's role as child bearer or the symbolic parallels between nature and female identity. (See Grace, "Quest for the Peaceable Kingdom"; Showalter; and Ortner.) Furthermore, it should be noted that Persephone's appearance with a son—the reborn Dionysus—is often seen as essential to the Eleusian mysteries, and the ancients celebrated the power located in childbirth. In the last analysis, demurrals about nature and babies miss the point because the source of the novel's power begins to appear when, approximately halfway through, the narrator's ostensible search for the father, the search that has brought her to this wilderness to begin with, gives way to an equally important search for the "wild space" of the mother and, through her, for her own rebirth.

From the beginning of her journey, and her story, the narrator's thoughts turn to her mother and the woman's mysterious power. On her death bed (pp. 23–24), the mother is associated with unplanted bulbs, snow, flowers, and some token or message for her daughter that the younger woman cannot find (p. 39). When the narrator and her friends arrive at the island cabin, one of the first things she sees is the dirty and cracked grey leather jacket that had belonged to her mother (p. 47), the jacket in which the mother fed the jays. This image cluster (woman/jacket/seeds/birds) will recur with increasing importance. Shortly after this, the narrator catches herself casting each of her companions as members of her own family—David and Joe as her father and brother, Anna (interestingly) as her younger self, she as her mother. She, however, does not know how to be this mother who, in the afternoons, would "simply vanish" into the forest:

> The only place left for me is that of my mother; a problem, what she did in the afternoons between the routines of lunch and supper. Sometimes she would take breadcrumbs or seeds out to the bird feeder tray and wait for the jays, standing quiet as a tree, or she would pull weeds in the garden; but on some days she would simply vanish, walk off by herself into the forest. Impossible to be like my mother, it would need a time warp; she was either ten thousand years behind the rest or fifty years ahead of them. (p. 56)

Slowly, image by image, without naming or locating, Atwood builds up, or better still *reveals,* the mother's power, which is so great that it enables her to fend off marauding bears (pp. 84–85) and to raise the narrator's brother from the dead (p. 79), and so great it lingers in her place after her death.

Even after she discovers her father's corpse, weighed down to the lake bottom by his camera (p. 152), the narrator's search has only begun. By the last quarter of the novel, she acknowledges that her quest is for herself, that she is on what Annis Pratt has called (in "*Surfacing* and the Rebirth Journey") a rebirth journey with life and sanity at stake. In order to free herself from her learned victimhood, from the silence, exile, and cunning that, unlike Stephen Dedalus's, serve only to cripple her, she must relocate "the power"—it is never more precisely named. This positive power can only be released through the mother whom she knows must have left "a legacy . . . simple as a hand . . . final" (p. 159). As she intensifies her search, feeling "the power" flood through her, she avoids the Death Angel mushroom, sprung up "from the earth, pure joy, pure death, burning white like snow" (p. 160) and confronts David, who seems to invade her space, "drawing away some of the power" (p. 161), as he tries to seduce her. She resists this obstacle to her rediscovery of power in the full knowledge that she must now find the mother's hidden gift because the father's cerebral knowledge is insufficient protection (p. 163).

What she seeks is in the scrapbooks, one of which radiates power (p. 167):

> I went into the other room and took the scrapbooks out from under the mattress. There was still enough light to see by but I closed my eyes,

touching the covers with my hand, fingertips. One of them was heavier and firmer; I lifted it, let it fall open. My mother's gift was there for me, I could look. [. . . T]he gift itself was a loose page, the edge torn, the figures drawn in crayon. On the left was a woman with a round stomach: the baby was sitting up inside her gazing out. Opposite her was a man with horns on his head like cow horns and a barbed tail.

The picture was mine, I had made it. The baby was myself before I was born, the man was God. (p. 169)

The last seven chapters bring the novel to its swift and spectacular conclusion: a creative act of ritual mating, a symbolic (and literal) act of destruction, and a deeper dive into hallucination and visionary ecstasy (all recognized stages in the Eleusian rites) that carry the narrator past language, past boundaries and fences of all kinds, until she and the god/baby (a type of Dionysus with shining fur?) she hopes she has conceived are one with everything: "I am not an animal or a tree, I am the thing in which the trees and animals move and grow, I am a place" (p. 195).

It is important, too, to note that in the closing moments of her ordeal—that is, after the narrator has surfaced (p. 195) but before she accepts the inevitability of return to society—she has two final visions: one of her mother feeding the jays the sunflower seeds from her leather jacket (p. 196) and one of another figure who appears to be her father but is "what my father saw, the thing you meet when you've stayed here too long alone" (p. 201). The mother-vision is positive, unthreatening, sustaining, simple, and human, though fully at one with the natural world; the father-vision is a warning, a danger, and an acknowledgment that "he was an intruder" an excluder ("as logic excludes love"), an image of penance and reparation with "wolf's eyes" but "crippled motion" (p. 201). In as much as the narrator is, mysteriously, this wild thing trapped in a human shape, as the footprints show, she too must make reparation for her past fear, failure to love, coldness, and lies, in short, for her logical misunderstanding of herself and the world. Her father shows her what she must not do; her mother shows her what she must be, and how.

Annis Pratt has claimed that in women's rebirth fiction the question of the heroine's reentry into society is much more problematic than it is in male rebirth quests because a woman's "assumed role in society is by necessity secondary or auxiliary and thus her elixir is not only devalued but a threat to civilization." Although there are as many ways around the problem as there are women's fictions, Pratt finds that *Surfacing* provides one of the most positive conclusions to the quest in that it affirms a feminine personality that is aware of its power and turns "patriarchal space inside out so that it can no longer limit her being" ("*Surfacing* and the Rebirth Journey," pp. 145, 156). Pratt goes on to acknowledge that the novel stops short of depicting the first steps of reentry, but perhaps, as Marie-Françoise Guédon explains in "*Surfacing:* Amerindian Themes and Shamanism," the novel is not primarily concerned with such a reentry. If we restrain our demand for this type of result (after all, we do not legitimately demand such answers of male artists) and hold our suspicions about nature and biology in abeyance, then we will see the real, positive force running through the narrative in the shape of a mother-daughter relationship and a mother-father polarity.

Paralleling the myth of Demeter and Persephone, the male in *Surfacing* (be he husband, father or would-be seducer) embodies a death principle; he is lord of the underworld. In "dying" or "going down" Persephone is impregnated, and yet, like our narrator, she can only be reborn through the intercession and life-giving power of the mother. Although they are opposite in their powers—the father bringing death, the mother life—in Atwood's system, both principles are essential to rebirth and integral to a fuller existence. Thus, the most unalloyed positive *result* of *Surfacing* is Atwood's *unearthing* of "double-voiced discourse," her use of both paternal and maternal codes, and her release of the initially "muted" search for the mother/self from within the familiar "dominant" search for the father. (She is still doing this, by the way, in "Unearthing Suite" from *Bluebeard's Egg,* which is dedicated to her parents.) Moreover, she weighs their relative merits and privileges the mother, without denying the father. What Atwood establishes here, she develops even more pointedly in later poems and stories. This is the knowledge that "sons branch out, but / one woman leads to another" (*Two-Headed Poems,* p. 37).[3] And it is the recognition that female power is expressed through life forces, continuity, and special rites, though the overcoming of rigid boundaries between things, people, nature, and culture, and through the condition of liminality.[4]

The controversial baby is a symbol of that knowledge and of the narrator's reconception of a powerful female self. This Persephone has been summoned from the depths of a sterile, living hell by an erring father to receive the mother's gift of renewed life, of "restored wholeness," and "a place and a meaning in the life of the generations" (Pratt, "*Surfacing* and the Rebirth Journey," p. 155). Here she passes her elixir on to us: if we can see how to find it, if we can recognize a "muted" within a "dominant" discourse, a daughter's search for a mother/self within the wilderness quest for a father.

In conclusion, let me return to the questions with which I began. Some of these have been answered simply by reading *Surfacing* as "double-voiced discourse" that recovers the "muted" story of Demeter and Persephone embedded in the more obvious "dominant" narrative. But one important question remains: to what extent can this text (and others like it, from Joy Kogawa's *Obasan* to Angelica Garnett's autobiography, *Deceived with Kindness*) be identified as feminist? To explore this question fully requires another essay, one in which I would look at some rebirth journeys by men where the Demeter-Persephone cathexis seems central—in Henry James's *The Bostonians,* say, or Robert Kroetsch's *Badlands.*

Although this is not the occasion to embark on such an extended analysis, I would like to hazard a few suggestions. It seems to me that *Surfacing* does not rely upon the primarily spatial and linear narrative "thrust" of the typical male quest, as we find it in *The Odyssey, The Studhorse Man, Don Quixote,* or *Deliverance.* It seems closer in form and structure to what Todorov equates with Grail literature and identifies as vertical and embedded narratives. Its purpose is not to march "onward" (as Atwood's Circe complains of Odysseus, *Selected Poems,* p. 206), but to "unhide the hidden" (Kroetsch, "Unhiding the Hidden"), to unveil, reveal, unearth. While drawing on the conventional formula of the male quest through external space (as Kroetsch portrays it in *Badlands*), *Surfacing* more importantly sifts through layers of time, peeling off deceptions, obfuscations, and camouflage, and opening hitherto closed documents. In short, it creates a "double-voiced discourse" that uses both male and female heritage, models, codes, and narrative strategies: one is the dominant, familiar trek through space—here a conventional North American wilderness—to overcome certain obstacles and conclude some business; the other is a muted story, a journey into time and "wild space," into the self in order to reveal and name something hidden there. And while dominant and muted stories are maintained throughout, the muted story gains impetus and power until it carries the speaker into the very center of illumination from which she is reborn. It might also be possible to argue that *Surfacing*, unlike the texts by men mentioned above, displays a "poetics of silence" (Freeman), leaving what is unsayable unsaid, while at the same time revealing through often-surreal image, gradual accretion of symbolic material, and indirect action, an immanence, plenitude, and female power.

Finally, I would like to consider why Persephone is searching for Demeter and why Demeter should be the one who is lost. In answer, one could refer to the myth where Demeter does wander, as if lost, in search of Persephone, or the daughter's search could be explained by conflating her with an Eleusian worshipper in search of the Great Mother. It is also true that in life the older woman usually dies first, and it could be further argued that, in accord with patriarchal conventions, we all lose our mothers when we are "given" by one man to another in marriage. But then *Surfacing* is not a simple realist text, and in any case to speak of Demeter as lost may be overstating and distorting the situation.

Although *Surfacing* depicts a young woman who has lost her mother through separation and death and is shown setting forth on a physical and psychological journey to rediscover her, it could also be argued that the mother has called to her daughter, awakening in her a desire to know, to be reborn–through dreams, natural cycles, signs, and pain. The jacket, seeds, and scrapbook are *left* by the mother in *Surfacing* just where the daughter will find them.

If this is the case, then Rachel Blau DuPlessis may be right in thinking of the mother figure as a necessary muse to whom the narrator owes her rebirth and her narrative.[5] Or, to go back to my initial hypothesis, Demeter may be lost because from the onset of patriarchy women have lived primarily in terms of their fathers and Father. The fact that the reunion seems so painful and arduous testifies to the force of patriarchal prohibition (in, for example, St. Paul), and points to the reasons for Atwood's choice of Persephone's point of view.

For centuries in Western culture, women have experienced themselves as "other," as powerless, or if powerful, as evil. Access to Demetrian power is denied them; therefore, today it may be more consistent with the "authority of experience" to begin with the daughter, the passive, powerless one, and only gradually, tentatively approach the more awesome force of the repressed, prohibited and scarcely imaginable Mother (see Landy). Moreover, to the degree that our literary and popular cultures encourage women to "identify against themselves as women," it has not been easy to welcome a powerful Mother figure. The many novels by women with daughters fleeing detestable mothers—rather like the hapless heroines of many fairy tales—testify to this syndrome; Doris Lessing's Martha Quest is a prime example, but even Atwood has been described (mistakenly, I think) by Lorna Irvine as depicting monster mothers in *Lady Oracle* (see "A Psychological Journey"). Interestingly, Atwood has acknowledged and accepted the terrible Mother as part of the Mother Goddess figure, implicitly in *Surfacing* but explicitly in poems like "Red Shirt" from *Two-Headed Poems* or, more recently, in "Letter from Persephone" from *Interlunar,* where Persephone resents those mothers who want only sons.

Indeed, it seems to me that Atwood has overcome the evil influence of the medusa (another aspect of Demeter) by transforming her power to turn a person into stone into a source of comfort. For Atwood, the black stone is an avatar of the goddess. And instead of allowing it to remain silent, Atwood privileges the mother's story, voices her speech, and reverences her power. In "The Stone," the once-muted is dominant:

> Have you had enough happiness? she says.
> Have you seen
> enough pain? enough
> cruelty? Have you had enough
> of what there is? This
> is as far as it goes.
> Now are you ready for me?

And the daughter answers:

> Dark mother, whom I have carried with me
> for years, a stone in my pocket,
> [. . . . . . . . . . . . . . . . . . . . . . . .]
> I will never deny you
> or believe in you
> only. Go back into your stone
> for now. Wait for me. (*Interlunar,* p. 25)

*Notes*

1. The figure of Persephone has been of interest to Atwood from her early chapbook *Double Persephone* (1961), which I examine in *Violent Duality* (1980), to *Interlunar.* I have found Paul Friedrich's discussion of Demeter in chapter 7 of *The Meaning of Aphrodite* most helpful. In addition to stressing the misogynistic Christian attack on the rites of Demeter at Eleusis, Friedrich notes many interesting features of the myth such as its orphic significance, the relationship between Demeter and Medusa, and the separation between Demeter and Aphrodite. Also of interest, of course, are studies by Erich Neumann, Carl Kerenyi, C. G. Jung, R. G. Wasson et al., and Mircea Eliade.

2. The notion of a feminine "wild zone" as the opposite of the masculine wilderness is discussed by Showalter in "Feminist Criticism in the Wilderness" and is central to my understanding of *Surfacing.* Although I cannot stop to explore it in this paper, I would note that "wild" in this context signifies imaginary or unreal from the masculine point of view as well. As Showalter explains, women know the male "wilderness" through legend and myth, whereas men "do not know what is in the wild," because it is excluded from culture and consciousness, rendered invisible and silenced. The task for women and women writers, then, is to recognize and articulate the "wild zone," and this acknowledgment is often inscribed in "quest fictions" where the heroine "travels to the 'mother country' of liberated desire and female authenticity" (see Showalter, pp. 29–31).

3. In "A Psychological Journey: Mothers and Daughters in English-Canadian Fiction," Lorna Irvine slips into a number of distorting generalizations regarding the literature. For example, she appears to confuse the mother-daughter issue in *Surfacing* when she claims that the leather jacket represents the stultifying past (p. 250). But it is not the past or the mother that damage the narrator; it is the narrator's attitudes (predominantly rationalist, like her father's) that stand in her way. What the narrator says is, "Leather smell, the smell of loss; irrecoverable" (p. 186), thus signifying the devastating nature of her motherless condition. Although Irvine chooses novels that appear to illustrate a daughter's struggle to be free of the mother (novels like *Lady Oracle, A Jest of God,* and *Lives of Girls and Women*), she does recognize that Canadian daughters do more than reject; they try to incorporate their mothers, and the past, in their present lives. And on this point Irvine is right. In a later article, "One Woman Leads to Another," Irvine correctly notes that in *Two-Headed Poems* Atwood moves conspicuously from angry attack on male gods to celebration of female gods. This trend is expanded and refined in *True Stories* (1981) and *Interlunar* (1984) and to some extent in *Bodily Harm* (1981), the stories in *Bluebeard's Egg* (1983), and *The Handmaid's Tale* (1985). In his recent study *Margaret Atwood: A Feminist Poetics,* Frank Davey seriously misreads Atwood's system in his effort to explain her "discourse" and its apparent rationalist bias. For Davey, femaleness is wordless chaos;

hence, the clarity, precision and, at times, abstractness of Atwood's language unsettles him.

4. The concept of liminality is discussed by Victor Turner in *The Ritual Process: Structure and Anti-Structure,* but Friedrich adapts and reapplies it to explain both Aphrodite and Demeter-Persephone as occupying "intermediary" positions that override "two categories that are opposed in the cultural system" (p. 147).

5. According to DuPlessis, "The daughter artist and the blocked, usually maternal, parent are . . . the central characters of twentieth-century women's *Künstlerromane.* The maternal or parental muse and the reparenting motifs are strategies that erode, transpose, and reject narratives of heterosexual love and romantic thralldom" (*Writing Beyond the Ending,* p. 94). In her self-styled autobiography, *Deceived with Kindness: A Bloomsbury Childhood* (1984), Angelica Garnett—daughter of Vanessa (Stephen) Bell and Duncan Grant, and niece of Virginia Woolf—describes and exorcises her "own ghosts." Chief among these "ghosts" is the silent, lost, yet still powerful Vanessa, the mother whose "image and personality had always obsessed me." Garnett's autobiography is, in fact, an attempt at biography; in telling her own story, she must tell her mother's (which includes identifying her father), and the act of telling is an arduous reconstruction, recovery, and recreation, as painful as birth itself. What intrigues me about this mother-daughter story is its structural and symbolic similarity with the central concerns of this paper and the implication that, whether as artist (the role DuPlessis privileges) or more generally as woman writer, *her*story has a narrative shape of its own. For another approach to this type of fiction see Patricia Merivale, "The Search for the Other Woman: Joan Didion and the Female Artist Parable." Merivale notes various mythic elements in the search for the other women—Orpheus motifs, Demeter and Persephone bondings (especially in Didion's *A Book of Common Prayer*), and Procne and Philomela paradigms.

# 5 *The Transforming Eye*

## Lady Oracle *and Gothic Tradition*

*Ann McMillan*

Gothic fantasy has for centuries romanticized the victimization of women. The typical paperback cover or book jacket of the modern Gothic novel shows "a terrified woman, clad in a long, swirling robe, who [is] fleeing from a darkened mansion lit only by a glow in an upper window" (Radway, "Utopian Impulse," p. 144). From such an illustration, one can "read" the story: the chaste young heroine; the mysterious house embodying vague dangers; the villain and hero, whose identities are confused until the penultimate moment. One can read, too, the inevitable happy ending: the mansion, purged of its threat, blazes with candles; the heroine takes her place beside the hero as its rightful mistress; the villain, unmasked, has been rendered harmless.

The victimization of the heroine serves a necessary function in the formulaic plot of Gothic fantasy. Although the heroine typically shows independence and courage, the pattern allows her to do very little for herself. As Janice Radway's study shows, "the heroine's stubborn refusal to be cautioned or aided by others places her in extreme danger. When she . . . is about to succumb, the hero conveniently arrives" (Radway, "Utopian Impulse," p. 159). The actions of the heroine in her own behalf only create the need for a savior.

In order to obtain her happy ending, the heroine must be able to bring both villain and hero out of the shadows, to distinguish between them. She does not simply recognize a hero, however; creation and recognition are simultaneous processes. Her need for salvation, her vulnerability, evokes heroic qualities in the man who rushes to her defense and thus becomes the hero. Her need and his response, in turn, enable her to recognize the man who comes to her aid as the hero (Radway, "Utopian Impulse"; *Reading Romance*).

Because perception and transformation take place together, this process may be called the "transforming eye." The author of the first true Gothic romances, Ann Radcliffe, uses the phrase in *The Mysteries of Udolpho* (1794) to denote the Romantic sense of human or superhuman meaning in nature (p. 15). She adapts this same power—neither truly visionary nor quite deceptive—to create her heroine's perception of Gothic horror. As I use it here, the phrase refers to the Gothic heroine's ability to "decode the erratic gestures" (Snitow, pp. 247–48) of a potential hero and mold him into heroic form. The transforming eye works outside the heroine's conscious awareness; her initial reaction to the not-yet-hero typically combines dislike and attraction. When, later, she becomes aware of his heroic qualities and admits her love for him, he is a hero because she has made him one. The transforming eye also works to create or exaggerate terrifying situations, in order to make it necessary for the heroine to be saved.

The Gothic tradition has two main branches. One branch, Gothic fantasy, employs the transforming eye as sketched above to procure a happy ending. In the second—less-known but well-established—tradition, Gothic naturalism, the heroine is acted upon by external societal forces she can neither understand nor control (Thrall, Hibbard, and Holman, p. 303). Works of Gothic naturalism inevitably end with the heroine's madness or death.

Margaret Atwood's *Lady Oracle*[1] relies explicitly on Gothic traditions; its heroine, Joan Foster, is a writer of Gothic romances who follows their promises of romantic escape in her own life. Yet the myth of woman as innocent victim carries a dangerous appeal for many of Atwood's heroines who are not explicitly linked with the Gothic. They, like Joan Foster, must begin their awakening to maturity by rejecting the notion that their passivity is innocence. Women's victimization and men's exploitation propel one other, as Atwood demonstrates repeatedly in her novels.

Nevertheless, the transforming eye is not merely an instrument of patriarchy. *Lady Oracle,* together with Jane Austen's *Northanger Abbey,* belongs to a third category, "mixed Gothic." In these novels, the transforming eye represents a transitional stage in the moral awareness of the heroines, who begin by naïvely modeling themselves on heroines of Gothic fantasy and, in so doing, narrowly miss the dismal fates allotted to heroines of Gothic naturalism. Austen and Atwood refuse the simpler resolutions of both Gothic traditions; for them, the transforming eye is neither malevolent nor benevolent but provides their heroines with opportunities for maturation and insight.

## I
## Chastity and the Transforming Eye

Janice Radway's study of Gothic novels written in the United States in the 1960s and 1970s details the inevitable process by which the heroine secures the help of a hero through chastity. First she feels a combined attraction and repulsion to the not-yet-hero; then the "special qualities shared by the heroine and [hero] . . . stand out as valuable" in contrast to other characters. Further, "the female foil . . . emphasizes the heroine's innocence and reserve because her passionate sexuality is . . . linked [to] her distasteful ambition, greed, ruthlessness, and vanity" ("Utopian Impulse," p. 149). The heroine's chastity also contrasts with the sexual experience of the hero and redeems him from a life of promiscuity or jaded abstinence (Radway, "Utopian Impulse," p. 149; *Reading Romance,* p. 126). Because he sees her as unique for this and other qualities, he responds to her need when "Gothic" dangers threaten. In the process, he is "converted," "made over," "transformed"—into a hero.

Traditionally, chastity (virginity or chaste married love) was "a woman's only virtue" (St. Jerome) and her exercise of it her only action. This sentiment was expressed by countless classical and medieval writers, often through images of enclosure: a fountain sealed up, an enclosed garden, a walled city, a jewel kept hidden. By the fifteenth century, at least one poet—perhaps a woman—had seen this emblematic enclosure as a maze. *The Assembly of Ladies* opens with its narrator and four other women walking in a maze:

> Some went inward and thought that they were going out; some stood in the center and looked around them; some were at first far behind and then all at once had caught up with the leaders; others were so confused that all paths seemed alike to them. . . . Thus they pressed forth and had

little rest; and some were so assailed with desire that for very wrath they stepped over the rails. (Pearsall, p. 105; my translation)[2]

Enclosure and the chastity it represents have long remained the ideal for women; in *The Handmaid's Tale,* for example, Atwood portrays a society in which the symbolic "maze" of constraints upon women's sexuality is made concrete and absolute. We recognize in this fictional society the facts of our culture's past as well as a warning of its present and future.

The "idea that it is at once absolutely necessary and extraordinarily difficult to keep a young woman in the home" (McNall, p. 3) permeates much popular fiction aimed at a female readership. The phrase "in the home" here is interchangeable with the words "virginal" and "chaste." Being "chaste" and being "in the home" are thought of as necessary protections for women. They can do nothing, however, to prevent violation by anyone unscrupulous enough to ignore these socially recognized boundaries. Thus, by giving women chastity as their protection, patriarchal society gives women a weapon effective only against those whom social constraints can bind.

One can imagine how this paradoxical situation came about. If a society places crucial value on a woman's chastity, it cannot risk letting her out of the house even to learn how to protect herself and make mature decisions in the world. The primacy of virginal or chaste reputation has served as an argument even against women's being educated to know good from evil. Being in the house—remaining chaste—must therefore act as its own defense. To prevent a woman from learning to defend herself or to recognize a threat is inexcusable otherwise. Chastity "protects" women by appealing to another cultural ideal—the chivalry of men. The transforming eye is Gothic fantasy's particular elaboration of this belief.

How could women's rebellion against enclosure and ignorance be expressed in literature without being encouraged in life? Horace Walpole unwittingly turned up an answer, which Ann Radcliffe and others made into a formula: the house is haunted. The house (castle, ruined abbey, maze) becomes a threat to be recognized and overcome. As Norman Holland and Leona Sherman point out, the Gothic castle "delineates a physical space that will accept many different projections of unconscious material," including—they cite Sade—"shame, agony, annihilation, . . . [and] desire" (p. 219). Women may project their fears of entrapment and violation into chamber doors that cannot be fastened from the inside, rooms in which other women may be imprisoned or dead, secluded passages from which vague threats materialize. Readers of Gothic romances thus experience, without risk, both desire for and fear of penetration, as their heroines overcome challenges without leaving the house (Moers, p. 191; see also Atwood, *Lady Oracle,* p. 146).

Gothic fantasy maintains, in general, a conservative relationship to social norms, advocating "submission to traditional gender arrangements," including female chastity, and "assumption of a typically female personality structure" (Radway, "Utopian Impulse," p. 155). Such fantasy excites fears of self-loss and violation; it then placates them, allowing readers to enjoy tantalizing yet fearful pleasures and to share in the heroine's rewarded virtue. Both Gothics and Harlequin romances, Ann Snitow says, "pretend that nothing has happened to unsettle the old conventional bargain between the sexes" (Snitow, p. 253). Gothic naturalism, however, shows that the bargain—remain powerless, and you'll be taken care of—has long failed to protect women. Its heroines also live in danger, not from exotic villains or supernatural powers but from forces in society and in themselves.

## II
## Gothic Fantasy

The transforming eye that reveals a mysterious communion between future lovers is a staple of romantic fiction. Its particular role in the Gothic, however, results partly from Mrs. Radcliffe's practicality. Unlike Walpole and "Monk" Lewis, Radcliffe never lets loose genuinely extrarational forces in *The Mysteries of Udolpho.* The supernatural occurrences and unnaturally horrid crimes witnessed by its heroine, Emily, turn out to be misperceptions of fairly commonplace horrors. Emily fears that her aunt has been murdered by her husband, when she is only ill from his mistreatment. Emily recoils from the undisclosed horror in the usually locked room; much later, we learn that she has mistaken a wax effigy for an actual worm-eaten corpse. The transforming eye functions correctly in warning her of evil, but what she "sees" is invariably worse than reality. Although the horrors are later explained away, they have worked their charm: "a terror of this nature, as it occupies and expands the mind, and elevates it to high expectation, is purely sublime, and leads us, by a kind of fascination, to seek even the object, from which we appear to shrink" (Radcliffe, p. 248).

The attractive power of fear and danger also makes the villain of *Udolpho,* Montoni, a far more vivid and sexually charged figure than its colorless hero, Valancourt. Radcliffe prudishly deflects Montoni's sexual threat: rather than attacking Emily himself, Montoni tries to sell her in marriage to Morano, whose similar name and relatively bland character suggest that he is a mere stand-in. Patricia Meyer Spacks describes Montoni as "the cruel stepfather, who marries the aunt but lusts for the girl (he claims to want her money) . . ." (p. 143). Emily first sees Montoni as "a man of about forty, of an uncommonly handsome person, with features manly and expressive, but whose countenance exhibited . . . more of the haughtiness of command, and the quickness of discernment, than of any other character" (Radcliffe, p. 23). Significantly, Emily and Montoni engage in those verbal battles that characterize later scenes between Gothic heroines and their wooers/tormenters. He storms; she resists and earns his grudging admiration. Because they are well-matched as adversaries, Emily and Montoni seem—though they never become—well-matched as lovers. Later readers were not fooled by Radcliffe's suppression of the sexual tension in their scenes together. Edward Fairfax Rochester and all the "thin-lipped and rapacious" (Atwood, *Lady Oracle,* p. 29) hero-villains to follow come from Montoni's mold. In *Lady Oracle,* for example, Joan endows each of her men in turn with the threatening appeal, or appealing threat, of Montoni.

Although Montoni is powerful and unscrupulous, Emily repeatedly eludes and finally escapes him. By remaining chaste, and yet refusing to act in her own behalf, Emily maintains an almost supernatural moral advantage. This superiority keeps her intact against Montoni's disguised sexual assaults. The efficacy of woman's innocent victimhood permeates Gothic fantasy. The balance of power shifts, and the villains begin their transformation into heroes at the hands of innocent, victimized femininity.

*Jane Eyre,* first printed in 1847, has a much more memorable heroine than *Udolpho*'s Emily. Jane Eyre's transforming eye perceives spiritual realities of danger and salvation that are not entirely dispelled by rational explanation. Jane's powerlessness also acts more forcefully in her behalf. Emily merely keeps Montoni at bay; Jane turns a near-Montoni into an adoring lover and completing alter ego. Jane first experiences her gift of imaginative insight when, at the age of ten, she suffers terror and a fainting fit in the red room. The moving light seen then later becomes a force for good, a presiding moon-goddess/mother. This force leads her away from Rochester at a time when their union would have destroyed her. It later leads her back when Rochester, cleansed by suffering, can share with her in an ideal union. As Sandra Gilbert and Susan Gubar demonstrate, the madwoman in the attic also acts to prevent and then to bring about the marriage. When Jane's entrapment in the role of governess or of bride disturb her peace of mind, the madwoman acts out her fears (Gilbert and Gubar, pp. 336–71, esp. p. 360). The madwoman represents the more terrifying aspects of Jane's transforming eye, placed outside her but still working for her good.

Brontë increases Jane's power manyfold by combining the villainous Montoni and romantic Valancourt in the more complex hero-villain Rochester. Later writers of Gothic fantasy follow Brontë's lead. Although their heroes may be falsely blamed for the deeds of their villains, the writers promote the mistake by making their heroes appear callous or even vicious until transformed by their heroines.

## III
## Gothic Naturalism

Wish fulfillment is the popular Gothic fantasy's stock-in-trade. A far different experience informs works of Gothic naturalism, in which the sterility and futility of women's lives drive them to escape into imagined worlds. For example, the heroine of Mary Wollstonecraft's *Maria* (published in 1798) escapes into romantic love. And *The Yellow Wallpaper* (1899), by Charlotte Perkins Gilman, narrates the mental disintegration of a sheltered wife left with nothing to do but turn her transforming eye upon the pattern in her wallpaper. Jean Rhys, in *Wide Sargasso Sea* (1966), tells the events leading up to *Jane Eyre* from the point of view of the first Mrs. Rochester, who falls in love with her stranger-husband, but whose passion evokes only fear in him. Despairing, unsure whether to blame him or herself, she falls deeper and deeper into madness. These heroines, by entering their various dream worlds, render real escape from confining circumstances impossible. They may rightly blame social convention for their circumstances, but they fail to recognize that their own perceptual and imaginative faculties also rely upon conventional notions of what women should be.

Mary Wollstonecraft deliberately wrote her didactic message about women's plight in the Gothic form although she despised it. She seems to have felt that by doing so she could reach the very women most reluctant to hear her message. She introduces her heroine as the inmate of a madhouse, and mocks such writers as Radcliffe, for whose heroines these horrors are imaginary. Wollstonecraft describes the inmates' "groans and shrieks" as "no unsubstantial sounds of whistling winds, or startled birds, modulated by a romantic fancy, which amuse while they affright; but such tones of misery as carry a dreadful certainty directly to the heart" (p. 23).

As we learn her story, we find that Maria has escaped from an uncaring childhood home into a worse marriage. Her husband has taken her money and attempted to sell his sexual rights over her to another man. She resists and tries to flee with their child but is caught and committed to the asylum, the child taken from her. A subplot reveals the plight of Jemima, a working-class victim of forced seduction who has become a keeper in the madhouse. Clearly, the ideal of chaste powerlessness has not saved these women. Their attempts to invoke women's right to protection have only led to sterner measures by their oppressors.

Wollstonecraft did not live to finish *Maria* (she died in 1797), but fragments make her general purpose clear. Her heroine, all but destroyed by her experiences, has a worse one yet in store. While in the madhouse, she meets and falls in love with the seemingly heroic Darnford. He shows her tenderness and consideration; her transforming eye does the rest: "what chance . . . had Maria of escaping [love], when pity, sorrow, and solitude all conspired to soften her mind, and nourish romantic wishes, and, from a natural progress, romantic expectations?" (p. 48). Her imagination "combined all the qualities of a hero's mind, and fate presented a statue in which she might enshrine them" (p. 49).

After they escape from the madhouse, Maria attempts to make her love for Darnford her whole world. Unknown to her, this passion forms her only inescapable prison: she depends upon him to give meaning to her life. He is fond of her for a time, but nothing more, and finally deserts her. Wollstonecraft makes Darnford not a calculating seducer but a well-meaning, though weak, human being. He is no more to blame for Maria's fate than the statue to which Wollstonecraft compares him. Because Maria has cast him as her savior, however, his loss of interest leads her to despair. One planned ending of the book shows Maria committing suicide.

*Maria* exposes the ideal of chastity as unable to protect women—as, rather, an instrument of their oppression. Maria's husband invokes it as a source of legal power over her, although he is openly unfaithful to her. Again and again, Maria meets men and women who condemn her as unchaste and illicit simply because she wants to leave this fiend of a husband. Yet Maria constrains herself by her own formulation of the ideal of chastity. Her love for Darnford must be complete, unreserved; any withholding or protection of self would seem to her "unchaste."

Wollstonecraft prefigures Atwood in her acute awareness that a woman becomes a heroine by giving up power, by refusing to act in her own behalf. Both show that this ideal of innocent victimhood is self-destructive: if total reliance upon a man fails to turn him into a hero, it turns him into a villain by default.

## IV
## Mixed Gothic: *Northanger Abbey* and *Lady Oracle*

*Northanger Abbey* (published in 1818) and *Lady Oracle* both combine aspects of Gothic fantasy and Gothic naturalism. Sherrill Grace quotes Atwood as using the term "anti-Gothic . . . for her third novel which she links to the treatment of Gothic in Jane Austen's *Northanger Abbey*" (*Violent Duality,* p. 111). Grace contrasts the two novels in terms of their narrators. Atwood's Joan Foster, relatively untrustworthy, tells her own story, leaving us in some doubt as to how seriously we should take any of it. By contrast, "Jane Austen's narrator never leaves us in any doubt as to her, and our, ironic distance from the naive Catherine [Morland]. We are invited to laugh, with the narrator, at Catherine's foolish confusions of Gothicism and real life" (*Violent Duality,* p. 124; see also Clara Thomas). While Grace's view is thoughtful, it oversimplifies the novels' treatments of Gothic themes, especially the transforming eye. In both novels, the heroines misapply the simple good-or-evil distinctions of Gothic fantasy in situations calling for more complex responses. Yet both novels also use the transforming eye, with its simple distinctions between hero and villain, as a significant part in the process of their heroines' maturations.

Undeniably, Catherine Morland of *Northanger Abbey* errs in many perceptions, especially in believing that General Tilney has killed his wife. Yet, after all, she is right to recoil from him. General Tilney's true villainy resembles that of Montoni: both wish to increase their wealth and power by arranging lucrative marriages for the young people in their charge. Catherine's initial naïvete prevents her from recognizing base motives in those around her, and she comes to see that her imputation of Gothic evil to General Tilney is foolish. However, her moments of Gothic fear enable her to move beyond her naïve vision of the world as black and white—the black relegated to fictional villains, the white to anyone she has met. She comes to a recognition of mixed virtue and vice in the best and worst of those around her. Catherine has in a sense repeated the mistakes of Radcliffe's Emily in seeing reality as worse than it is, but Catherine learns from her misperceptions. As Patricia Meyer Spacks says, Catherine, "having used her derivative fantasies to express hostility and rebellious impulse . . . surmounts her need for them" (p. 163).

Austen briefly but clearly states the importance of what Catherine has learned to her increased sense of moral complexity:

> Among the English . . . there was a general though unequal mixture of good and bad. Upon this conviction, she would not be surprized [*sic*] if even in Henry and Eleanor Tilney, some slight imperfection might hereafter appear; and upon this conviction she need not fear to acknowledge some actual specks in the character of their father, who, though cleared from the grossly injurious suspicions which she must ever blush to have entertained, she did believe, upon serious consideration, to be not perfectly amiable. (p. 202)

*Lady Oracle*'s heroine, Joan Foster, like Catherine Morland, learns from her transforming eye only after it has led her into serious mistakes. For Joan, the mistakes are much more serious. Like Wollstonecraft's Maria and other heroines of Gothic naturalism, she fabricates prisons of romantic self-deception. In discussing Joan Foster, Grace aptly quotes Margaret Atwood's description of heroines who "have become their own prisons" (*Violent Duality,* p. 5). With each man, Joan follows her transforming eye toward the happy ending it envisions ahead. She can never reach it, never complete the recognition-transformation process, because her world is not the world of Gothic fantasy.

Each of the men important to Joan seems first hero, then villain. She envisions them sometimes as double-natured (p. 325), sometimes as many-natured in a sequence (p. 236), sometimes as masked—good by evil, evil by good (p. 300). She flees from a lonely and banal existence into the arms of Paul, her first lover. Her life with him turns out to be hardly less lonely and even more banal. Her growing uneasiness with him necessitates her casting of Arthur in the role of hero. From Arthur she escapes to the Royal Porcupine, whose eccentric appearance promises material for heroic transformation. To her horror, though, she transforms him backwards, into the antiheroic Chuck Brewer. Clean-shaven and T-shirted, Chuck is too much reality for Joan, who flees back to Arthur. When mysterious incidents make her fear that her life is in danger, she plans the ultimate escape by faking her own death.

Atwood's first-person, past-tense narration shows Joan reflecting upon her experiences, recalling that "every man I'd been involved with . . . had two selves" (p. 325). She suspects them all of deliberately hiding one under the other in order to trap her, but the "two selves" are actually projections of her transforming eye. Like most oracles, the contradictory messages she receives from her transforming eye elude helpful interpretation. Her attempts to decipher and act upon them enmesh her, as similar attempts enmeshed Oedipus, even more deeply in danger. Since Joan, following the Gothic pattern, believes that she can only escape by finding a hero-rescuer, her attempts leave her increasingly dependent upon the next man. The Gothic novels Joan writes endorse the view that women, who cannot protect themselves, must be able to recognize and secure the devotion of men who can protect them. Although Joan does not share her Gothic heroines' literal chastity, she models her role as an innocent victim on theirs, and she, too, looks for a man to be made into her savior.

Joan Foster needs a change of perception in order to move beyond passivity and self-imposed victimization. Like a heroine of Gothic fantasy, her fears make her dependent upon a hero. Unlike the fantasy heroine who faces actual danger, Joan's fears stem not so much from external threats as from within herself. On her escapes into love Joan carries with her a heavy load of guilt, shame, and deception regarding her past and her "real self." Her need to see men as heroes, to escape into them, results from her desire to escape the unglamorous facts about herself. Her desire for one or another man is heightened by her fear that he will learn the truth about her. The transforming eye creates fear that, at first, incites her to escape, enhances her desire for the men she thinks will make her a heroine. Her transforming eye does not let her rest there, however. Each escape involves a further "sacrifice of complexity" (Rosowski, p. 92), since it forces Joan to deny aspects of herself not acceptable in a heroine. These denials create "ghosts," terrors resembling those of Gothic fantasy, but these ghosts are suppressed selves that return to haunt her: "I wanted to forget the past, but it refused to forget me; it waited for sleep, then cornered me" (p. 239).

Paradoxically, modeling herself on the innocent, passive heroines of Gothic fantasy leaves Joan more and more haunted by guilt. Her habit of deception can be seen as a form of self-destruction, making "confusion and fear" (Rosowski, p. 95) increase until they become intolerable. Finally, Joan must either destroy her selves completely (as she has tried and failed to do) or enter the maze and face the ghosts she herself has created.

The scene in which Felicia, the "female foil" of Joan's Gothic novel, enters the maze dramatizes Joan's "confusion and fear." Half fearful, half fascinated, Joan imagines her simplified projection Felicia being drawn into the maze. The path closes behind her, and she is trapped with Joan's other alter egos. When she asks the way back, one Joan-self replies, " 'We have all tried to go back. That was our mistake.' " The way in which Joan's simplified, partial selves have entered the maze prevents them from getting out without further destruction. These selves are caught because her way of escape, time after time, is to tell another lie, "kill" another self, enter another maze—another man. The mysterious door they point to as the "only way out" of the maze opens to reveal Redmond, the Gothic hero-villain, then a series of other hero-villains: Joan's father, Paul, the Royal Porcupine, the man with icicle teeth, Arthur, then Redmond again. When Joan/Felicia refuses to enter the door, saying " 'I know who you are,' " the figure turns into a skeleton reaching for her throat (p. 377).

Although Joan does not share the literal chastity of her Gothic heroines, she believes in its passive power. Her "chastity" resembles Maria's. Both try to give themselves a form of chastity—sexual wholeness—by giving themselves wholeheartedly to one man. When the attempt fails for Maria, she commits suicide. When it fails for Joan, she tries again, with yet another escape into yet another man. Her transforming eye recasts as a villain each man who fails to be her rescuer, while creating for her another rescuer in the wings. This frenzied flight from one transformation, one escape route, to the next forms both the entrapping maze and the destructive "way back." Rather than attempting to save herself by creating and entering another maze, Joan must break free of the pattern of mazemaking.

Freeing herself from the transforming eye does not come about through a simple process of facing reality. Margaret Atwood makes clear that "reality" and perception cannot be fully disentangled (Grace, *Violent Duality,* pp. 2–3). Her novels show again and again that one does not break out of a destructive pattern by applying reason. Her heroines typically follow a downward spiral, falling deeper and deeper into their private visions.

Joan Foster, the narrator of *Surfacing,* Marian in *The Edible Woman,* and Rennie in *Bodily Harm* have all been, in some sense, victimized by men. Their recognition of this fact is a first step in recovery; they must regain enough feeling to know that they hurt. All lose themselves for a time in complete identification with victims: plundered nature, slaughtered animals, exploited peoples, and above all, victimized women. The enemy appears clearly defined: "Americans," prison guards, and, above all, men. Yet soon this clarity is obscured by recognition of complicity. There can be no villains without victims.

Paradoxically, in the process of discovering their own guilt, Atwood's heroines gain a new strength. Simply stated, that strength comes from having glimpsed the responsibility of interrelatedness. Seeing their own victimization as fueling a system of exploitation frees Atwood's heroines from their paralyzing need to remain innocent. In each case, too, they have gone as far as they can in making themselves victims. Cornered, physically and spiritually, they must succumb to their own destruction and, by extension, to the pattern of destruction. Or they must refuse to do so. Having seen the pattern for what it is, they can no longer remain innocent by remaining passive; they must fight (see Christ, p. 44).

*Lady Oracle* casts this same movement in the "mixed Gothic" tradition. Joan's romantic and sexual response to men is prefigured—some would say formed—by her early experience of her father and of the exhibitionist "daffodil man," who may or may not have rescued her from a schoolgirl prank. Of the latter, she asks herself whether he was "a rescuer or a villain . . . or . . . both at once?" (p. 67) This romantic/sexual response is mirrored in that of her Gothic heroines. Like them, Joan is drawn to men who offer both the appeal of danger and the promise of security. Because these qualities are intangible and subjective, she relies upon her transforming eye, but its transformations become more frustrating than satisfying. Joan enters the maze, where all her hero-villains in turn appear to offer her an escape that conceals destruction. Her Gothic fantasies have deluded her, just as Catherine Morland's did. She has not been able to see the consequences of her refusal to take responsibility for her own life; instead, she has seen men on whom to project both hope and blame.

Also like Austen's Catherine, though, Joan learns from her transforming eye. When carried to its extreme, her identification with Gothic victims empowers her to free herself from this pattern, represented by the maze. Gothic fears, unrealistic as they may be, keep her from resting comfortably in her state of self-deception and irresponsibility. When she can no longer tolerate being haunted by selves she has denied, she can begin to face them directly. Atwood uses the ghosts created by the transforming eye to carry a "potential for morality" (Rosowski, p. 95). The guilt created by deception and duplicity becomes the motivating force for her acceptance of responsibility.

Joan is distracted from her fantasy of the maze by the sound of "real footsteps" and prepares "to face the man who stood waiting for me, for my life." She says, "I knew who it would be." Though she realizes the footsteps are real, she is still following the transforming eye in its visions of Gothic horror. Her eye tells her who "he" is and what he intends, but it is mistaken. Her next words make that clear: "I didn't really mean to hit him with the Cinzano bottle. I mean, I meant to hit someone, but it wasn't personal. I guess I just got carried away: he looked like someone else" (p. 377). The fact that she has actually injured a complete stranger because, to her transforming eye, he "looked like someone else" at last frees Joan from her self-created maze.

It is no coincidence that Joan has broken out of the maze by acting like one of her own Gothic heroines, who often defend their virtue in similar ways. We see them fend off attackers with such weapons as a hatpin and Boswell's *Life of Johnson.* Joan's weapon, a bottle, recalls these humorously ineffectual ones. On one level, Joan is again acting out one of her own plots. Yet crucial differences suggest that this act also represents something new and potentially freeing. First of all, her heroines are not really defending themselves with hatpins and heavy books. No real attackers are deterred by such means. The heroines are in the process of converting these men to heroes, and what really saves them is their old standby, chaste helplessness. " 'I beg you to remember, sir,' " says Joan's heroine Charlotte, " 'that I am alone and unprotected under your roof. Remember your duty!' " True to heroic form, "Redmond looked at her with a new respect . . ." (p. 143). Joan acts out of identification with her chaste heroines. Unlike them, however, she makes no speeches and wields her bottle powerfully enough to do real damage. In so doing, she crosses the line between habitual victim and potential destroyer. Moreover, as Clara Thomas points out, she "can . . . recognize and act in her own area of choice," and "she chooses the future . . ." (Clara Thomas, p. 172).

Like Atwood's other heroines, Joan strikes out for herself and for all those other victims, other selves: Aunt Lou, the symbolic "fat lady," the pallid heroines, and Felicia. In actually doing harm, Joan moves from the passive guilt of lying and concealment to the active responsibility of facing what she has done. Her genuinely harmful act of anger and rebellion is potentially healthier than her heroines' manipulative adherence to the code. Perhaps she realizes that if she can be both innocent and destructive, so can the men she has reduced to one or the other category. Moreover, what her transforming eye has been revealing to her indirectly turns out to be true. It has been right in presenting the different faces of each man, leaving no one man a hero. No human being is entirely a hero or a villain. No man is; neither is she. For her, honesty and maturity will be possible only when she is free to respond to a person or situation in all its complexity and without suppressing one or more selves. Like Catherine, she has learned to face a mistake and to forgive herself. Joan has, in the last lines of the novel, gained at least some self-knowledge and self-acceptance. The man she hit, she says, is

> the only person who knows anything about me. Maybe because I've never hit anyone else with a bottle, so they never got to see that part of me. Neither did I, come to think of it.
>
> It did make a mess; but then, I don't think I'll ever be a very tidy person. (p. 380)

At the end of the novel, Joan seems to stand clear of the maze at last. She may, however, create another maze for herself, if she lets her transforming eye cast yet another man as her savior. Her remark about the reporter she hit with the bottle—"there is something about a man in a bandage" (p. 379)—leaves this danger open. Her self-revelation may contain a good deal of deception and even self-deception: "I didn't tell any lies. Well, not very many. Some of the names and a few other things, but nothing major." Sherrill Grace points out that, because Joan is so untrustworthy a narrator, the whole story may be a fabrication (*Violent Duality,* p. 124). But if Joan has fabricated the story, at least she has made up for herself neither an unrealistic happy ending nor a dramatic tragic one, but an ending which is ambiguous yet hopeful. We cannot rule out any possibility, and this openness is one of the novel's greatest strengths. Any attempt at a resolution, good or bad, would put us back in the realm of the Gothic novel in its fantastic or naturalistic mode.

At the end, however, we can see better possibilities for Joan than the pattern of escape attempts. Even her thought of going on to write science fiction instead of Gothics can appear hopeful. "The future doesn't appeal to me as much as the past," she says, "but I'm sure it's better for you" (p. 379). In writing Gothic fantasy, Joan has shared the guilt of those writers who assure women that conventional female virtue will receive tangible rewards. She has helped to keep the house haunted with romantic fears, distracting those trapped in it from seeing any way out save through a hero. Although writing about the future may represent another form of escape, it would at least allow her to create alternatives to the ideal of victimization. Without victims—to paraphrase Hélène Cixous—patriarchy's "little circus no longer runs" (see Gallop, p. 133).

## *Notes*

1. Page references in the text are to *Lady Oracle* (New York: Avon, 1976).
2. *Corage,* translated here as "desire," may also mean "courage" or "boldness." For discussion, see McMillan, pp. 27–42.

# 6 Life Before Man

## *"Can Anything Be Saved?"*

*Gayle Greene*

All she wants is for both of them to be different. Not very different, a little would do it. Same molecules, different arrangement. All she wants is a miracle, because anything else is hopeless.

Atwood
*Life Before Man*

Margaret Atwood describes *Life Before Man*[1] in somewhat dispiriting terms as a "mainline social novel" and as such of "limited appeal" to her: "It takes place in the actual middle of a middling city, in the middle class, in the middle of their lives, and everything about it is right in the middle, and it's very claustrophobic" (Schreiber, p. 209). Many readers have responded to the novel with a lack of enthusiasm like Atwood's own. Sherrill Grace calls it "Atwood's first attempt at social and domestic realism" and sees the characters as "devoid of drama or interest" in inner as well as outer lives: "Their responses to life, their indecisiveness and triviality, envelop them like a gray blanket. . . . And seen against the claustrophobia of Toronto and the Royal Ontario Museum, these lives mirror the monotony and emptiness surrounding them." Grace describes Atwood's subject—the "vacuity of private and public contemporary life, the empty inconclusiveness of modern marriage and urban existence"—as "more tedious than terrifying"; and she uses the same terms Atwood does to characterize the novel, "claustrophobic" and "gray," associating these qualities (as Atwood does) with "realist" fiction (*Violent Duality,* pp. 135–37).

Faced with these responses to a novel I find so powerful and haunting, I am reminded of the observation by one of the novel's major characters that "one woman's demon lover is another's worn-out shoe" (p. 213).[2] Furthermore, even though *Life Before Man* has certain qualities of social realism—its social setting is tangibly rendered, its characters are precisely delineated in relation to their environments, and "nobody reappears from the dead," as Atwood says (Schreiber, p. 209)—in other respects it has more affinities with modernist than with realist fiction: the structure problematizes time and reality; events are filtered through three consciousnesses in a way that draws attention to problems of interpretation; and Atwood's lyrically and imagistically textured style draws attention to itself rather than offering a transparent medium on a knowable reality.

Externally, nothing much happens. We begin at one point in time, Friday, 29 October 1976, and end at a later point in time, Friday, 18 August 1978. The novel is structured as a series of short sections, each precisely dated, each describing an event or experience, actual or emotional, that occupies a discrete "chunk of time" (p. 308). The sections cover several days over a period of nearly two years; except for two flashbacks, they proceed chronologically. Each section is told from the point of view of one of the main characters, Elizabeth, Nate, and Lesje; each section begins with a precise delineation of the posture or activity of the character whose perspective we're in—for example, "Elizabeth sits," "Nate is running." Since these actions and postures are characteristic—we encounter them again and again—the sense is one of stasis.

The action is unremarkable and unmarked by "events" that provide the customary framework of narrative. As Lesje reflects when she returns home for Christmas and finds herself unable to tell her parents that she's moved out of William's because she never told them she moved in, "Marriage is an event, a fact, it can be discussed at the dinner table. So is divorce. They create a framework, a beginning, an ending. Without them everything is amorphous, an endless middle ground, stretching like a prairie on either side of each day." Though Lesje herself has "moved herself physically from one place to another [she] has no clear sense of anything having ended or of anything else having begun" (p. 192). The one big event, Chris's suicide, has occurred before the novel begins; and it is an "event"—this is Lesje's term for it (p. 293)—that not only compels attention, but raises the ultimate question of existence. The present action, however, occupies an "amorphous middle ground" where nothing much happens—"everything right in the middle," as Atwood says. There are no marriages or divorces, and though relationships dissolve and re-form, change occurs imperceptibly, with little sense of anything ending or beginning. The plot, such as it is, involves a series of shifting love triangles: initially, the triangles consist of Nate, Elizabeth, and third persons Chris and Martha; Chris kills himself and Lesje supplants Martha as the "other woman" then supplants Elizabeth as the "main woman" in Nate's life; a triangle forms briefly around Nate, Lesje, and William, and another around Lesje, William, and Elizabeth. But this description makes the novel sound like "Atwoodian soap opera." (Rosenberg, *Margaret Atwood,* p. 126). It conveys little of the novel's real interest—for what Elizabeth, Nate, and Lesje really do as they go about their unremarkable and all-too-familiar activities, is think, and as their minds roam time and eternity what the novel really concerns is change, change which is imperceptible but constant and profound.

Atwood has pared action down to a minimum, and though neither she nor her critics seem to appreciate this, she has actually accomplished what Woolf and other modernists strive for: she has freed the narrative from plot so that she can focus on the inner events that are the real adventures. Assessments of this novel as drab and mundane (including Atwood's own) are based on the assumption that action is the main measure of interest in a work. In *Life Before Man* the absence of event releases Atwood's imagination from the constraints of plot to create a work as consistently effective as her poetry is. She has freed herself from the clumsy machinery of Caribbean revolutions, searches for missing persons, and returns from the dead—though "hooked on plots" as she is (as she says of the protagonist of *Lady Oracle* [p. 342]), she does not seem to appreciate her own accomplishment.[3]

## I

Atwood's structure draws attention both to time as the medium of life and to the way we experience time. Though each "chunk of time" seems static and unconnected to other chunks, the sections cumulatively give a sense of inexorable process: "time will flow on; soon everyone will be one day older" (p. 83). "Time hasn't stood still," as the characters are made to realize more than once (pp. 139, 151); "it goes on" (p. 13). Two flashbacks—one to the moment when Nate realizes that Elizabeth and Chris are having an affair, the other to the moment when Elizabeth tells Nate that the affair is over—disrupt the chronological sequence in a surprising way and make the point that change has occurred. While we are living through time, we are unaware that processes are occurring; only later can we name them and frame them. As Lesje reflects, "The dinosaurs didn't know they were in the Mesozoic. They didn't know they were in the middle" (p. 290). And she wonders if her boss, Dr. Van Vleet, who uses the phrase, "in my day," "knew it was his day at the time," "even though she herself does not feel that the time through which she's presently living is particularly hers" (p. 237). While we are young we see people and things as constant; thus Lesje cannot imagine her grandmothers, any more than Nate can imagine his mother, as ever being other than they are. Only when we are older can we see that everything is always changing: when Lesje returns to the neighborhood she grew up in, she is made to realize that it was "not a settled neighborhood there for eternity . . . but a way station, a campground" (p. 268). To understand this is to know that we are mortal: Nate, meeting Martha after a time and seeing that she has changed, is made to realize that "the world exists apart from him. . . . It follows that his body is an object in space and that someday he will die" (p. 276).

The title of the novel, which specifies a time "before man," raises the question of evolution: if humankind is not yet "man" (that is, "human"), can it perhaps become human at some future time? (I dislike using *man* to mean *human,* but Atwood's use of it makes this unavoidable.) Time itself, furthermore, presides over the novel, oppressive, menacing: "the past yawns around [Elizabeth], a cavern filled with menacing echoes" (p. 263). Elizabeth has an image of her body as an hourglass with sand running through it—"When it's all gone she'll be dead" (p. 89)—and of "every second a pulsebeat, countdown" (p. 251). Nate, with his children in the Royal Ontario Museum, has a vision of time closing in on them: "Run . . . or time will overtake you, you too will be caught and frozen" (p. 82). The museum is more than a microcosmic community that brings the characters together on account of their work; it is a storehouse and symbol of the past, itself a presence in the novel, a weight on the present. Atwood evokes a sense of determinism—biological, psychological, and historical—as oppressive as "the nightmare repetition" that haunts Doris Lessing's Martha Quest.[4] Actions are produced by "childhood imprintings" (p. 98) that are produced by family histories that are produced by history; and behind history, the past stretches back millenia, to prehistory and beyond, to the vast stellar spaces. The central question of the novel, then, is how can people change for the better when we are so burdened by the past? How can we make time an ally rather than an enemy?

Elizabeth has the strongest sense of the nightmare repetition, of the sins of the elders being inflicted on the younger: "There's a small deadening voice in her [that] cancels choice" (p. 58). It is she who best understands "childhood imprintings" (p. 98) and that "nothing ever finishes" (p. 188): "My mother, my father, my aunt and my sister did not go away. Chris won't go away either" (p. 99). She has a bleak sense of herself becoming "*Mummy,*" source of pain and guilt to her children: "She will become their background . . . explanation for everything they find idiosyncratic or painful about themselves. If she makes them feel guilty enough they'll come and visit her on weekends. . . . [S]he will become *My Mother,* pronounced with a sigh" (p. 250).

If Elizabeth sees humanity as psychologically determined, Lesje sees it as evolutionarily determined, "a mere dot" on "the tree of evolution" (p. 308). Lesje's view of humankind as a form of "mischievous ape" (p. 293), "a modern mammal" (p. 211), is corroborated by Atwood's descriptions of the way the characters behave, their adherence to "territorial imperatives": they mark boundaries, claim space, "take possession" (p. 207), exclude others and are themselves excluded by their markings; they "violate," "transgress," and "trespass" on one another's territories (see, for example, pp. 159, 169, 200, 251). After her confrontation with Elizabeth, who fills up the space in Lesje's office as she has taken over her life. Lesje recalls hearing how the dominant ape stares and the other lowers its eyes ("it avoids murders") and wishes she had spent more time studying "modern mammals" (p. 211).[5]

Nate, who believes that "things have to be viewed in a historical context" (p. 67), believes in historical determinism. Atwood provides some support for this perspective by showing family histories in historical contexts: Nate lost his father in the war and Lesje's grandmothers hated one another because of Balkan politics and antisemitism. But Atwood also evokes a longer view of time, an anthropological rather than a historical view, from which contemporary Canadian society is like a "primitive" society, engaged in attempts to control nature through rites and magic. Frequent references to ritual and ceremony, along with the descriptions of holidays (Halloween, Remembrance Day, Christmas, a birthday) that are the settings of sections, make the point that this is a society with its own rites and rituals. It is also a society that defines itself by excluding outsiders, as "primitive" societies do (according to anthropologist Mary Douglas[6]), and its politics are the collective expression of territoriality. The newspaper headlines Nate comes on as he is packing to leave Elizabeth, "old stories which come to him across time as one long blurred howl of rage and pain," all have to do with Canadians defending themselves against the encroachments of Pakistanis, Portuguese, Greeks, French, and "Balkanization" (pp. 201–2). Lesje, who as a foreigner and outsider has firsthand experience of this xenophobia, suspects nationalism of any sort and argues that World War II was a matter of "grab and counter-grab," against William's defense of it in moral terms (p. 28). Elizabeth also sees politics as a mask for territoriality, as "contests between men . . . in which she's expected to be at best a cheerleader" (p. 59); and Nate cannot understand how she can sleep through the election returns, which he finds the most exciting event since the first Russian-Canadian hockey series (p. 70). (Though Elizabeth and Lesje are critical of male power-grabs, Atwood shows the women to be more territorial, in personal terms, than the men: whereas Nate refuses to fight with Chris over Elizabeth as if she were "a female dog," viewing it instead as "a matter of human dignity" [pp. 174–75], Elizabeth thinks of Nate as a bone [p. 203] and contests Lesje for possession of him.)

The long view of time evoked by the novel produces a complex effect. On the one hand, it reduces human life, showing the characters to be determined by forces so huge that they can barely begin to comprehend them. They are the sum total of their pasts, their own and others', the "sediment" (p. 308) or "repository" of the past: Robert Rubenstein describes them as "fossilized," "mounted specimens," like "museum exhibits" (pp. 101–2). On the other hand, this view of time widens the scope of the novel and gives a sense of the range and power of the human imagination. As Elizabeth sits and Nate runs and Lesje goes about her daily activities, their minds move through time, through various pasts and possible futures, evoking a universe of potential. Though their actions fix them in consequences, their imaginations are not so confined: they are free to construct alternatives, to consider roads not taken (as when Nate imagines a time before his marriage, "when all directions still seemed possible" [p. 199]) and to imaginatively explore roads that might have been taken or still might be taken (as when Elizabeth imagines various funerals and possible "futures" for Chris [pp. 158–60] or when she "walks through the future, step by step," thinking "it can go two ways . . ." [p. 204]).

We follow their imaginations as they explore their own pasts and futures and construct possible pasts and futures for the species. Nate's is the shortest view; his realm, history, is the shallowest and least significant dimension of life. Lesje provides a longer view, with her understanding of prehistory, a perspective from which humanity is a small part of the large process of evolution, and whether we survive is not all that important: "the dinosaurs didn't survive and it wasn't the end of the world" (p. 27). Elizabeth provides the longest perspective, with her intimations of eternity. Her proximity to Chris's suicide puts her closest to the ultimate question of existence and brings the possibility of extinction—"that piece of outer space he'd carried" (p. 301)—into the novel. She hears voices and feels Chris's breath on her neck; and on her visit to the planetarium, she is not surprised to learn that "someday our sun will explode" (p. 72). In the opening scene, Elizabeth is lying on her bed, staring at the ceiling: "Nothing will happen, nothing will open, the crack will not widen and split and nothing will come through it. All it means is that the ceiling needs to be repainted" (p. 12). In Lessing's *Memoirs of a Survivor* (published five years earlier), the wall does open to reveal a transcendent realm, but in *Life Before Man* there seemingly is nothing on the other side. As Elizabeth knows, however, there is *nothingness* on the other side, a nothing so menacing as to be something, an absence so strong as to be a presence: "She knows about the vacuum on the other side of the ceiling," the "black vacuum" into which she could be pulled "like smoke" (p. 12). Elizabeth's imagination is finely tuned to the void, to "the rushing of wind, the summoning voices she can hear from underground, the dissolving trees, the chasms that open at her feet. . . . She has no difficulty seeing the visible world as a transparent veil or a whirlwind. The miracle is to make it solid" (p. 302).

Thus, time is the novel's subject and setting: the "middle ground" that the characters occupy is the present time, the "way station" we pass through on our way from birth to death, our mortal lives. Far from being claustrophobic, *Life Before Man* opens out on all time and eternity. Far from being uneventful, it concerns the movement of life through time and addresses the subject of change, the possibility of creating "something new" against the weight of the past. Though the social, psychological, and biological determinism Atwood suggests in the novel makes "human dignity" or "freedom" improbable, these characters do attain freedom and dignity. Nate's mother sees people as "products of their environment . . . [but] manages to combine this view with a belief in human dignity and free will"; and though "Nate doesn't feel capable of this logical contradiction" (p. 273), Atwood is capable of it. Against all odds, in spite of the causality to which events are chained, people "nevertheless" change; and the world *nevertheless* recurs, to suggest the improbably, "illogical," "miraculous" nature of change.

## II

At the outset, the novel's three main characters are stuck in situations that leave them repeating the patterns of the past, locked into old defenses, and (though they are in relationships) unconnected and alone. Each character is delineated in relation to a family that has made her or him what s/he is, thus accounting for present actions and attitudes. Each is fixed in a backward-looking, unproductive relation to time: Elizabeth, needing all her energies to cope with the past, cannot imagine a future; Nate is nostalgic for "former times," which he thinks of as the "olden days, like a bygone romantic era" (p. 15); and Lesje "is wandering in prehistory," her "idea of a restful fantasy," knowing that "she's regressing" (pp. 18–19). As the love triangles shift, though, Nate and Lesje move out of relationships that prevent them from changing and into relationships that liberate them to larger possibilities; and though Elizabeth is left alone, she too arrives at a place where she can realize her better potential. Each makes a connection of some sort; each learns to go with time, to accept its forward movement, to make time an ally; and each of the women develops a capacity for compassion that counters the processes by which the sins of one generation are inflicted on the next.

Elizabeth is the most damaged and damaging of the three, which is why she has the strongest sense of "the nightmare repetition." Her childhood was sufficiently horrendous to destroy her only sibling, her sister Caroline. Their father walked out when they were children, "was suddenly not there anymore" (p. 136), at which point "space became discontinuous" (p. 150); their mother gave up and also disappeared. Auntie Muriel stepped in and took over "and worked at developing those parts of Elizabeth that most resembled Auntie Muriel and suppressing or punishing the other parts" (p. 137).

Elizabeth's relations with people are defenses against her terror of the void. She marries Nate for safety and becomes involved with Chris "to be the center" (p. 161). When Nate begins to move out of the position assigned him, outer space again threatens: "Stay in your place, Nate, I will not tolerate that void" (p. 162). The ceiling that was ripped off by Chris's death has begun to "heal over" (p. 162), but when Nate moves out of place, the cracks between the boards widen; "gray light wells from them, cold. Dry ice, gas, she can hear it, a hushing sound, moving towards her face. It eats color"; "somewhere out there [in the dark of outer space] the collapsed body floats . . . tugging at her with immense gravity. Irresistible. She falls towards it, space filling her ears" (p. 205).

Elizabeth has so strong a sense of determinism because she sees herself becoming the Auntie Muriel she has always feared and hated. In her better moments, Elizabeth can be quite clear about this. She knows that Auntie Muriel was destructive because of what was done to her: "Auntie Muriel was thwarted in her youth. She had a domineering father who stunted her and wouldn't let her go to college because college was for boys. . . . Auntie Muriel had a strong personality and a good mind and she was not pretty, and patriarchal society punished her. These things are all true" (p. 120). Still, Elizabeth insists that Auntie Muriel is accountable for the damage she has done: "Nevertheless . . . given her own sufferings, why has Auntie Muriel chosen to transfer them, whenever possible, to others?" (p. 120). In an imaginary conversation Elizabeth has with a psychologist she decides against seeing, she tries to accept responsibility for herself: "I am an adult and I do not think I am merely the sum of my past. I can make choices and I suffer the consequences" (p. 99). Nevertheless, she finds herself incapable of preventing herself from doing to others what has been done to her.

If Auntie Muriel plays chess with her dead relatives (p. 123), Elizabeth makes pawns of everyone in her life. Imagery relating to games and war is associated with her movements, as she maneuvers people into positions that empower her (pp. 180, 204, 213, 260–61, 263). She treats Martha like the "kitchen help" (p. 34), Chris like the chauffeur (p. 97); she makes Lesje feel like "a kind of governess" just "hired for a job she hasn't applied for" (p. 211); she tries to "supervise" Nate's affair with Lesje as she had his affair with Martha (p. 147). She assumes the powers, actual and imaginary, of Auntie Muriel, and others have fantasies about her like hers of Auntie Muriel: Nate imagines her dissolving, just as she imagined Auntie Muriel disintegrating like the wicked witch of Oz (pp. 139, 279; 218, 258); Lesje imagines Elizabeth as a prehistoric monster just as Elizabeth's children see Auntie Muriel as "a mammoth or a mastadon" (pp. 265, 120). Whereas Auntie Muriel was the spider in Elizabeth's version of the spider and the fly (p. 119), spider imagery accrues to Elizabeth in the spider plants that surround her: and now Elizabeth sits in "her parlor" and draws people into "her net" (p. 258) (in this parlor are carefully selected and exquisite things, Auntie Muriel having taught Elizabeth that "money counts" [p. 137]). Elizabeth finds herself "using Auntie Muriel's phrases," speaking "the doctrine according to Auntie Muriel" ("if you really love someone you're willing to make certain sacrifices" [p. 262]); and she even expresses Auntie Muriel's xenophobia when she patronizes Lesje as "someone with unusual interests" (Lesje has the impression that she meant "something like *foreigner*" [p. 211]).

Doing to others what was done to her, she uses her children as "counters in the bargaining process with Nate" (p. 204). She wants the best for them, but she also manipulates them: "she wants them to be happy. At the same time she wants to hear of injuries, atrocities, so she can virtuously rage" (p. 250). She has pride in them—they are her accomplishments—but she also would like to eradicate Nate's part in them as Auntie Muriel tried to eradicate her mother's part in her.

What enables Elizabeth to change is partly Nate's leaving, and partly a change in her relation to Auntie Muriel—a perception of her as a person, that releases a new capacity for forgiveness in her. As Auntie Muriel is dying, Elizabeth sees feelingly what she has known all along, that behind Auntie Muriel's cruelty was a cruelty done to her (" 'your mother was always the favorite,' " Auntie Muriel tells her), and in this scene, "to Elizabeth's horror," Auntie Muriel begins to cry, "a reversal of nature, a bleeding statue, a miracle." Although Elizabeth hates Auntie Muriel and will not forgive her, and although Elizabeth is "no priest" and unable to "give absolution," "nevertheless, nevertheless, she whispers: It's all right. It's all right" (pp. 281–82). At the funeral, the bizarre service Auntie Muriel has arranged ("the result of premature senility" or "a joke?") makes Elizabeth wonder if Auntie Muriel "might be other than what she seemed" (p. 299). Torn by conflicting emotions, Elizabeth giggles hysterically, then faints; and when she comes to, "she feels the horrified relief of someone who has stopped just in time to watch an opponent topple in slow motion over the edge" (p. 301). Though this episode has been read as signifying the rebirth of Auntie Muriel in Elizabeth (Hutcheon, p. 24), actually, the Auntie Muriel in her is the defeated "opponent." Elizabeth has salvaged something "despite the wreckage": "she's still alive . . . she holds down a job even. She has two children"; "she's managed to accomplish a house. . . . She's built a dwelling over the abyss, but where else was there to build it? So far, it stands" (pp. 301–2).

That what has been reborn is Elizabeth's better potential is corroborated by the last section of the novel, where her imagination is released to a fantasy, not of horror, but of a better life, a fantasy prompted by the Chinese art exhibition she's curated. When she first reads the catalog about the China exhibition, she can't bring herself to care (p. 86), but at the end, looking at the pictures, she is moved: "Elizabeth blinks back tears: foolishness, to be moved by this. This is propaganda" (p. 316). For the first time, she realizes how alone she has been and has a vision of a connection with others. She knows "China does not exist. Nevertheless, she longs to be there." Whereas in the first line of the novel Elizabeth is thinking "I don't know how I should live," the last line—"Nevertheless she longs to be there"—offers a possible "should," a communal ideal that she knows is utopian but longs for "nevertheless." In terms of external event, nothing good happens to Elizabeth: her husband leaves her and her aunt dies. But again, plot is no measure of what actually happens, for the most significant events are internal; and there are stirrings of new life in Elizabeth as important as those in Lesje, as her imagination and compassion come to life.

Lesje knows that in any competition with Elizabeth for unhappy childhoods, she would lose (p. 292). Lesje is the daughter of a mother who wants only her happiness; in fact, "Lesje's happiness is her mother's justification" (p. 196). Though this puts a burden of another sort on her, it leaves her less damaged than Elizabeth, less defended, and more capable of change. (Thus, Lesje walks down the street glancing "into the windows of dress shops," "looking for something that might become her, something she might become" [p. 26], whereas Elizabeth "knows what she looks like and she doesn't indulge in fantasies of looking any other way. She doesn't need her own reflection or the reflections of other people's ideas of her or of themselves" [p. 57]). But Lesje, too, has been subject to the manipulation of elders: Lesje's Christian Ukrainian and Jewish Lithuanian grandmothers fight for possession of her, cursing one another and trying to wipe out the other's part in her—"each thought she should scrap half her chromosomes, repair herself, by some miracle" (p. 65). This has left her divided and weakened: though it "should have made her trilingual . . . instead she was . . . bad at English, plodding, a poor speller" (p. 94), left without any language until she discovers the language of science—"the names [of the rocks] were a language. . . . The names of the dinosaurs . . . were even more satisfactory" (p. 94). And though Lesje is a foreigner and Elizabeth appears to be "*haute Wasp,*" both women have a sense of impermanence, and Lesje seeks the sort of security in William that Elizabeth sought in Nate. Whereas Elizabeth's intimation of the universe as whirlwind is terrifying (p. 302), though, Lesje finds it "soothing" that "she is only a pattern. She is not an immutable object. There are no immutable objects. Some day she will dissolve" (p. 169). Lesje's imagination puts her in touch not with the abyss, but with a prehistory which is beautiful and serene.

What Lesje "accomplishes" is not a house, but an edifice of another sort—"a palace built in the pursuit of truth," with herself a "guardian" of the past (p. 308). Paleontology is not "the bone business," as her father calls it (p. 194), but something imaginative and alive. Her fantasy life is the most creative and original of all the characters'; and though it is sometimes "flight," it is more often "exploration"—and she understands the distinction (p. 264). As she wonders, the day Nate's children come to the museum, how she can explain "why she does this, why she loves doing this," she recalls when "they found the Albertosaurus, a thigh, a vertebra," and "she'd wanted to cry," "*Live Again!* . . . like some Old Testament prophet, like God, throwing up her arms, willing thunderbolts; and the strange flesh would grow again, cover the bones, the badlands would moisten and flower" (pp. 80–81). She wants to discover a new kind of dinosaur that she'll name "*Aliceosaurus*" (p. 194), a new land that she'll name "*Lesjeland,*" "tropical, rich and crawling with wondrous life forms" (p. 92). The night they play Lifeboat at Elizabeth's dinner party, a game that requires each character to describe why she or he deserves to be saved, Lesje, panicking at a sense of her own superfluousness ("what is she good for?" [p. 156]), "clutching for lucidity," defends the study of bones:

> Everyone has a certain number of bones. . . . Not their own but someone else's and the bones have to named, you have to know what to call them, otherwise what they are, they're lost, cut adrift from their own meanings, they may as well not have been saved for you. You can't name them all, there are too many, the world is full of them, it's made of them, so you have to choose which ones. Everything that's gone before has left its bones for you and you'll leave yours in turn. (p. 157)

Though this doesn't make entirely good sense, Lesje manages to suggest that the naming of bones is a way of retrieving, redeeming the past—lest it, and we, be "lost."

At the outset, Lesje is in a relationship that is "settled": William "sees no reason why anything should ever change" (p. 19), and she is no more able than Elizabeth or Nate to dislodge herself from her situation. But she does have the saving instinct to respond to

Nate's advances, attracted to the "adult world" he represents, "where choices had consequences, significant, irreversible" (p. 221). When Nate remains in his marriage, she is initiated into an adult world where she learns "more than she ever intended to, more than she wants" (p. 295), and is made more miserable by her love for Nate than she was by her lack of feeling for William: she "feels she's blundered into something tangled and complex, tenuous, hopelessly snarled" (p. 208). As Nate remains entangled in his domestic mess and unable to shift his allegiances, Lesje's sense of unbelonging increases and she finds herself wishing "to be endorsed, sanctified, she doesn't care who by. She wants a mother's blessing" (p. 269). She also comes to understand why Chris killed himself: "it was the anger and the other thing, much worse, the fear of being nothing. People like Elizabeth could do that to you, blot you out; people like Nate, merely by going about their own concerns. Other peoples' habits could kill you. Chris hadn't died for love. He'd wanted to be an event" (p. 293). Backed into a corner by Nate's behavior, she considers killing herself, but rather than committing suicide, she flushes her birth control pills down the toilet—committing this action "with some deliberation" (p. 293).

As ambiguous an action as this is, it is also a way of asserting her existence, her identity, by making a connection: "If children were the key, if having them was the way she could stop being invisible, then she would goddamn well have some herself" (p. 293). Though she thinks "surely no child conceived in such rage could come to much good," she is nevertheless "unrepentant" (p. 293). She has joined the adult world where actions have consequences, by doing something of consequence: "It's hard to believe that such a negligible act of hers can have measurable consequences for other people. . . . She's not used to being a cause of anything at all." But it is a creative rather than a destructive "event," an acceptance of forward-looking processes, a going with time rather than regressing; she could "stop time" by having an abortion, but this is not what she wants (p. 308).

Moreover, she has a "new idea" at the end of the novel that suggests that she will be capable of meeting the situation she has created. Coming upon Elizabeth unexpectedly, seeing her standing alone and gazing over the balustrade into the rotunda of the museum, she has a glimpse of her as "ordinary, mortal"; though "she's used to thinking of Elizabeth as permanent, like an icon," she suddenly sees her as part of the processes to which all of them, including the children, are subject. This makes her wonder if she and Elizabeth will still be warring twenty years hence: "It occurs to her, a new idea, that this tension between them is a difficulty for the children. They ought to stop" (p. 309). Lesje's understanding of processes enables her to stop doing to others what her grandmothers did to her, and her "new idea" is a first sign of compassion toward others, a first step in countering the processes by which pain is transmitted from one generation to the next. On her way home to tell Nate, Lesje wonders if he will forgive her: though "she would prefer instead to forgive, someone, somehow, for something . . . she isn't sure where to begin" (p. 311). She has begun: she has set in motion the process by which curses are transformed to blessings, and made a beginning to the end of the "nightmare repetition"; and since she is about to become a mother, this is "a mother's blessing."

Of the three main characters, Nate changes the least. But then he needs to change least, since he is the least damaged: he already has a "mother's blessing." In absence of a father (who supposedly died a "war hero" though actually died of hepatitis), he has been doted on by a loving mother, the "apple of her eye," "the perpetual spotlight in which he's always lived, alone on stage, the star performer" (p. 134). Nate's mother combines—another of her illogicalities—a cheerful nature with a belief in disaster: "Nevertheless . . . crusader, dauntless astronomer, charting new atrocities, sending out her communications . . . unaware of the futility of what she is doing" (p. 42). Nate is a shallower character than any of the women in the novel. Whereas all the women, including his mother, have contemplated suicide, Nate never does confront that ultimate question; as Elizabeth knows, he does not know about "that freedom, that exit" (p. 261). His fantasy life is the most banal, which is in a way appropriate—since history is where "he lives," his thought is the most culturally determined. His idea of domestic bliss is "left over from some Christmas cards of the forties" (p. 232); his fantasy of escape is a raft trip down the Amazon (p. 255); his paradise is a grade B movie, "late-movie scenarios" (p. 235), rather than the ideal of communal effort that Elizabeth glimpses. Yet he is also the most sympathetic male in Atwood's fiction, and the most fully depicted.[7]

Nate's vision of Lesje is taken from "a Saturday matinee of *She*" (p. 71). Though this vision is clichèd, it is powerful and creative: "by seeing how beautiful she is he's made her beautiful" (p. 246); and Lesje becomes "addicted to Nate's version of her" though she knows "that the picture he's devised of her is untrue" (p. 267). It is his vision of her and hers of him that enable both of them to change. But though Nate turns to her seeking "salvation" and "blessing" (p. 25), he is also drawn to her because he wants to protect her—which is unusual for him, as Elizabeth realizes: "Before, he wanted to be protected. . . . But this time he wants to protect" (p. 162).

Nate is also changed by a revelation—like Elizabeth's—that enables him to see a parent as a person. In a scene toward the end of the novel, his mother amazes him by revealing that she turned to political work not from hope but from despair—as an alternative to suicide after his father died. Nate is made to realize that she is more complex and cynical, more like himself, then he had ever imagined: "It's not only the revelation but the unexpected similarity to himself that appalls him. He has thought her incapable of such despair" (p. 287). This new perspective on the past jolts him into a new view of time, a vision of a future when his daughters will be women, "demanding," "rejecting," "blaming," "criticizing," "judging" him (p. 287). Nate's response is characteristic—he runs. This time, however, he also does something uncharacteristic—he leaps, "aim[ing] for . . . that nonexistent spot where he longs to be" (p. 288), a place he had formerly feared being, "in mid-air, hurtling toward a future he can't imagine" (p. 163).

Though Nate has despaired of political action, he is, in the course of the novel, drawn back into political work—partly because of this new sense of kinship with his mother, and partly because he is feeling more hopeful. He is hailed as

> What he's spent so much effort to avoid becoming: his mother's son. Which maybe he is.
>
> But not only, not only. He refuses to be defined. He's not shut, time carries him on, other things may happen. . . . (pp. 305–6)

He is, at the end, ever hopeful ("his mother's son"), expecting "some news," some message, from the evening's news: "Perhaps there will finally be some news. A small part of him still waits, still expects, longs for a message, a messenger" (p. 306)

He will get a message that night, for (we know what he does not) Lesje is about to tell him she's pregnant. In his last scene, he is running, thinking about meeting Lesje: "He anticipates this moment, which he cannot predict, which leaves room for hope and also for disaster" (p. 314)—the terms indicating his surrender to processes of change. It is true that he is—as he sees himself—"helplessly molded by the . . . demands and . . . disapprovals of the women he can't help being involved with" (p. 41). The women are the stronger characters, their imaginations the more powerful, and their strengths are connected with maternity and the territoriality it entails (as Hutcheon say, the creative act of Lesje's pregnancy becomes the paradigmatic act of creation in the novel [p. 29]). But Nate is also liberated from a relationship with someone who sees him as a failure into a relationship with someone who takes him seriously; and, as the novel ends he and Lesje are moving toward one another, accepting the forward movement of time and a new connection.

## III

Nate is not the only character who has difficulty reconciling the logical contradiction of his mother's position that people are the products of their environments but are "nevertheless" capable of dignity; that people are the products of their pasts but are nevertheless responsible for who they are and what they do. Against the determinism that Atwood evokes, however, the characters do attain a degree of freedom and dignity. My sense of the novel's ending differs from that of Sherrill Grace, who reads it as hopeless ("Elizabeth, Nate, and Lesje will simply go on, unable to feel and unaware that they are already museum pieces, gray dinosaurs. The lesson . . . is that history repeats itself" [*Violent Duality,* p. 138]), and from that of Linda Hutcheon, who suggests that "nothing has changed" (p. 26).[8] I see the characters as changing and countering the processes of repetition. To the challenge of Lifeboat, to Elizabeth's question about the marriage—"Can anything be saved? Meaning this wreck" (p. 100)—the answer is yes, something has been saved. The characters salvage something from the wreck, from the "shrapnel" of an "exploding family" (p. 266). Elizabeth "accomplishes" a house and children and attains a glimmer of a better life; Lesje, who has been "guardian" of the past, has a "new idea" that will enable her to provide for the future as well. Nate and Lesje move out of dead-end relationships and into relationships with people who have larger images of them; and though Elizabeth ends alone, she too is liberated—from Nate's view of her; she has gained "freedom from . . . that constant pained look which is worse than nagging . . . like a huge mirror in which her flaws are magnified and distorted. . . . She'll be free of that. . . . It will mean she'll have to carry out the garbage bags herself on garbage day, but she thinks she can live with that" (p. 206). Her imagination is liberated to conceive of better possibilities. Even Martha shows signs of progress. Each ends with the capacity to imagine better things and to make new connections. Their changes counter the relentless nightmare of repetition and are steps in the slow, painful process toward becoming human.

If there is hope on an individual level, is there hope for the species? Can anything be salvaged from the wreckage of the world, the "howl of pain and rage" that rises from the newspapers? The echoes of Eliot's *The Waste Land* and "The Hollow Men" point to this central question. Elizabeth recalls a line that sounds like a misquote of "The Hollow Men": "*We are the numb. Long years ago / We did this or that. And now we sit*" (p. 100); Nate feels like "a tin man, his heart stuffed with sawdust" (p. 241); Lesje's desire to make the dinosaur bones live recalls Tiresias's metaphors and the central question of *The Waste Land*—"Shall these bones live?" Can the contemporary world be redeemed? To this question, Atwood offers little hope. For the social injustices Nate and his mother contemplate, there is no remedy; if change is possible, it will not be accomplished through political action. In this sense I would have to agree with other readers that Atwood's vision is hopeless—though these are not the terms in which they have read the novel, or the terms in which Atwood encourages us to consider the novel. Change may occur on the personal level, but there is no suggestion that the personal is political; and this dissociation is characteristic of the late seventies when *Life Before Man* was written, the "post-feminist" generation in which (as Elizabeth and others have noted) "women's lib is on the wane" (p. 275). The most we can hope for is a separate peace, a private salvation, some connection to another human being, some shelter from the void. Build houses, cultivate our gardens, raise families to stem the tide; do unto others as we would have them do unto us rather than as they *have* done to us; harness our imaginations to creative rather than destructive uses—and perhaps do some political work in the hopes of making a better world, knowing that our efforts will be futile. Perhaps the species will evolve, and evolution will occur as a kind of sum total of the type of individual change that occurs in the novel—"or not, as the case may be" (p. 27).

*Notes*

1. Page references in the text are to the following: *Life Before Man* (New York: Simon and Schuster, 1979); *Lady Oracle* (New York: Avon, 1976).

2. Arnold E. Davidson and Cathy N. Davidson also call the novel bleak ("Prospect and Retrospect in *Life Before Man,*" p. 205). There does seem to be something forbidding about it which makes it the least liked of Atwood's novels—"astringent" is Roberta Rubenstein's term for it in *Boundaries of the Self* (p. 108). It is also the least written about: the most recent anthology, *Margaret Atwood: Reflection and Reality,* edited by Barbara Mendez-Egle, contains essays on all the novels except this one.

3. Frank Davey reveals a similar confusion of external with internal event when he suggests that *Life Before Man,* unlike Atwood's other novels, "has no climactic moment"; elsewhere in Atwood's fiction, Davey argues, "climaxes give each character a sense of deep change, and conviction that something new awaits them," a "cathartic breakthrough to new hope," whereas this novel affirms "the continuing power of the past" (*Margaret Atwood,* pp. 85–86). Actually the novel shows "breakthrough" to "something new" yet dissociates internal development from external event in a way that minimizes dependence on plot.

4. Martha Quest is overwhelmed by a sense that her behavior is determined by repetitive cycles—biological, psychological, social, historical—which she terms "the nightmare *repetition*" in Lessing's *A Proper Marriage* (pp. 77, 95); and she thinks "it was time to move on to something new" in *Martha Quest* (pp. 7–8). The phrase "something new" recurs throughout *The Children of Violence* (see, for example, *Martha Quest,* pp. 53, 141, 216; *Landlocked,* p. 117) and *The Golden Notebook* (pp. 61, 353, 472–73, 479), and it points to the central concern of Lessing's fiction—which is a central focus of Atwood's fiction as well.

5. Lesje also sees herself as a herbivore (p. 19) and an "appeaser" (p. 62); she thinks of the children in the museum who throw things at the dinosaur exhibits as "mammal cubs, jeering their old enemies" (p. 183).

6. Mary Douglas suggests that "ideas about separating, purifying, demarcating and punishing transgressions have as their main function to

impose system on an inherently untidy experience. It is only by exaggerating the difference between within and without, above and below, male and female, with and against, that a semblance of order is created" (p. 4).

7. This is the first time Atwood represents a male character from within, and the last time, since her subsequent novels return to the female perspective. Whereas in her other novels, we are within the perspective of one female consciousness, here we move among three consciousnesses, one of which is male. This gives the novel a breadth her other novels lack—which is another reason I do not find it "claustrophobic."

8. Davey suggests that Nate has moved from one doomed relationship to another and that "for all three characters the novel has barely moved past its opening lines" (*Margaret Atwood,* pp. 81–82). Davidson and Davidson read it as an old-fashioned, closed ending, which counters the promise or at least the possibilities implicit in twentieth-century fictional indefiniteness ("Prospects and Retrospect," pp. 219–20). Grace sees it as an open ending—"*Life Before Man* has a final page, but no conclusion, no finality, no *anagnorisis*" (*Violent Duality,* p. 138)—but as hopeless nevertheless.

# 7 *The Here and Now of* Bodily Harm

*Lorna Irvine*

> I think "feminine literature" is an organic, translated writing . . . translated from blackness, from darkness. Women have been in darkness for centuries. They don't know themselves. Or only poorly. And when women write, they translate darkness.
>
> Marguerite Duras
> From an interview by Susan Husserl-Kapit

> Isn't the final goal of writing to articulate the body? For me the sensual juxtaposition of words has one function: to liberate a living past, to liberate matter.
>
> Chantal Chawaf
> "Linguistic Flesh"

With the opening words of Margaret Atwood's novel *Bodily Harm,* "this is how I got here,"[1] the reader, along with the main character, Rennie, is drawn into a labyrinthine plot that uses the themes and images of earlier Atwood novels, poems, and criticism in order to make a radical statement about female sexuality, the political body, and the female text. It is a terrifying novel, a mystery that systematically confuses characterization, plot development, setting, and even genre. Surrealism embues the story, making ambiguous its temporal orientation as well as its location. Although the opening sentence implies a specific time (the present) and space (here), the novel in fact refuses clarification in favor of a nightmarish literary landscape that condenses the characters and displaces the affects. Throughout, plots and subplots intermingle, and the repetition of both words and images creates a ritualistic pattern that often suspends movement. A number of italicized language fragments, seemingly disembodied, pierce the text, drawing to the reader's attention the peculiar balance between first- and third-person narration while, at the same time, signaling a possible here and now. It is a heavily coded novel, yet a novel that painfully articulates the female body, that perhaps even liberates it.

The novel's major code is the superficial plot that gives an apparent, although highly deceptive, order of development to a number of recorded events. A central character is presented—Rennie Wilford, a free-lance journalist of only mediocre ability. The novel appears to be her story, a story told sometimes in the first person, sometimes in the third, a splitting of subject and object that is of considerable importance to the mystery of the novel. The story begins with Rennie's recounting of an attempted crime against her body. A man has entered her apartment and as a reminder of his visit has left a coil of rope on her bed. Like the game of Clue, the episode establishes a series of similar patterns that are also based on clues. Not long after this episode, Rennie is offered a chance to do a story for *Visor,* a magazine directed toward male readers. She accepts the assignment, flies to the Caribbean island where she is to do the travel piece and arrives at Sunset Inn, a place more ominously named than at first appears. For the next six days, she travels around the island, meeting people and becoming inadvertently involved in the island's current revolution. During the early morning of her seventh day on the island, and following a night of violent revolutionary outbreak, she is arrested. She then suffers, for about two weeks, in a poorly run Central American prison, from which she is finally rescued by a member of the Canadian diplomatic corps. She is put on a plane back to Canada where, as Audrey Thomas comments in a review of the novel, she has become, like the Ancient Mariner, "a sadder but wiser person" (pp. 9–12). An acceptable, upbeat, Harlequin plot: another story about a victimized woman who wins in the end. A deceptive story!

Of course, we learn much more about Rennie than this plot summary suggests. Because she constantly reflects on the past, large segments of the novel present other stories, other lives. One such story is that of her relationship with Jake, a man with whom she has been living but who has moved out of the apartment shortly before the novel begins. Another story is that of her operation, a partial mastectomy. Daniel, the doctor who performed the operation, figures dominantly in her fantasy life; as she suggests, he has been imprinted on her, the first face she saw when emerging from the anaesthetic. Rennie also talks about her early life in the small town of Griswold, where she and her mother lived with her mother's parents. Memories of her grandmother flit in and out of her consciousness. As well, the stories of two other women are included, one told by Jocasta, a Toronto friend of Rennie's, and, on five separate occasions, those told by Lora, a woman whom Rennie meets on the island and who becomes her cell mate in the last section of the novel. Throughout, the present events and characters of the novel merge with those of the past. Thus, segments of alternating stories are condensed and displaced so that the operation, the grandmothers of the island, the sexually violent men, the doctors, the brutal beating of Lora, all have the resonance of recurrence rather than singularity. As a result, the texture of the novel is peculiarly dense.

Certainly the themes and images of the superficial stories of *Bodily Harm* allow a coherent literary critique and satisfy contemporary demands for extended analysis. The novel addresses itself to the nature of violence, to victimization, to women. The epigraph from John Berger's *Ways of Seeing* focuses immediate attention on these themes: "A man's presence suggests what he is capable of doing to you and for you. By contrast, a woman's presence . . . defines what can and cannot be done to her." Newspaper articles describe "those women they were always finding strewn about ravines or scattered here and there" (p. 23); Jake gets sexually excited by imagining intercourse as pretended rape; taxi drivers and policemen make constant sexual innuendos; a deaf and dumb man on the island seems on the verge of attacking Rennie; the Toronto policemen's pornography museum displays women's bodies as maps of violence; on the island, men freely beat up their wives; attacked by the male guards in the prison, guards to whom she has been giving sexual favors in return for help, Lora is mutilated and possibly killed. Rennie's summary of the situation is inspired by her sexual involvement with Paul, whose boyish pride in his gun fills Rennie with terror: "She's afraid of men and it's simple. It's rational, she's afraid of men because men are frightening" (p. 290).

The sexual battlefield with its various power plays is paralleled in certain nationalistic themes that appear from quite a different perspective in the opening section of *Survival,* Atwood's early book of criticism. There, Atwood discusses the ways in which victimization seems to dominate the Canadian imagination and offers her thematic study as a "map of the territory" (p. 18). More important, she uses as a dominating question Northrop Frye's frequently quoted statement about Canadian literature, that the major question is "Where is here?" The opening sentence of *Bodily Harm* thus alerts the reader to the novel's interest in Canadian nationalism and to certain of its political intentions. The refrain, "the sweet Canadians," reiterated by the shrunken Fisher King, Dr. Minnow, means different things at different points in the novel. Sometimes, it implies the naïvete of Canadians, a theme given physical representation through the character of Rennie, who, like the narrator of *Surfacing,* represents the country in which she lives. Like Canada, Rennie is perceived by many different characters as naïve, as politically uncomplicated, as obscurely old-fashioned. Towards the end of the novel, Paul says about her: " 'For one thing you're nice. . . . You'd rather be something else, tough or sharp or something like that, but you're nice, you can't help it. Naive. But you think you have to prove you're not merely nice, so you get into things you shouldn't' " (p. 15). At another point, an old couple questions Rennie: " 'You're Canadian, aren't you? We always find the Canadians so nice, they're almost like members of the family. No crime rate to speak of. We always feel quite safe when we go up there' " (p. 186). In this respect, then, the novel ironically attacks Canadian simplicity by dramatizing the massive involvement of Rennie in the political affairs of a country she knows so little about. Far from keeping her safe, her naïvete is responsible for her ultimate victimization. No one, not even the Canadians, can stay outside contemporary political violence or placidly castigate other countries for encouraging such violence. As Dr. Minnow says to Rennie: " 'Everyone is in politics here, my friend. . . . All the time. Not like the sweet Canadians' " (p. 124) and, later, " 'There is no longer any place that is not of general interest. . . . The Sweet Canadians have not learned this yet' " (p. 135). Furthermore, even Rennie, who at the beginning emphasizes her own neutrality ("she needs it for her work. . . . Invisibility" [p. 15]) is embarrassed by the Canadian official with his safari jacket and attempted neutrality. As she watches him following Dr. Minnow out of the room, she can think of him only as "the neutral-coloured Canadian" (p. 191). Strikingly enough, the text itself represents the colors of the Canadian flag—red and white—by reiterating them in all kinds of different combinations.

*Bodily Harm* also self-consciously investigates the act of writing, even dramatizes the creative process. Because Rennie is a writer, the spatial and temporal ambiguity that permeates the novel evokes the actual space and time of the writing act. Small spaces and moments of time punctuate the novel like clockwork, suggesting the painful physical problems that accompany composition. Furthermore, at the beginning of the novel, masculine and feminine readers, and by extension writers, are contrasted. Rennie has been associated with the "Relationships" column of a magazine called *Pandora,* and allusions to Pandora's box (thinly disguised as Lora's box) keep constantly before the reader the implications of the myth. Her present employment is with the magazine *Visor,* a magazine whose readership is predominantly male. As for the writer herself, she refuses to be taken seriously, insisting that she is merely interested in writing trendy articles. Her frivolity is, of course, misleading. Like every other stance in this novel, it is a defense. One of the poems from Atwood's *True Stories,* a collection published the same year as *Bodily Harm,* also emphasizes the shift that Rennie experiences, a shift from belief in a "real story" (*Bodily Harm,* p. 64) to a recognition of the unreliability of narrative:

> The true story lies
> among the other stories
> . . . . . . . . . . . . . . . . . . .
> the true story is vicious
> and multiple and untrue. (p. 11)

The themes that emerge from the stories of *Bodily Harm*—victimization of women, nationalism, writing—are certainly important and can be related by readers and critics to all of Atwood's work and to that of many other writers. Yet, having said this much, I now insist that they do not, at least in their apparent form, explain this novel, do not clarify its geography and history, do not situate the italicized voice, do not account for the peculiarly evasive shifts of perspective, do not explain the emphasis on the unreliability of narrative, do not, finally, unmask the truly radical statement at the novel's core. In somewhat the same way as suggested by Frank Kermode in his analysis of Conrad's *Under*

*Western Eyes,* "Secrets and Narrative Sequence," *Bodily Harm* is replete with secrets that pull against straightforward interpretation and cloud the major themes. Rennie admits that "she no longer trusts surfaces" (p. 48) and announces that "almost nobody here is who they say they are at first" (p. 150). Her fear of the "faceless stranger" moves in and out of consciousness, sometimes associated with specific characters, for example Paul, at other times merely a focus for free-floating anxiety. Although Rennie's stories dominate the text, as the novel progresses, it becomes increasingly clear that her reading of events is erroneous. In some fundamental way, she is blind. She plays Clue poorly: "What has she done, she's not guilty, this is happening to her for no reason at all" (p. 286). Thus, the reader has great difficulty in accumulating the clues that will lead to the discovery of the space, the victim, and the weapon of the crime. Even the crime itself is unclear.

Most problematic is the time of the novel's action. Partly, as with many novels, this temporal ambiguity results from a reliance on recollection. In *Bodily Harm,* recollected stories interfere with the forward narrative movement and even break up the written page. Like the dismembered bodies referred to, the text itself seems repeatedly deconstructed. But the temporal ambiguity is not only a structural problem; it is also contextually important. Early in the novel, Rennie admits that she has "stopped thinking in years" (p. 11). Indeed, as the novel progresses, it seems likely that she has stopped thinking in terms of time at all. Unable to assume a future (" 'I'll tell you about it sometime,' he says, assuming the future; which is more than she can do" [p. 47]), near the end, she admits: "There's the past, the present, the future: none of them will do" (p. 282). Time, always critical for the constructor of stories, disintegrates completely. The opening sentence with its apparently assured present tense is therefore merely a cover, a secret. The concluding "this is what will happen" (p. 293) that parallels the opening "this is how I got here" insists on temporal confusion right to the stopping of the novel by casting the narrative into the future tense. Indeed, even such narrative closure as is allowed by projected fantasy is questioned, for present, past, and future continue to cross through each other: "She will never be rescued. She has already been rescued" (p. 301). Time is like the time of dreams. In "Postcard," similar ambiguities exist:

> Time comes in waves here, a sickness, one
> day after the other rolling on;
> I move up, it's called
> awake, then down into the uneasy
> nights, but never
> forward. (*True Stories,* p. 18)

Vertical rather than horizontal movement perplexes the novel throughout.

This last observation introduces the other principal ambiguity of *Bodily Harm,* its space. To repeat the question asked of Canadian literature by Frye and Atwood: "Where is here?"[2] Certainly, the reader's attention to space is visually insisted on by repeated references to enclosed spaces that are being threatened or that reflect damage. The small apartment bedroom that contains the first of the novel's stories has been violated, a violation that is emphasized by Rennie's offering to show the investigating policemen her mastectomy scar. The enclosed cabin of the plane to the island is also connected with Rennie's damaged body for, as she enters, "she's afraid to look down, she's afraid she'll see blood, leakage, her stuffing coming out" (p. 22). Lying in her room in the Sunset Inn, her hands across her chest, Rennie listens to the sounds from the next room, an eavesdropping insisted on by spatial constriction. The neighboring couple's lovemaking eerily combines torture and sex, a sado-masochistic ritual that is emphasized here by the disembodied, italicized "*Oh please,*" a cry repeated in other places in the novel, an ambiguous fragment (Who is speaking? To whom? From what space? At what time?) that becomes an important clue in the clarifying of the novel's locale. Other confined spaces—the cellar Rennie recalls being locked into by her grandmother, the basement apartment that Lora describes—condense into references to boxes (Pandora's, Lora's) and into statements such as Jake's, that women "should all be locked in cages" (p. 73).[3]

Furthermore, the fear of enclosure invokes a claustrophobia that reflects death. Asked by Rennie what he dreams about, Paul answers, "a hole in the ground" (p. 249). Dr. Minnow's coffin is yet another "box." The gravelike jail cell, five feet by seven feet, in which Lora and Rennie are incarcerated also figures dominantly in the measurements of the novel. Here is a space from which the stories of the text often seem to emerge, a central space in the novel. Such a space would help to account for the kind of story telling that occurs in *Bodily Harm* and also for the confusion of time: virtually unpunctuated days, one space, the creating of stories the only protection against insanity. It would account, too, for the thematic centrality of physical brutality, dominantly the fear of rape, and would explain the insistence on the spatial metaphors that connect enclosure and death. The ambiguous italicized words are given terrifying resonance if the reader answers the confusions and false leads of the novel by believing that *Bodily Harm* culminates with Rennie's physical crises, brought on by seeing a man (Paul? the Prince of Peace? the deaf and dumb man?) being tortured by the prison guards in the yard of the prison: "She has been turned inside out, there's no longer a *here* and a *there.* Rennie understands for the first time that this is not necessarily a place she will get out of, ever. She is not exempt. Nobody is exempt from anything" (p. 290). If the novel's spatial parameters are the prison cell and its temporal parameters the day of Lora's beating, Lora's dismemberment would become the dominant metaphor of the novel, and Rennie's inability to separate here and there, inside and outside would help to account for the way in which she reports Lora's beating. Furthermore, such a scenario also implies a combination for the textual Clue game: the guards in the prison with the penis/gun; the victim, Lora; or, in a possible displacement, Rennie.

Yet the disembodied voice of the novel, its splits, its mysteries, its secrecy, remains insistent. "This is how I got here." Is it possible for there to be another space, another time, another story? Certainly, one other space figures dominantly in the stories of the novel—the hospital room where Rennie undergoes her operation for breast cancer. So pervasive is this space in the themes and images of the novel that it gives considerable resonance to the ambiguous "here." It gives resonance also to the novel's time, and helps to account for the repeating of dreams, the recurrence of the question, "What do you dream about," the dreamlike organization.

Rennie's stories seem, then, to imply a slipping in and out of consciousness that roughly corresponds to her experiences in the operating room. Even her dreams condense and displace anxieties about the operation. Her grandmother, a major actor in these dreams, looking for her hands, becomes a projection of Rennie herself, a foremother who, like Rennie, suffers fears about dismemberment. For example, in a dream occurring apparently at the Sunset Inn, Rennie dreams of gardens, of her mother (who "can't take care of everything" p. 115), of hummingbirds, and, most important, of her grandmother. As she struggles to wake from the dream, she describes herself in "a long white cotton gown," although she insists that she is not in a hospital. Like her grandmother, she is looking for her hands. Again, she drifts into sleep, and again struggles into consciousness: "It's dawn; this time she's really awake, the mosquito netting hangs around her in the warm air like mist. She sees where she is, she's here, by herself, she's stranded in the future. She doesn't know how to get back" (p. 116). Such combinations of waking and sleeping, of dreaming and experiencing, of sensory condensation and displacement disguise absolutely both time and space. The anaesthetic, the mosquito netting, and the mist illustrate Rennie's confused senses and clouded eyes. Furthermore, the sign system used implies yet another variation on the metaphoric game of Clue: the doctor in the hospital room with the knife, the victim Rennie.

Like the "picture-puzzles" of Freud's dream texts in *The Interpretation of Dreams, Bodily Harm* thus creates perplexity by disguising time and space and by representing the same thoughts in a number of different ways. Lost gardens and grandmothers, somewhere in the past, mingle with an indecipherable present and future. Towards the end, space and time become increasingly ambiguous and the characters condense, split, and reform with ever greater frequency. Apparently in the jail cell, Rennie allows her thoughts to wander wildly; she wants to end her stories. She thinks of Paul, then of the doctor, Daniel, of Daniel's hands, of "Daniel enclosed in a glass bubble" (p. 284), herself on the "outside looking in" (p. 284): "From here it's hard to believe that Daniel really exists" (p. 284). But the real focus of her attention is, once again, her body, her "nibbled flesh"; she assures her reader-listener that "nothing has happened to her yet, nobody has done anything to her, she is unharmed. She may be dying, true, but if so she's doing it slowly, relatively speaking. Other people are doing it faster: at night there are screams" (p. 284). I do not need to point out the ways in which this passage, like many other passages in the novel, simultaneously evokes the hospital bed and the jail cell; nor do I need to emphasize the obsession with the body. The concluding comments in these thoughts about Daniel are so much like the dream of her grandmother as to seem like an insistent accumulation of clues: "Rennie opens her eyes. Nothing in here has changed. Directly above her, up on the high ceiling, some wasps are building a nest. . . . Pretend you're really here, she thinks. Now: what would you do?" (p. 284). Where is here? Obviously, the passage does not answer that question. Yet, whether in a hospital bed or a jail cell, Rennie needs to distance herself from her body, to pretend. In these respects, she behaves like a writer.

Such condensed images inevitably create a surrealistic, rather than a realistic, landscape. The hummingbirds in the dream of her grandmother, the wasps building their nest on the ceiling, the sounds of the air-conditioner in the hospital room (and the draughts from open windows that keep occurring in Rennie's dreams), the concluding ride in the airplane where "there's too much air conditioning, wind from outer space flowing in through the small nozzles" (p. 301) merge into one image—something cold and humming somewhere above Rennie's head. The clothing of the various characters also blends together: the safari jacket worn by the Canadian government official looks like a doctor's uniform; the outfits of the stewardesses on the plane, pink satin with white aprons, and the blue and white uniforms of the waitresses at the Sunset Inn are outfits similar to those worn by nurses. Whenever Rennie mentions her clothing, it is usually white, "a plain white cotton dress" (p. 59), a "white shirt and wrap skirt, also white" (p. 203). The bed she sleeps in with Paul has been "expertly made, hospital corners tucked firmly in" (p. 203). Recalling a dream she has had during her night with Paul, Rennie describes "another man in bed with them; something white, a stocking or a gauze bandage, wrapped around his head" (p. 217). The mosquito netting around her bed at the Sunset Inn blends with her description of crawling through "the grey folds of netting" (p. 173) as she lies on the hospital bed and with the threatened suffocation she describes just before escaping to St. Antoine: "Rennie closes her eyes. Something with enormous weight comes down on them" (p. 259). Daniel's hands blend with those of her grandmother. Her fantasized leaving of the jail corresponds with a patient's leaving a hospital: "Rennie will be taken to a small room, painted apple green. On the wall there will be a calendar with a picture of a sunset on it. There will be a desk with a phone and some papers on it"

(p. 293). The recurring italicized words, "*malignant,*" "*massive involvement,*" "*terminal,*" and the italicized statement overheard at Dr. Minnow's funeral, "*What did she die of? Cancer, praise the lord,*" combine to give, in the disembodied voice of the novel, political and bodily correspondence. Blood colors the text.

*Bodily Harm* seems, therefore, a considerably more complicated text than at first appeared. Although the story as told by Rennie superficially follows narrative logic and gives the reader a plot to hold on to, that plot is in fact profoundly ambiguous. Unlike the cover story, the submerged stories follow no specific chronology nor do they make clear their space. Yet, from the clues gathered and the dreams interpreted, a here and now do emerge: it seems possible that the novel presents Rennie's drugged reflections in the hospital.

But what does the reader gain by discovering that the ambiguous here and now of the novel are in fact its subject? Furthermore, what point is there in establishing the connection between jail cell and hospital bed? The title helps our search for an answer. The novel is predominantly concerned with bodies, most notably, with Rennie's. It is also concerned with harm, the symbol of which, on the body, is the mark of castration. Can we therefore discover, on a woman's body, the marks that will allow us to read her story? For much of the novel, Rennie reveals herself to be a thoroughly manipulated writer, and repeatedly emphasizes that she is *not* writing. Nonetheless, that her body is to be imagined as potential material for inscription is abundantly clear. After Daniel operates on her, he says: "Think of your life as a clean page. You can write whatever you like on it" (p. 84). Later, buying postcards to send home, Rennie recalls this conversation with Daniel and reflects that "empty is not the same as clean" (p. 85). She also recalls herself complaining to Jake: "Sometimes I feel like a blank sheet of paper. . . . For you to doodle on" (p. 105). Rennie even establishes a physical difference between phallic penetration and female passivity when she wonders "what it was like to be able to throw yourself into another person, another body, a darkness like that. Women could not do it. Instead they had darkness thrown into them" (pp. 235–36). In many of the ways elucidated by Gilbert and Gubar, for Rennie the pen is phallic, the page the female body.[4]

The powerlessness of women's inscribing is certainly attacked by Hélène Cixous in "The Laugh of the Medusa," when she insists that "woman must write her self: must write about women and bring women to writing, from which they have been driven away as violently as from their bodies—for the same reasons, by the same law, with the same fatal goal. Women must put herself into the text—as into the world and into history—by her own movement" (p. 875). And, later: "Here they are, returning, occurring over and again, because the unconscious is impregnable. They have wandered around in circles *confined to the narrow room* in which they've been given a deadly brainwashing" (p. 877, my italics). Perhaps, then, Atwood's novel illustrates, ironically, inscription of the female body and, by connecting hospital room and jail cell, dramatically presents the injury to the female body that results from its confinement. Similar bodily harm is described in another of the poems from *True Stories:*

> But power like this is not abstract, it's not concerned
> with politics and free will, it's beyond slogans
> and as for passion, this
> is its intricate denial.
> the knife that cuts lovers
> out of your flesh like tumours,
> leaving you breastless
> and without a name,
> flattened, bloodless, even your voice
> cauterized by too much pain.
>
> a flayed body untangled
> string by string and hung
> to the wall, an agonized banner
> displayed for the same reason
> flags are. (p. 51)

The metaphoric relationship between the female body and the country, Canada, here, as in *Bodily Harm,* insists on the connection of the politics of sexual power with the politics of colonial domination, for, like women, Canada is only now emerging from a "deadly brainwashing." Atwood seems to suggest that such a brainwashing has clearly interfered with both Canada's history and her literature.

Up to a point, the novel therefore appears to be an intricate analysis of female history (with underlying allusions to Canada), and a record of the dismembering of the female body. Inside and outside are radically confused. Rennie's divided consciousness, like the split space and time of the narrative, seems to represent both disrupted female history and a confused sense of self. Early in the novel, she imagines "herself from the outside, as if she were a moving target in someone else's binoculars" (p. 40). Both inside and outside are subjects in this novel; so too are the conflicts between appearance and actuality, stereotypes and realistic characters, woman's superficial exterior and the interior text of her self. Rennie struggles with repression. "Her real fear, irrational but a fear, is that the scar will come undone in the water, split open like a faulty zipper, and she will turn inside out" (p. 80). She is physically revolted by Lora's hand: "She doesn't like the sight of ravage, damage, the edge between inside and outside blurred like that" (p. 86). The operation thus seems a metaphor for a radical split in consciousness and for the repression that results:

> There's a line between being asleep and awake which Rennie is finding harder and harder to cross. Now she's up near the ceiling, in the corner of a white room, beside the air-conditioning unit, which is giving out a steady hum. She can see everything, clear and sharp, under glass, her body is down there on the table, covered in green cloth. There are figures around her in masks, they're in the middle of a performance, an incision, but it's not skin-deep, it's the heart they're after, in there somewhere, squeezing away, a fist opening and closing around a ball of blood. (pp. 172–73)

The separation between consciousness and the female body-text is here dramatically described. So too is the act of writing. Like all the other hands of the novel (Lora's, the grandmother's, Daniel's, the deaf and dumb man's), the fist that opens and closes around "a ball of blood" seems a metaphor for painful inscription.

Nonetheless, *Bodily Harm* is not, finally, a negative text. As the sign of the father is recognized ("she's afraid of men. . . . because men are frightening" [p. 290]), a new sign begins to emerge. For women, this sign seems to be that of the mother, the sign of creativity, freedom, even flight. Thus, this novel also describes the joining of splits that have dominated texts by women. Rennie first imagines joining through positive sexual intercourse, an experience that is paralleled with the separation experienced on the operating table:

> Nobody lives forever, who said you could? This much will have to do, this much is enough. She's open now, she's been opened, she's being drawn back down, she enters her body again, and there's a moment of pain, incarnation, this may be only the body's desperation, a flareup, a last clutch at the world before the long slide into final illness and death; but meanwhile she's solid after all, she's still here on the earth, she's grateful, he's touching her, she can still be touched. (p. 204)

But it is not enough. Sexual joining does not give woman control of the pen. Instead, Rennie has to go further; she has to give birth to herself. In a powerful doubling towards the end of the novel, Lora and Rennie become one: "She turns Lora over, her body is limp and thick, a dead weight. . . . She's holding Lora's left hand, between both of her own, perfectly still, nothing is moving, and yet she knows she is pulling on the hand as hard as she can, there's an invisible hole in the air, Lora is on the other side of it and she has to pull her through, she's gritting her teeth with the effort" (pp. 298–99). A birth indeed!

A three-part movement seems, then, to define the production of a female text: a recognition of the silence imposed on the castrated body by patriarchal rules; an illustration of the use the male pen has made of the female body as text; a final enlightenment that gives birth to an independent and complete female body. When this birth occurs, the female text is ready to be written. Only then, as Cixous suggests, can women "take pleasure in jumbling the order of space, in dissolving it, in changing around the furniture, dislocating things and values, breaking them all up, emptying structures" (p. 887). Flying becomes "woman's gesture—flying in language and making it fly" (p. 887). When Rennie describes flight at the end of the novel, she stops being text and becomes writer. She can now inscribe herself.

According to Marks and de Courtivron, French feminists "poke fun at the male erection, the male preoccupation with getting it up, keeping it up, and the ways in which the life and death of the penis are projected into other aspects of culture: in the need for immortality and posterity, in the fear of death, in the centralized organization of political systems, in the impossibility of living in the here and now" (p. 36). To a considerable degree, Atwood's text does "poke fun" at the penis, although the humor is very black, and the knowledge of the depths of its destructiveness is paramount. Throughout, the game of Clue implies a kind of conjunction between play and torture, between fun and terror. Yet Rennie can imagine extricating herself from its various combinations, even from the one that most damages her own writing: man with the pen in the text, the victim the female body. She learns how to write herself and about herself. Furthermore, she learns to deal with the fear of death ("Zero is waiting somewhere, whoever said there was life everlasting; so why feel grateful? She doesn't have much time left, for anything. But neither does anyone else. She's paying attention, that's all" [p. 301]), to question "the centralized organization of political systems," to live in "the here and now." Luce Irigaray insists that woman's dominant pleasure is touching rather than seeing. Rennie learns the importance of touching: "she can feel the shape of a hand in hers, both of hers, there but not there, like the afterglow of a match that's gone out. It will always be there now" (p. 300).

In *Archetypal Patterns in Women's Fiction,* Annis Pratt writes: "Since women are alienated from time and space, their plots take on cyclical, rather than linear, form and their houses and landscapes surreal properties" (p. 11). Spatial and temporal alienation dominates much of Atwood's novel and its landscape, as Rennie herself emphasizes, is insistently surreal. Yet, at the same time, in this moving dramatization of the female body-text, the novel arrives somewhere. Although the time and the space of the novel are limited (a confined area, one day), by the end Rennie has become her own mother, has given birth to herself. Dismembered, fragmented, victimized, the female body has regrouped, has become its own subject. No longer the blank page, it is prepared to write itself, to report. Thus, in a fundamental way, the title, *Bodily Harm,* has been canceled, the sign of castration (the former sign of the female sex) refused.[5] Not surprisingly, Rennie "for the first time in her life . . . can't think of a title" (p. 301). She has discovered herself through a new and subversive language.

## *Notes*

I would like to thank the National Endowment for the Humanities for the grant that made the writing of this paper possible.

1. Page references in the text are to the following editions: *Bodily Harm* (Toronto: McClelland and Stewart, 1981); *True Stories* (Toronto: Oxford Univ. Press, 1981). A shorter version of this essay was presented at the National Women's Studies Association Conference in 1983; a longer,

slightly different version constitutes chapter 2 of *Sub/Version,* my study of Canadian women writers published in 1986. Since working through various of the themes in the novel, I have read Elaine Tuttle Hansen's "Fiction and (Post) Feminism in Atwood's *Bodily Harm.*" As I do, Hansen pays close attention to the opening sentence of *Bodily Harm,* to the subversive feminist argument throughout, and to the connections between politics and narrative. Hansen's emphasis on consciousness raising and on metaphors of healing foregrounds important elements in the text to which I have paid less attention.

2. A number of titles reflect the importance of this question to Canadian literature, for example, Frank Davey's *From There to Here: A Guide to English Canadian Literature Since 1960;* John Moss's *The Canadian Novel Here and Now;* Sandra Djwa's "The Where of Here: Margaret Atwood and a Canadian Tradition."

3. In *The Wacousta Syndrome,* Gaile McGregor argues that, at least from the evidence of their cultural artifacts, Canadians distrust transcendence. Her discussion of Jack Hodgins's *The Invention of the World* strikingly reflects what I have just said about *Bodily Harm:* "In Hodgins's fictional universe, for example, life is a closed system, a *box,* from which—as from the reception hall that stands as its symbolic correlative at the end of the novel—there is only one exit, under the aegis of the Horseman, death" (p. 82). Later, McGregor writes: "From one point of view the 'box' makes a mockery of human aspirations. From another, a demythicized landscape says that anything is possible—at least 'inside.' Canadian literature in the twentieth century has largely addressed itself to the task of negotiating if not often actually reconciling these two extremes" (p. 90).

4. The whole first section of *The Madwoman in the Attic* is introduced by the now famous question: "Is the pen a metaphorical penis?" Also relevant is Susan Gubar's " 'The Blank Page' and the Issues of Female Creativity," in *Critical Inquiry.* She writes that Dinesen's story "can be used to illustrate how women's image of herself as text and artifact has affected her attitudes toward her physicality and how these attitudes in turn shape the metaphors through which she imagines her creativity" (p. 247).

5. In *Communities of Women,* Auerbach describes Monique Wittig's work symbolically as follows: "The apparent zero of the vulva, token of traditional and Freudian visions of female incompleteness, is transmuted by female art into the circle of eternity" (p. 186).

# 8 *Nature and Nurture in Dystopia*
## The Handmaid's Tale
*Roberta Rubenstein*

I

One might say that Margaret Atwood has always been concerned with issues of survival—first as a condition of Canadian experience and, more recently, as a condition of female experience. In her latest fiction and poetry, she connects the personal and political dimensions of victimization and survival in explicitly female and feminist terms. Moreover, in the course of her fiction the terms of survival have become increasingly problematic. In her fablelike *The Handmaid's Tale,*[1] she stunningly extends, recasts, and inverts two of the most persistent clusters of theme and imagery that originate in her earlier concern with survival: *nature* and *nurture.*

As a number of her commentators have pointed out, Atwood uses the imagery of nature in her poetry and fiction in complex ways, delineating the terms of survival and growth as well as oppression and death. Concurrently, from the beginning of her fictional oeuvre in particular, *nurture*—I use the term here as ironic shorthand for motherhood and procreation—is viewed in problematic terms. In *The Edible Woman,* Marian MacAlpin's female friends dramatize extreme attitudes toward procreation as a "natural" function of female identity: Ainsley is obsessed with becoming pregnant while Clara is virtually engulfed by maternity. Marian views both women with scepticism and anxiety. A central problem for the narrator of *Surfacing* is the necessity to come to terms with her denied abortion; the somewhat ambiguous sign of her psychological recovery is her desire to be impregnated by her primitive lover, Joe.

Joan Foster of *Lady Oracle* also feels anxiety about motherhood, principally because for much of her life (as revealed in her story) she has remained psychologically merged with her destructive mother. Her childhood obesity and her adult fantasies of the sideshow "Fat Lady" are grotesque exaggerations of anxieties about maternity. In *Life Before Man* Elizabeth Schoenhof and Lesje Green represent complementary views of motherhood. Elizabeth has appreciative but rather remote relationships with her two daughters; Lesje, unmarried but perhaps pregnant (by Elizabeth's husband, Nate) by the end of the narrative, seeks maternity to confirm her fragile female identity. Rennie Wilford of *Bodily Harm* worries that the cancer in her body, which has already resulted in the loss of part of a breast, will fundamentally alter her reproductive capacity.

In *The Handmaid's Tale,* female anxieties associated with fertility, procreation, and maternity are projected as feminist nightmare and cultural catastrophe. Atwood demonstrates the way in which the profound and irreconcilable split between "pro-life" and "pro-choice" ideologies of reproduction in contemporary social experience corroborate female ambivalence about childbearing in patriarchy. She imagines a world in which women are explicitly defined by their potential fertility (or its absence); procreation and maternity are simultaneously idealized and dehumanized.

Atwood has recently acknowledged her increasingly explicit ideological focus, noting that there is a vital connection between the function of the novel as a "moral instrument," the responsibility of the writer to "bear witness," and politics. As she elaborates, "By 'political' I mean having to do with power: who's got it, who wants it, how it operates; in a word, who's allowed to do what to whom, who gets what from whom, who gets away with it and how" ("An End to Audience?" *Second Words,* p. 353). In her most recent novel to date, the correspondences between "personal" and "political" find brilliant and disturbing expression. Both public and private worlds are radically altered, exaggerating the unresolved cultural and ideological controversy over the circumstances of procreation.

In the Republic of Gilead the "natural" world is utterly denatured. Pollution of the environment has resulted in adult sterility and genetic mutation and deformity of offspring; generativity itself is at risk. Hence, fertile females are made vessels for procreation; anatomy is indeed destiny. The physically confining rooms, walls, and other actual boundaries of the Republic of Gilead corroborate the condition of reproductive "confinement" to which the handmaids are subject. Maternity is both wish (handmaids are discarded after three unsuccessful attempts at pregnancy) and fear (the baby, unless deformed and declared an "Unbaby," becomes the property of the handmaid's Commander and his wife). The surrogate mother's function ceases after a brief lactation period following delivery of a healthy child.

The handmaid Offred (the narrator), subjected to sexual exploitation masquerading as religious fervor and worship of procreation, experiences herself as utterly subordinated to the procreative function. In her former life she had regarded her body as an "instrument" under her own control—with "limits . . . but nevertheless lithe, single, solid, one with me" (p. 84). In Gilead, her body, like that of her coequal "handmaids," exists literally to be used against her: "Now the flesh rearranges itself differently. I'm a cloud, congealed around a central object, the shape of a pear, which is hard and more real than I am and glows red within its translucent wrapping. Inside it is a space, huge as the sky at night . . ." (p. 84). Under the pressure of terrifying alternatives, Offred (whose name encodes her indentured sexuality: both "offered" and the property "Of-Fred") "resign[s her] body freely, to the uses of others. They can do what they like with me. I am abject" (p. 298)—and object.

## II

From the central issue of procreation to the language and imagery that form the substructure of Offred's narrative, *The Handmaid's Tale* demonstrates multiple inversions and violations of ***nature*** and ***natural***. Not only is the female body used as a tool for reproduction, but bodies in general are objectified and described in terms of parts rather than as wholes. In *Bodily Harm*

Atwood implied that the reduction of the body to a "thing" is connected to its violation; in *The Handmaid's Tale* torture and mutilation as well as less extreme forms of manipulation underscore the ruthless and repressive values that shape Gilead. Both men and women who are identified as political "enemies" of the state—guilty of such crimes as "gender treachery" (p. 53)—are sacrificed at public ceremonies called "Salvagings" (the word resonates ironically with *salvage, salvation,* and *savaging*) in which they are mutilated and hanged in public view.

Other images throughout the narrative reinforce the symbolism of disembodiment and dismemberment. When Offred tries to recall her visceral connections to the husband and daughter from whom she has been so abruptly separated, she mourns, "Nobody dies from lack of sex. It's lack of love we die from. There's nobody here I can love. . . . Who knows where they are or what their names are now? They might as well be nowhere, as I am for them. I too am a missing person. . . . Can I be blamed for wanting a real body, to put my arms around? Without it I too am disembodied" (p. 113). Most obviously, Offred and other handmaids are, to those in power in Gilead, merely parts of bodies: "two-legged wombs" (p. 146). The doctor who examines them periodically for signs of pregnancy never even sees their faces; he "deals with a torso only" (p. 70). The ceiling ornament in Offred's room resembles "the place in a face where the eye has been taken out" (p. 17); in fact, there are Eyes—the network of informants (C-Eye-A?)—everywhere. The grappling hooks on the large Berlin Wall–like structure where criminals are hanged look like "appliances for the armless" (p. 42). An image of people with "no legs" (p. 143) resonates with the unknown but terrible torture to which the rebel handmaid Moira is subjected (p. 102) and with Offred's first intimation of the changing dispensation that has culminated in the Republic of Gilead. When she and other women were fired from their jobs and summarily stripped of political and legal rights, she felt as if someone had "cut off [her] feet" (p. 188). In these latter instances of literal or symbolic mutilation of female feet, the image of Chinese footbinding—another form of social control of women—comes to mind.

In Gilead, Aunt Lydia (one of the "Aunts," who retain power in the puritanical state through their role as indoctrinators of the handmaids) speaks distastefully of women in the recent past who cultivated suntans, "oiling themselves like roast meat on a spit . . ." (p. 65). In her former life, Offred had been aware of the self-mutilations practiced by women who, desperate to attract men, had "starved themselves thin or pumped their breasts full of silicone, had their noses cut off" (p. 231). She also recalls more violent crimes against the (implicitly female) body, as expressed in newspaper stories of "corpses in ditches or the woods, bludgeoned to death or mutilated, interfered with as they used to say . . ." (p. 66). In Gilead the handmaids, as part of their "re-education" in submission, are made to watch old pornographic films from the seventies and eighties in which women appear in various attitudes of submission, brutalization, and grotesque mutilation. Extrapolating from these contemporary realities, Atwood extends into the future her critique of female brutalization articulated in *Bodily Harm* and in recent essays.

The imagery of mutilation and dismemberment permeates the narrator's own language. Offred struggles to "reconstruct" (p. 144) her fragmented selfhood and to justify the choices she has made (or which have been imposed on her) under the circumstances she describes. Her past experiences, apparently severed from the "present" time of Gileadean tyranny, are in fact linked by these very images of female brutalization. The terse words she exchanges with other handmaids, who may or may not be trustworthy confidantes, are "amputated speech" (p. 211). Late in her story Offred apologizes to an unknown audience in whom she must believe for her own survival; her story is an act of self-generation that opposes the oppressive obligations of procreation. She describes her narrative as if it were herself, "a body caught in crossfire or pulled apart by force . . . this sad and hungry and sordid, this limping and mutilated story" (p. 279).

## III

Among the multiple inversions of normalcy in *The Handmaid's Tale* are frequent references to animals, plants, smells, and other objects or experiences typically associated with "nature." In Gilead the changing seasons bring no solace; spring is "undergone" (p. 160). The month of May, however, is linked with the one possibility of freedom: the password of the resistance movement, "Mayday," with its coded message of "*M'aidez*" (p. 54).

Flowers are among the few objects of the natural world whose symbolic associations have not been entirely corrupted. Offred frequently describes them in terms of color and variety and, late in her narrative, confesses that they are among the "good things" she has tried to put in her sordid story (p. 279). More often, flowers and plants suggest the confining circumstances of sexuality and reproduction. Offred struggles to keep the image of crimson tulips (also the color of the nunlike robes worn by the handmaids) free from association with blood. The blossoms worn by Serena Joy (the ironic name of Offred's Commander's wife) are withered, like her sexuality; flowers are, Offred reminds herself, merely "the genital organs of plants" (p. 91). Elsewhere she describes the reeking "stink" of "pollen thrown into the wind in handfuls, like oyster spawn into the sea. All this prodigal breeding" (p. 190). Handmaids are told to think of themselves as seeds (p. 28); their password to each other is "Blessed be the fruit" (p. 29)—yet seeds and fruit are associated with manipulated, not natural, reproduction.

The narrative is studded with such references to plant and animal life—generally primitive or lower forms—which are often juxtaposed with aspects of the human body and/or sexuality. The animals in Gilead are, for the most part, repugnant. A virtual menagerie of insects, fish, fowl, and beasts parades, figuratively, through the narrative: ant, beetle, spider, fly, worm, oyster, mollusk, rat, mouse, fish, frog, snake, pigeon, hawk, vulture, chicken, turkey, pig, sheep, horse, cat, dog, elephant. The handmaids are treated like brood livestock: tattooed with "cattle brands" (p. 266), they are kept in line by women called Aunts who wield electric cattleprods.

The "livestock" of the narrative is partly of the zoo, partly of the barnyard—the latter figures recalling Orwell's satiric *Animal Farm.* Offred thinks of herself, in the eyes of the powers of Gilead, as a "prize pig" (p. 79); another handmaid takes mincing steps like a "trained pig" (p. 29). Both usages resonate ironically with the other-gendered "chauvinist pig[s]" (p. 131) and "fucking pigs" (p. 190) of Offred's mother's generation. A number of the animal images are associated with confinement: caged rats in mazes (pp. 79, 174), "held birds" (p. 80) or birds with wings clipped or "stopped in flight" (pp. 289, 305), and the predatory relationship of spider to fly (p. 89). Handmaids are both sexual "bait" and "baited," as in the sense of "fishbait" (p. 164) or "throwing peanuts at elephants" (p. 212).

Often, the animal references suggest the debased, denatured, dismembered human body as mere flesh. Offred, walking after a rainy night on a path through the back lawn that suggests "a hair parting" (p. 27), observes half-dead worms, "flexible and pink, like lips" (p. 27). In the dehumanized sexual act (a ménage à trois in the service of insemination: the Commander, his Wife, and the Handmaid), the penis is disembodied: the male "tentacle, his delicate stalked slug's eye, which extrudes, expands, winces, and shrivels back into himself when touched wrongly, grows big again, bulging a little at the tip, travelling forward as if along a leaf, into [the women], avid for vision" (p. 98). Elsewhere Offred imagines sexual encounters between "Angels" and their brides (insipid young men and women of Gilead who actually marry) as "furry encounters . . . cocks like three-week-old carrots, anguished fumblings upon flesh cold and unresponding as uncooked fish" (p. 234). Similarly, she imagines a balding Commander with his wife and handmaid, "fertilizing away like mad, like a rutting salmon . . ." (p. 230).

Thus, in the perverse relations of Gilead, the distinctions between "natural" and "unnatural," between human and nonhuman, are grotesquely inverted or reduced. In a central passage Atwood suggestively links these levels of imagery and theme, clustering the ideas of institutionalized reproduction, environmental pollution, and the inversions between animal, vermin, and human that result from these perversions of normalcy. As Offred explains,

> The air got too full, once, of chemicals, rays, radiation, the water swarmed with toxic molecules, all of that takes years to clean up, and meanwhile they creep into your body, camp out in your fatty cells. Who knows, your very flesh may be polluted, dirty as an oily beach, sure death to shore birds and unborn babies. Maybe a vulture would die of eating you. Maybe you light up in the dark, like an old-fashioned watch. Death watch. That's a kind of beetle, it buries carrion.
>
> I can't think of myself, my body, sometimes, without seeing the skeleton: how I must appear to an electron. A cradle of life made of bones; and within, hazards, warped proteins, bad crystal jagged as glass. Women took medicines, pills, men sprayed trees, cows ate grass, all that

souped-up piss flowed into the rivers. Not to mention the exploding atomic power plants, along the San Andreas fault, nobody's fault, during the earthquakes, and the mutant strain of syphilis no mould could touch. Some did it themselves, had themselves tied shut with catgut or scarred with chemicals. (p. 122)

The chances of giving birth to a deformed infant are, the handmaids learn during their indoctrination, one in four. Yet Gileadean ideology prohibits birth control and abortion under any circumstances as "unnatural" and obliges the handmaids to submit to "natural" childbirth without medication. The pregnancy that culminates in birth during Offred's narrative is a manifestation of this revolt by nature, the blurring of categories of living forms. Before the handmaid Janine delivers, Offred speculates on whether the baby will be normal or "an Unbaby, with a pinhead or a snout like a dog's, or two bodies, or a hole in its heart or no arms, or webbed hands and feet" (p. 122). In fact the baby initially seems normal, but is later discovered to be deformed and is mysteriously disposed of. Despite the obsessive focus on procreation, actual children are notably absent from Gilead. The only child described in the narrative is the young daughter from whom Offred has been painfully separated.

As part of the inversion of "natural" in the unnatural Republic of Gilead, Atwood demonstrates the assault on the senses as well as the body and the psyche. In keeping with the implicit barnyard references, Gilead *stinks.* The stench of rotting flesh from the corpses of executed political enemies—including doctors who practiced abortion—masks the equally humanmade but relatively less repugnant odors of "Pine and Floral" deodorizing sprays. As Offred phrases it, "people retain the taste" for these artificial scents as the expression of "purity" (p. 174)—embodying the false connection between cleanliness and godliness.

Conversely, uncleanliness is associated with sin and—since sex is evil in Gilead apart from procreation—sexuality. The servant Marthas express distaste toward the handmaids, objecting to their smell; the handmaids, to whom baths are permitted as a luxury rather than as a hygienic routine, are regarded as unclean not only in the literal but in the moral sense.[2] Nuns who are forced to renounce celibacy and become reproductive objects have "an odour of witch about them, something mysterious and exotic . . ." (p. 232). When Offred first observes Nick, her Commander's chauffeur who later becomes her lover, she wonders whether or not he supports the status quo arrangements between the sexes. As she expresses her doubts, "Smells fishy, they used to say; or, I smell a rat. Misfit as odour" (p. 28). Yet, instead, she thinks of "how he might smell. Not fish or decaying rat: tanned skin, moist in the sun, filmed with smoke. I sigh, inhaling" (p. 28). When Offred tries to (and tries not to) imagine what might have happened to her husband, Luke, she thinks of him "surrounded by a smell, his own, the smell of a cooped-up animal in a dirty cage" (p. 115). Later the rebel handmaid Moira describes her contact with the underground resistance movement in similar terms. " 'I almost made it out. They got me up as far as Salem, then in a truck full of chickens into Maine. I almost puked from the smell' " (p. 259).

The air of Gilead is stagnant, suffocating, oppressive: literally, the polluted atmosphere; symbolically, the claustrophobia and oppression experienced by its unwilling female captives. Offred describes the atmosphere of a "birthing"—a collective ceremony, attended by both handmaids and wives who coach the delivering handmaid—in language that reverberates with other images derived from animals and nature: "the smell is of our own flesh, an organic smell, sweat and a tinge of iron, from the blood on the sheet, and another smell, more animal, that's coming, it must be, from Janine: a smell of dens, of inhabited caves. . . . Smell of matrix" (p. 133).

As the sense of smell is more typically assaulted by the unnatural, so is the sense of taste and the experience of hunger. References to the smells of food also demonstrate the perverse connection—or disconnection—between sensory stimuli and their objects. The odor of nail polish, improbably, stimulates Offred's appetite (p. 39). Recalling the sexual violation termed "date rape" in her former life, she remembers that the term sounded like "some kind of dessert. *Date Rapé*" (p. 48).

In fact, like sex in Gilead, food serves only functional, not emotional, appetites. In a parody of the Lord's Prayer, Offred makes the connection between bread and spiritual sustenance, observing, "I have enough daily bread. . . . The problem is getting it down without choking on it" (p. 204). The yeasty aroma of baking bread, one of the few pleasant smells in Gilead, also recalls comfortable kitchens and "mothers": both Offred's own mother and herself as a mother. Accordingly, it is a "treacherous smell"

(p. 57) that she must resist in order not to be overwhelmed by loss. Later she provides another context for these ambiguous associations as she recalls her childhood confusion about the extermination of the Jews: "In ovens, my mother said; but there weren't any pictures of the ovens, so I got some confused notion that these deaths had taken place in kitchens. There is something especially terrifying to a child in that idea. Ovens mean cooking, and cooking comes before eating. I thought these people had been eaten. Which in a way I suppose they had been" (pp. 154–55).

Late in the narrative, Offred extends this link between eating and sacrifice. She describes another "Salvaging," the public execution of handmaids accused of treason and sacrificed before breakfast; she and the other handmaids grip a rope that reeks of tar, the other end of which is used to hang the offending women. Offred's reaction to her compulsory complicity in the horrifying event discloses the extent of her emotional numbing and deprivation. The tar odor makes her feel sick; yet at the same time,

> Death makes me hungry. Maybe it's because I've been emptied; or maybe it's the body's way of seeing to it that I remain alive, continue to repeat its bedrock prayer: ***I am, I am.*** I am, still.
> I want to go to bed, make love, right now.
> I think of the word ***relish.***
> I could eat a horse. (p. 293, Atwood's italics)

Offred's hungers are both literal and symbolic. Earlier, she had been "ravenous for news" (p. 29). When her Commander, having sought her out for forbidden companionship, allows her the proscribed act of reading, she reads like a starving person finally given food—"voraciously, almost skimming, trying to get as much into my head as possible before the next long starvation. If it were eating it would be the gluttony of the famished, if it were sex it would be a swift furtive stand-up in an alley somewhere" (p. 194). The pieces in the Scrabble game she plays with her Commander remind her of candies: peppermint, lime, "delicious" (p. 149). In Gilead, the act of intellectual intercourse is the equivalent of sin; as Offred puns, "Quick, eat those words" (p. 191).

"Nature" is also invoked in Gilead as justification for male sexual dominance and female oppression. Offred's Commander advises her that the era of romantic courtship and marriages based on love—the older dispensation—was "an anomaly, historically speaking. . . . All we've done is return things to Nature's norm" (p. 232). This "norm," however, leaves something to be desired for men who still prefer sex in the old manner, as conquest rather than duty. Those with power have access to a nightclub–brothel called Jezebel's. Resembling a Playboy Bunny Club, it is stocked with women in provocative costumes (primarily females "unassimilated" into other Gileadean roles) and private rooms for sexual assignations. To Offred's assumption that such things are "strictly forbidden," the Commander rejoins, " 'but everyone's human, after all. . . . [Y]ou can't cheat Nature. . . . Nature demands variety, for men. . . . [I]t's part of the procreational strategy. It's Nature's plan' " (pp. 248–49).[3] Even at Jezebel's, the ubiquitous cattle-prod-wielding Aunts preside, supervising the women's "rest breaks" and reinforcing the sense of sexual slavery that prevails in Gilead. The "forbidden" is accommodated, but only to serve traditional assumptions about male, not female, sexuality.

Offred's dark story of female exploitation concludes with an ambiguous event. A van arrives for her and—like an experience described by one of Kafka's characters—she has no way of knowing whether she is approaching her own "salvaging" or her salvation: whether she is being delivered into the hands of spies or rescuers. Entering the vehicle, she faces either her "end or a new beginning. . . . I have given myself over into the hands of strangers, because it can't be helped" (p. 307). The ambiguity corroborates the earlier conflations of death and birth: "And so I step up, into the darkness within; or else the light" (p. 307).

In the narrative's ironic coda, "Historical Notes on The Handmaid's Tale," the reader discovers that Offred's story was originally spoken onto audio tapes, presumably after her escape from the Republic of Gilead. From the distant perspective of the year 2195, at the Twelfth Symposium on Gileadean Studies held in Nunavit ("None-Of-It"—presumably somewhere in the Arctic reaches of Canada), anthropologists and historians meet to debate the chronology and authenticity of events detailed in Offred's story. (One imagines Atwood wryly anticipating her commentators at the annual rites of MLA!) In this pseudo-pedantic coda, the imagery of nature that is so consistently inverted in the handmaid's own narrative is briefly parodied. The conference facilitators bear names (presumably analogous to Canadian Inuit) with associations with nature: Professors Maryann Crescent Moon and Johnny Running Dog. Program participants can avail themselves of special activities, including a fishing expedition and a Nature Walk (p. 311).

From the more "objective" perspective of scholarly research, Professor Pieixoto, an archivist whose remarks comprise most of the coda, focuses less on the details of Offred's life than on the *men* who shaped it. Yet, as he concludes, "the past is a great darkness, and filled with echoes. Voices may reach us from it; but what they say to us is imbued with the obscurity of the matrix out of which they come. . . ." (p. 324).

Along with the professor's concessions to the limits of interpretation, his choice of words is particularly resonant, given the narrative that precedes his remarks. The "matrix" of Offred's experiences—with its linguistic associations with mother and matter—is the matrix out of which Atwood has written her dystopian fantasy of female oppression. If "nature" and "nurture" are the matrices out of which we come, *The Handmaid's Tale,* by inverting both, demonstrates the "broad outlines of the moment in history" (p. 317) in which we live: the inhospitable environment in which female identity must discover itself. Appropriately, the narrative ends with the interrogative, " 'Are there any questions?' " (p. 324).

## *Notes*

1. Atwood, *The Handmaid's Tale* (Toronto: McClelland and Stewart, 1985). Page references in the text are to this edition.

2. I am grateful to Annette Kolodny for pointing out the "literality" of this detail.

3. In a brilliant and influential essay, "Is Female to Male as Nature Is to Culture," Ortner has traced the phenomenological linkages between "female" and "nature" in terms that illuminate Atwood's narrative. According to Ortner, women are perceived, in virtually all societies, as "closer" to nature. This proximity derives from physiological functions, domestic roles (including childrearing), and psychic makeup. The consequences of the cultural attribution of women as "intermediate" between culture and nature can be interpreted as "middle status" in a hierarchy, as "mediating" between the two categories, or as ambiguous (both "above" and "below" culture).

# 9 *Future Tense*
## *Making History in* The Handmaid's Tale

*Arnold E. Davidson*

Margaret Atwood in *The Handmaid's Tale* conjoins two different projected futures. The first, distinctly dystopian, is Gilead, a fundamentally tyrannical order the author envisions for the Northeastern United States. The handmaid Offred's secret account (the women of Gilead are not even to have thoughts of their own, much less stories) gives us the measure of Gilead and particularly emphasizes—as even Offred's name attests—its use and abuse of women. This same account gives us, too, Gilead's genealogy, the story of its rapid rise in the last years of the twentieth century. Understandably alleviating her devastating assessment of her life in Gilead with memories of a different past, Offred records the traumatic transition from one order of things to a radically different order, all of which takes place within the limited span of her childbearing years.

Or perhaps Gilead embodies not such a radically different order after all. In fact, *The Handmaid's Tale* portrays the advent of that society as an easy slide into "final solutions" only slightly less brutal than those attempted in Nazi Germany (but solutions given a thoroughly American habitation and name) and thereby fulfills the traditional function of the dystopia. By envisioning an appalling future already implicit in the contemporary world, Atwood condemns just those present propensities that make a Gilead possible and does so on every level, even the comic. There is something humorously appropriate, for example, when the Commander's wife, formerly a spokesperson for women in the

Phyllis Schlafly mode, gets exactly the life that she earlier advocated for others and does not find it good. And there is something tragically wrong when others, such as Offred, who ask for little get so much less, not even the children they are forced to bear for the state (if they are lucky enough to conceive them, since, for handmaids, the alternative to fertility is death).

Yet Offred's perturbing narration does not comprise the whole of *The Handmaid's Tale.* Appended to the fifteen titled sections that constitute her account and the bulk of the novel is a final part not numbered as another section nor even designated as a separate chapter. These "Historical Notes" give us both a second future (a future to Gilead) and the genealogy of Offred's account, which up to that point we have been reading. The resultant disjunction might well seem disconcerting. After an appalling story of tyranny, genocide, and gynocide in late twentieth-century America, we are, in effect, brought fast-forward to June 25, 2195, to the University of Denay in Nunavit and an International Historical Association's rather placid (if pompous) intellectual foray back into the Gilead Regime.

This unequal division of the text serves several narrative functions. On a most immediate level, the second part provides, as previously noted, the history of Offred's history and an account of how her private record has become a public document, the object of future historians' attention. That attention, moreover, supplements Offred's story by the very act of subjecting it to academic scrutiny. Whereas Offred describes the practices of Gilead, the Twelfth Symposium on Gileadean Studies can provide some of the theory that underlies those practices. Thus, we are given the analysis of the use of the "Aunts" as especially "cost-effective" or the observation that Gilead itself was partly the product of earlier theories such as the sociobiology of Wilfred Limpkin. A retrospective symposium attests, too, that Gilead was survived and as such constitutes a distinct note of hope for the future. But that note is countered by another consideration. The historical notes, like any scholarly afterword, also serve to validate the text that they follow, and there is something ominous in that claiming of the right to have the last word.

Retrospective analysis by a Cambridge don—male, of course—is ostensibly more authoritative than a participant woman's eyewitness account. Furthermore, the supposed "objectivity" of the scholarly enterprise of the Twelfth Symposium on Gileadean Studies is a chilling postscript to a story in which women (and others too: blacks, Jews, homosexuals, Quakers, Baptists) have been totally *objectified,* rendered into objects by the State. Is the process beginning again? And implicit in that question is a more immediate one. Do we, as scholars, contribute to the dehumanizations of society by our own critical work, especially when, as according to the distinguished professor of the novel, "our job is not to censure but to understand"?[1] Atwood's epilogue loops back through the text that precedes it to suggest that the ways in which scholars (present as well as future) assemble the text of the past confirms the present and thereby helps to predict the future, even the horrific future endured by Offred. In short, Atwood does not let intellectuals off the hook—and the hook is a loaded metaphor in *The Handmaid's Tale.* How we *choose* to construct history partly determines the history we are likely to get.

Another version of this same problematics of history is implicit in the textual question posed by the epilogue. "The Handmaid's Tale" in its present form is not the only possible ordering of the "some thirty tapes" (we are never told exactly how many) that have been transcribed (we are never told how directly) into text. The editors, we are specifically informed, have intervened to make choices about the structure of the tale. Moreover, Professor Knotly Wade of Cambridge and Professor James Darcy Pieixoto, Director of the Twentieth and Twenty-First Century Archives at Cambridge, have ordered thirty or so tapes into an extremely intricate structure—forty-six untitled chapters arranged in fifteen labeled sections, with the heading "Night" used seven times (and the only heading repeated). Professor Pieixoto admits that "all such arrangements are based on some guesswork and are to be regarded as approximate, pending further research" (p. 314). But that pro forma disclaimer does not acknowledge how much the very process of assembling a text (or writing the history of any age from its surviving traces) means *creating* a fiction. Where, then, is the boundary between novel and history? This textual question becomes all the more pertinent when juxtaposed against Atwood's insistence that everything in the book is "true," has, in some form in some society, already been done (Cathy N. Davidson, "A Feminist *1984,*" p. 24).

In a very real sense, the future presaged by "The Handmaid's Tale" is already *our* history, just as the meeting of the Gileadean Symposium of 2195 could readily be incorporated into a contemporary literature or history convention.[2] The relentlessness of history is partly what makes *The Handmaid's Tale* (like any successful dystopia) plausible. The plot of the novel also plays to our sense of the familiar. As Peter S. Prescott has observed, Atwood borrows the standard format of the dystopia (p. 70). First, the narrator experiences hopeless despair in the face of the brutal regime, then feels some hope through discovering the possibility of resistance (the Mayday Underground and the Underground Femaleroad) and begins to perceive cracks in what seemed to be the unassailable power of Gilead (the lapses of the Commander, Fred). This political hope is strengthened by personal hope in the form of a love affair, a testament to continuing human emotion in the face of the dehumanization of the regime. Finally, there is the possibility of escape. Within the tale itself, Offred's end is uncertain, yet the very existence of the tapes suggests that, aided by Nick, she did elude the rule of Gilead.

Even the most idiosyncratic feature of this dystopia, its female narrator, is tellingly domesticated. Offred's reconstructed narration embodies the same sexual dualities that Gilead exhibits in their starkest form. She is essentially passive and in need of rescue by a man, a gender cliché underscored by Professor Pieixoto's distinction between the "quasi military" Mayday Underground as opposed to the nurturing and escapist enterprise of the Underground Femaleroad. This distinction (supported with remarkably little data, it must be emphasized) posits men aggressively striving to destroy the regime and women merely reacting to it in a compassionate capacity. This distinction is further underscored by another of the professor's little jokes, his reduction of the Underground Femaleroad to "The Underground Frailroad." And of course, the whole title of the narration is appended by Professor Wade, "partly in homage to the great Geoffrey Chaucer" but also as an intentional pun on "the archaic vulgar signification of the word *tail*" (p. 313). Yet it is those little jokes that give the larger game away. The grotesque transformation of women's bodies into passive receptacles for the perpetuation of the genes of the Regime's Commanders is itself grotesquely transmogrified, in the twenty-second century, into silly sexist jests. As Atwood has noted to Cathy N. Davidson in an interview, this is "what happens to history—something that's a very intense experience for the people who are living it becomes a subject of speculation, often of witticism, and rather detached analysis two hundred years later."

The countering academic text is intended to condition future readings of the Gilead regime, just as Biblical commentaries (of any era or religion) condition readings of the Bible. Nor is that analogy gratuitous. Indeed, the Biblical fundamentalism of Gilead poses crucial questions about the interpretive use of literary texts, for that society's most appalling practices all have their scriptural justification. Chapter and verse can be cited for every atrocity, but who privileges those particular chapters and verses and decides how they should be read? And more important, how does that right to textual authority itself write the larger text of the society? The novel presents us with versions of this process in the Gileadean reading of the Bible and the professional reading of Gilead:

> If I may be permitted an editorial aside, allow me to say that in my opinion we must be cautious about passing moral judgement upon the Gileadeans. Surely we have learned by now that such judgements are of necessity culture-specific. Also, Gileadean society was under a good deal of pressure, demographic and otherwise, and was subject to factors from which we ourselves are happily more free. Our job is not to censure but to understand. (pp. 314–15)

Again an ostensibly marginal aside situates us right in the center of the professor's own moral judging and his society's "hypocritical self-congratulation." The conferees at the Twelfth Symposium on Gileadean Studies assent to Professor Pieixoto's remarks by a round of applause.

One imagines that "The Handmaid's Tale" could provide the scholars of the twenty-second century with a crucial text from the Gilead regime. Very little remains of Gilead, for destroying information—obliterating marks of the past—was part of the many purges that marked this unstable society. We are told that, besides Offred's tapes, anthropologists have discovered "The A. B. Memoirs" in a garage in a Seattle suburb and "The Diary of P." "excavated by accident during the erection of a new meeting house in the vicinity of what was once Syracuse, New York" (p.

313). Aside from offering us a tantalizing glimpse of what life might be like in the United States in 2195—does the new meeting house recapitulate the town structure of an earlier Puritan or Quaker theocracy?—the very scantiness of the evidence underscores how much history is the product of historians. The only other guide to the era is a "diary kept in cipher" by sociobiologist Wilfred Limpkin, a political insider whose theories of natural polygamy served as the "scientific justification for some of the odder practices of the regime, just as Darwinism was used by earlier ideologies" (p. 318).[3]

If social Darwinism supports rampant laissez-faire capitalism and sociobiology justifies the theocratic totalitarianism of Gilead, then, we must ask, what ideologies are supported by the seemingly innocuous exercise in literary history indulged in by those at the Twelfth Symposium on Gilead Studies? The form of historical analysis assayed by Pieixoto is, essentially, a pre-Foucault, pre–de Beauvoir form of historical criticism, which pretends to "objectivity," to placing texts within their historical "contexts" with little awareness that context itself is a construct. As Mary Wilson Carpenter has pointed out, Pieixoto continually trivializes the status of "The Handmaid's Tale" as document precisely because he trivializes women's role in society—in Gilead society, in his own society (p. 5). In fact, much of his narration is concerned not with the text itself but with attempting to discover the identity of Fred, the Commander to whom the narrator of "The Handmaid's Tale" is assigned. "What would we not give, now," Pieixoto laments, "for even twenty pages or so of printout from [the Commander's] private computer!" (p. 322).

The professor's desire for what he has not and the concomitant disregard for all that he has (if he could only read it better) is finally parodic. Other comic inversions also characterize the enterprise of these future scholars. For example, Professor Gopal Chatterjee, of the Department of Western Philosophy, University of Baroda, India, is scheduled to speak on "Krishna and Kali Elements in the State Religion in the Early Gilead Period." Or the session on "The Handmaid's Tale" is chaired by Professor Maryann Crescent Moon, of the Department of Caucasian Anthropology, University of Denay, Nunavit. And even Denay, the future nation in the north that a number of native peoples in Canada currently wish to form—a nation in which the traditional ways of the natives will replace the Western ways of their oppressors—embodies obvious contradictions. With most of the United States contaminated by radioactivity and other industrial and nuclear disasters, the far north has apparently become the seat of power in North America, and with power comes a society that mimes the very Western ways it was intended to oppose. Although the existence of a Department of Caucasian Anthropology reverses the usual hierarchies—who is studied, who studies—there still *are* such hierarchies and the institutions that embody them.

Maryann Crescent Moon's role as chair of the conference session on "The Handmaid's Tale" does not prove an egalitarian future. On the contrary, as soon as the keynote speaker ascends to the podium, we are shown the real distribution of textual and sexual power. The eminent Professor Pieixoto of Cambridge (another enduring hegemony despite his non-Anglo name) begins his talk with the standard speaker's ploy of breaking the ice with a joke. Yet his opening comment, ostensibly marginal to the topic at hand, effectively centers the professor's discourse, and from the very first he sounds his key note. A most dubious note it is. His joke turns upon a bad pun conjoining the "charming Arctic Char" that "we all enjoyed" last night at dinner and the current "Arctic Chair" that "we are [now] enjoying" (p. 312). Lest the full racist and sexist implications of that equation go unappreciated, he also spells out the different senses of "enjoy" and thereby elicits his audience's laughter. The chairwoman/charwoman thus assumes her marginal place as mere handmaiden to Pieixoto's central text.

Pieixoto's discourse mirrors, then, the structure of the novel of which it is a part, and by that mirroring it also claims the part it would play. "The Handmaid's Tale" as text serves as handmaiden to the career-enhancing epilogue provided by the academics. Is this what history is for? To round out the vitae of historians? Or does the asserted marginalization of one text set forth itself still another text and a context in which to read it? We know—from both Offred's narration and Pieixoto's speech—that the Caucasian birthrate declined disastrously in Gilead, thanks to such factors as radioactive fallout, chemical pollution, and a backfired plan for gene warfare against the Russians. Women who could bear children were therefore vital (literally) to the survival of the regime. But prospective mothers were nevertheless the most controlled, powerless, and demeaned members of that society. In short, there is no necessary relationship between one's importance to the perpetuation of society and one's privilege within that society. Significance and status are both constructs manipulated by those in power. Just as the conference chair in 2195 is peripheral to the proceedings themselves, so is Offred merely a marginal (and ultimately disposable) tool of the patriarchy that cannot exist without her.[4] What Atwood has written is not just a history of patriarchy but a metahistory, an analysis of how patriarchal imperatives are encoded within the various intellectual methods we bring to bear on history.

The historical notes with which *The Handmaid's Tale* ends provide comic relief from the grotesque text of Gilead. Yet in crucial ways the epilogue is the most pessimistic part of the book. Even with the lesson Gilead readily at hand, the intellectuals of 2195 seem to be preparing the way for Gilead again. In this projection of past, present, and future, the academic community is shown to have a role, not simply an "academic" role (passive, accommodating) but an active one in recreating the values of the past—which is, Atwood suggests, the way to create the values of the future. Professor Pieixoto's title is "Problems of Authentication in Reference to *The Handmaid's Tale,*" and his very mode of speaking authenticates her tale by retrospectively duplicating the suppression her society inflicted upon her, by claiming the right to determine the meaning of her experience. But because his reading of her experience verges back towards Gilead again, our reading of his reading can authenticate Offred's account in a different sense than the professor intended and can also show how insidious are the horrors at the heart of his dark narrative.

The professor, too, concludes with mixed metaphors of light and dark: "As all historians know, the past is a great darkness, and filled with echoes. Voices may reach us from it; but what they say to us is imbued with the obscurity of the matrix out of which they come; and, try as we may, we cannot always decipher them precisely in the clearer light of our own day" (p. 324). It is a brief peroration that elicits his audience's applause and prepares the way for any discussion that might follow. Indeed, when he ends, with again a standard ploy—"Are there any questions?" (p. 324)—that question itself well may be rhetorical. And even if it is not, the speaker has already indicated what he thinks the questions are. His questions, however, need not be our questions, especially when we consider the matrix out of which his asking comes. His persistent assertion of gender prerogatives darkens his claimed "clearer light of [his] own day" and conjoins his world with Gilead's and ours.

## *Notes*

1. Atwood, ***The Handmaid's Tale*** (Toronto: McClelland and Stewart, 1985), p. 315. Page references in the text are to this edition.

2. An old-fashioned "historical" critic searching for the "sources" of the novel might find a particularly germane item in Atwood's attending the 1984 Modern Language Association Convention, which, incidentally, included a special session on Atwood.

3. Annette Kolodny has pointed out (in private correspondence) that Wilfred Limpkin well might be based on Harvard sociobiologist F. O. Wilson, which would, of course, help to further ground Gilead in what was once Cambridge, Massachusetts. Obviously more is at stake than a Puritan past.

4. And of the historian, too, it might be added. As Offred at one point in her narration observes: "From the point of view of future history . . . we'll be invisible" (p. 24). Professor Pieixoto hardly refutes that claim.

# 10 *Weaving Her Version*
## *The Homeric Model and Gender Politics in* Selected Poems

*David Buchbinder*

Margaret Atwood's *Selected Poems*[1] offers the reader an overview of her work from 1966 (*The Circle Game*) to 1974 (*You Are Happy*). Such a collection is useful from several points of view, not the least of which are the opportunities to observe development in the poet's skill and technical accomplishment, and to trace her thematic preoccupations. These sorts of studies have been undertaken elsewhere (in, for example, Linda W. Wagner, "The Making of *Selected Poems,* the Process of Surfacing," and Sherrill E. Grace, "The Poetics of Duplicity"). What has not been demonstrated has been the way that thematic preoccupations such as Atwood's concern with gender politics also allow *Selected Poems* to be read as a unified text, independent of chronologies of composition. In this essay I propose to examine how the presence of a number of classical allusions unifies *Selected Poems,* bestowing upon the selection a continuity not usually assumed of such compilations.

Particularly, I wish to single out the intertextual references to Homer's *Odyssey,* as well as to the related myths from sources other than Homer. (I will call this group the Homeric model.) "Circe/Mud Poems" (pp. 201–23) form one such reference, as do the associated "Songs of the Transformed" (pp. 188–200), which includes a "Siren Song" (pp. 195–96). I shall argue that reading Atwood against Homer in this way uncovers a central unity of her poetry and invites the decoding of the poems as part of an intertexual as well as an intratextual discourse concerned with the nature of gender roles in the moves and countermoves of sexual politics. Such a reading establishes both gender-political and literary antecedents for Atwood's work and enables us to see how Atwood uses the Homeric model to resolve the problems generated in her poetry by the dynamic of gender politics with which she is concerned.

## I

The presence of a specifically Homeric model in the latter part of *Selected Poems* need not be defined as a late development in the chronology of Atwood's work. Rather, we can say that Atwood's choice of poems presupposes, at least from the reader's point of view, that this model is also to be found or at least foreshadowed in the earlier part of the collection. Support for this kind of reading is to be found in the discoveries made in polysystem theory with regard to the dynamics of literary evolution. In his article "Polysystem Theory," Itamar Even-Zohar develops a thesis concerning the nature of semiotic elements and systems in a culture, and their dynamic interrelationships. A key notion in this theory is the idea of the model, which Even-Zohar defines as "a potential combination selected from a given repertory upon which 'proper textual relations' (order, concatenation and positions [matrix] . . . ) have already been imposed . . ." (pp. 304–5). This definition of the model proves fruitful when applied to the individual text.[2]

To argue that *The Odyssey* provides a model for *Selected Poems* in this sense does not therefore imply that Homer's text has been imitated slavishly in terms of either its narrative or its poetic structure. Rather, it means that Homer's poem contains certain features that, *abstracted* from the Homeric text, may become available to other writers and other poems as a model. This has several important implications, for *The Odyssey* and *Selected Poems* belong to different cultures and hence to different polysystems. The use of the Homeric model transfers to Atwood's poetry a number of relevant or desired properties or features (Even-Zohar, "Polysystem Theory," pp. 302–3). These include particular traditional or conventional stances of the woman in gender politics, as defined in Homer's poem.

The transferred features make up a set of relations whose constellations we may call "Circe," "Siren," and "Penelope," and which represent in the Homeric model three kinds of female role. The last constellation remains unnamed in Atwood's poetry, although its identity is indirectly alluded to in a number of poems (see, for example, "When you look at nothing" [p. 218]; or "At first I was given centuries" [pp. 154–55]). Finally, included by implication in the Homeric model constituted in *Selected Poems* is Odysseus, who stands for a male addressee of the relevant poems and is the male Other who helps to define the female roles in the poems.

The polysystems implied by Homer's *Odyssey* and Atwood's *Selected Poems* act as two loosely, though hierarchically, connected sets of relations and functions, each set having a particular value for the other.[3] In this way, the Homeric polysystem provides through the model abstracted in *Selected Poems* a structure of attitudes, values, and practices that may at times function as oppositional to the contemporary polysystem or, at other times, as analogous with it.

Homer's poem thus may be seen to contain a discourse on sexual politics that Atwood's poems systematically foreground. Modern readers are likely to perceive in the structures of *The Odyssey* principally an underwriting of the ideologies of male supremacy and of patriarchal values. Nonetheless, some investigation and explanation is needed to explain the facts that Odysseus's departure from and return to Ithaca are conditioned by the presence and action of two female figures (Helen and Penelope); that his return journey begins only at the instigation of another female figure (Athene); and that he is propelled or impeded by an array of yet other female characters. Whether one argues that the text somehow contains relics of a matriarchal social order far older than Homer's patriarchal culture, or finds another way of accounting for these literary fact in *The Odyssey,* the point is that the text reflects a polysystemic discourse on gender and that this discourse is made available to other texts. Of special significance to Atwood is the suggestive ambiguity in the Homeric model of female figures who are simultaneously subordinate to male ones, yet powerful.

II

In order to understand how the Homeric model operates in *Selected Poems,* we should first briefly consider *The Odyssey* as it relates to Atwood's poetry. Odysseus's departure from and return to Ithaca are conditioned by the infidelity of Helen of Sparta on the one hand and on the other by the fidelity and patience of his wife Penelope. Between these poles of female fidelity other female figures range themselves paradigmatically as positive or negative mediators, helpers or hinderers, creators or destroyers. The most interesting of these is Circe, whose function in the poem is ambiguous: an enchantress (creator) whose powers are dangerous (that is, potentially destructive) to mortals, she also aids Odysseus (after the failure of her attempt to transform him [Homer, pp. 175–76]). She occupies, therefore, a position intermediate between the two poles and shares qualities of each.

The three female figures that concern us in Homer's poem each represent a threat or an insecurity to Odysseus: Circe's role as an enchantress is ambivalent, as is her role as Odysseus's lover, which is in effect forced upon her; the Siren (there are only two in Homer's poem, but other myths tell of three, and it is as a member of a "trio" that Atwood's Siren speaks) is a clear threat to the unwary; and Penelope, dubious about Odysseus's identity, seeks to prove it in a test that causes Odysseus to doubt his wife's fidelity and trustworthiness.

In *Selected Poems* the members of this triad are rearranged in a particular configuration, so that certain qualities of each of these figures are seen in relationship to each other. Those qualities include sexual attraction and attractiveness, accessibility, betrayal, bitterness, suspicion, revenge, and so on—the various aspects of human emotional and sexual relationships condensed into particular roles. These roles may be described as the positions of the victim, the victimizer, and the victor. The first two, victim and victimizer, are in Atwood passive positions by which the female subject is locked into an unchanging and unchangeable role; the position of victor is by contrast an active one, permitting change, renewal, or termination of the role. These correspond in *Selected Poems* roughly to the identities of Circe, the Siren, and (the implicit) Penelope respectively. I wish, though, to emphasize that these are only approximate correspondences, because Atwood's poems often construct their female subjects dynamically in at least two of these positions.

Circe functions as a victim because in the negotiations of emotions and relationships in "Circe/Mud Poems" she knows that she will be abandoned by Atwood's Odysseus (see, for example, the prose poem "It's the story that counts" [p. 221]); however, the intertext informs us that she is also a victimizer—she enchants unwary travelers. The Siren, too, is an obvious victimizer in the intertext, but, as we shall see in Atwood's poem, she is also a victim of her own function and mode of existence. Finally, Penelope in *The Odyssey* is both victim and victor: abandoned (like Circe, in Atwood's poems) by Odysseus, she finally both regains her husband and retains her position in Ithaca (defined as both sexual and political: to become Penelope's husband is to become Ithaca's king). Indeed, in *Selected Poems* Penelope is constructed chiefly as a victor, though her victories, however persuasive, are always temporary and subject to renegotiation.

Circe, the Siren, and Penelope are all literally isolated, Circe on Aiaia, the Siren on an unnamed island, and Penelope on Ithaca. This isolation implies limitation, yet all three figures possess the power to attract and affect males: Circe and the Siren exert a baleful or at least ambiguous allure, while Penelope, apparently widowed, both attracts suitors and acts as a sort of homing beacon for Odysseus, and thus indirectly brings about the destruction of the suitors. In *Selected Poems,* however, only those poems centered on Circe and the Siren foreground the fact of the island habitation and thus of the spiritual or emotional isolation, as well as the implied primitive existence. The Siren does not "enjoy it here / squatting on this island" (p. 194), while the prologue poem to "Circe/Mud Poems" specifies the arrival of Odysseus "*on the dry shore*" (p. 201; Atwood's italics); another (prose) poem describes Circe's context as "this island with its complement of scrubby trees, picturesque bedrock, ample weather and sunsets, lavish white sand beaches and so on" (p. 207). By contrast, although the poems associated with Penelope remain indeterminate with regard to geographical settings, their speakers and addressees are evidently envisioned as continentally enclosed, and sheltered by culture—the settings, whether implicitly as explicitly, include a lake ("Four Auguries" [pp. 230–31]), bedrooms ("Head Against White" [pp. 232–35]; "Late August" [p. 237]), a kitchen ("There Is

Only One of Everything" [p. 236]), and a living-room ("Book of Ancestors" [pp. 238–40]). The relative familiarity and the domesticity of her physical location differentiate Penelope's role from those of the isolated and deprived Siren and Circe.

The geographical stasis in which Circe and the Siren are held are complemented by the temporal loops that also imprison them. In Homer's narrative we learn about these characters during Odysseus's recitation at the court of Alcinous, *after* he has escaped Calypso, encountered Circe, and avoided the treachery of the Sirens, but *before* he undertakes the final stage of his voyage home to Ithaca and to Penelope. Circe and the Sirens are thus a past tense of the Homeric narrative, Penelope a future tense. In *Selected Poems,* these three figures are also placed in a particular temporal matrix. Circe, who knows the Homeric intertext, is caught up in a temporal loop that causes the known past to become the predictable future: "Don't evade, don't pretend you won't leave after all: you leave in the story and the story is ruthless" (p. 221). Thus the rhetoric of "Circe/Mud Poems" is essentially oriented toward a known and recurring past, which gives a particular value and meaning to the present and future tenses of this group of poems. Similarly, the Siren knows what the outcome of her song will be because it always has the same outcome. She is caught in a different temporal loop in which the future is always transformed into the past, for the result of her cry for help is always the same. In this way, the present tense of "Siren Song," as of "Circe/Mud Poems," is effaced. By contrast, the poems associated (implicitly) with Penelope—the closing poems of *Selected Poems,* from "Is/Not" to "Book of Ancestors" (pp. 224–40)—take place in a present whose provisional nature is stressed. Penelope's situation needs constantly to be redefined and reaffirmed.

## III

The Siren and Circe, each at once victim and victimizer, remain trapped within the predicament created in the articulation of their positions. Each tries somehow to control reality, particularly in relation to an implicit Odysseus, by shaping that reality through language. Each then must confront the intractability of reality, registered by a doubling of the signified, which then becomes self-contradictory. The ambiguity that results perpetuates the roles of victim and victimizer.

Analogies between Circe and the Siren are to be found in the Homeric model, analogies that are put to interesting use in *Selected Poems.* Both women are, to varying degrees, monstrous females: the Siren, a destroyer and, according to some versions of the myth, a devourer of males; Circe, a deceiver and transformer of males. According to classical mythology, the Siren is part human, part bird (Graves, vol. 2, p. 249) and is endowed with an alluring voice by means of which she entices the sailor to his death. The apparent signified of the Siren's utterance is thus not its real signified: her invitation is in fact an act of aggression, leading to her victim's death.

This duplicity—a trap which consists of the doubling of the signified—is put to interesting use in *Selected Poems,* and can be seen at work in "Siren Song." To the Homeric myth of the Siren, Atwood adds the notion of the loneliness of the Siren:

> I don't enjoy it here
> squatting on this island
> looking picturesque and mythical
>
> with these two feathery maniacs,
> I don't enjoy singing
> this trio, fatal and valuable
>
> . . . . . . . . . . . . . . . . . . . . . .
> This song
>
> is a cry for help: Help me! (pp. 195–96)

That the expression of this loneliness is part of the alluring verbal (as well as musical) trap of the Siren does not in the least invalidate it as an actual condition of existence. It is the same cry as voiced, for example, by the speaker of *The Journals of Susanna Moodie,* where the loneliness is defined as constituted not merely by location or number of inhabitants, but by language itself:

> I am a word
> in a foreign language. ("Disembarking at Quebec," p. 80)

> . . . this area where my damaged
> knowing of the language means
> prediction is forever impossible ("First Neighbours," p. 83)

The radical disjunction between what is *said* and what *is* (the Siren's trap) produces a radical disjunction within the self:

> . . . I felt I ought to love
> this country.
> I said I loved it
> and my mind saw double.
>
> I began to forget myself
> in the middle
> of sentences. Events
> were split apart ("Thoughts from Underground," p. 111)

The severed relation between event and word leads to a modification of the relation between signified and signifier. As with the mechanism of the Siren's trap, the subject is caught in her attempt to shape fact through language by language itself.

Like Susanna Moodie, the Siren too finds that events are split apart: she is no longer an integral member of "this trio." She desires rescue and articulates that desire, her song expressing frustration, loneliness, and hope; but that same song is, of course, also a trap for her victim. In this kind of text, desire and the trap are mutually implicit. The reader is constructed as an Odysseus, the male Other included implicitly in the Homeric model, who then becomes the victim of the poem, led by the verbal texture first to one seemingly innocent signification, and then, too late, realizing that it conceals another, inimical and dangerous:

> I will tell the secret to you,
> to you, only to you.
> Come closer. This song
>
> is a cry for help: Help me!
> Only you, only you can,
> you are unique
>
> at last. Alas
> it is a boring song
> but it works every time. (p. 196)

The irony of this verbal strategy is multiple: it includes not only the entrapment of readers as they learn of the very mechanism of the Siren's verbal duplicity at all levels but also the entrapment of the Siren herself, whose utterances, whether or not *intended* to draw victims, must always *create* such a victim. The Siren's verbal duplicity, unlike Susanna Moodie's, thus makes prediction forever possible because the future event she creates through language is always identical with her past experience. The whole notion of prediction is thus rendered absurd.

The Siren, as a particular female role, shows that in the politics of gender the victimizer's victim is, finally, the self. Each apparent success of her alluring verbal trap is a confirmation of the Siren's essential isolation. She is defined by her function as victimizer; her verbal ambiguities, intended to disguise that function, or to express dissatisfaction with it, serve merely to reinforce it.

A similar irony of predictability characterizes the Circe of *Selected Poems.* Like the Siren, she is a double-dealer in words, yet in the Homeric model her business is with truth—its exposure, in her capacity as a seeress, as well as its concealment or reworking, in her role as sorceress. Like the Siren, Circe has a "beguiling voice" by means of which she both attracts her victims and commands their metamorphosis (Homer, pp. 171, 175). Circe can thus be understood as a transform of the Siren, in Atwood as well as in Homer.

If the Siren ironically employs the process of signification in language as a blind and a trap, Circe uses it both to expose the truth of "*what there is*" (p. 201; Atwood's italics) and to try to transform that truth, unacceptable to her, into a different one. The transformations of Circe's victims and their deaths come about through language, through its double power either to name or to refuse to name:

> I did not add the shaggy
> rugs, the tusked masks,
> they happened
>
> I did not say anything, I sat
> and watched, they happened
> because I did not say anything. (p. 203)

To Circe's concern with her fate ("Is this what you would like me to be, this mud woman?" [p. 214]), the Odysseus-addressee displays indifference. As in the Siren's role of victimizer, this is a definition of Circe's role (as victim) in terms of the male one: "In the story the boat disappears one day over the horizon, just disappears, and it doesn't say what happens then. On the island, that is. . . . Don't evade, don't pretend you won't leave after all: you leave in the story and the story is ruthless" (p. 221).

Circe's fate is determined by other words, another text—that of Homer's poem.

> *There are two islands*
> *at least, they do not exclude each other*
>
> *On the first I am right*
> *the events run themselves through*
> *almost without us*
>
> . . . . . . . . . . . . .
>
> *it is over,*
> *I am right, it starts again. . . .* (p. 222; Atwood's italics)

This first island is that of the intertext, Homer's prior poem, which predetermines the actions and moves performed by Circe and Odysseus. It repeats itself ("*it starts again, / jerkier this time and faster*") like a movie on a faulty projector, or like a silent movie in which the actors are rendered absurd by repetition and the jerkiness and speed by which their actions are accomplished (compare "You take my hand" [p. 142], in which the relationship also "goes on and on" like "a bad movie").

In the first world created—or rather re-created—by Circe's words, experience is repetitive, and through repetition both immortal and predictable.

> *The second I know nothing about*
> *because it has never happened:*
> *this land is not finished,*
> *this body is not reversible. . . .* (pp. 222–23; Atwood's italics)

This second world has an open structure, and is the world of love desired by Circe, as opposed to the eternal world of narrative already known to her. Experience in this second world is unique and therefore mortal. "Circe/Mud Poems" thus concludes by facing simultaneously in two directions: towards an intertext that determines events and gender relations in the present text, and towards a desired ideal text that would permit redefinition of situation and gender relations. The latter, however, is impossible, since Circe is a literary construct derived from an intertext. She is thus committed to an existence that defines her in only one way, despite her own desires and intentions.

Circe's trademark, the principle of transformation or metamorphosis, is to be found throughout *Selected Poems* (see, for example, in "Against Still Life" [p. 37], "The Settlers" [pp. 45–46], "The Animals in That Country" [pp. 48–49], "Axiom" [p. 78], "Wish: Metamorphosis to Heraldic Emblem" [p. 107], and "She Considers Evading Him" [p. 143]). In each, the transformation lends definition and meaning to the object or subject undergoing the change: what it *is* has significance and signification only when compared to what it *was,* and vice versa. Like the two worlds of desire and actuality that Circe simultaneously inhabits, this is a mode of the doubled signified that we saw in the Siren's song.

The Siren and Circe together constitute a subject in the poems who seeks for an absolute or an essence of some kind—uniqueness, authenticity of experience, truth of love. This subject is set in a temporal matrix in which the future always promises delivery of this essence; this matrix, however, is so structured as to make the future identical with a past that has always been deprived of the desired essentiality.

## IV

Atwood's poems, though, do not construct the roles of victim and victimizer as the only possibilities for the female subject. Transforms of each other, the Siren and Circe are set in an oppositional relation to Penelope. Like Atwood's Siren, she desires rescue in the Homeric model; like Circe, she wants Odysseus by her side. However, unlike either of them, her wishes are granted and legitimized. First, however, her passive identity as constructed by the Homeric model must be neutralized. She may be identified as the silent (that is, unspecified) archetype of the faithful wife in "At first I was given centuries" (pp. 154–55), who waits for a succession of men throughout human history, men who quest for glory and return maimed, if, indeed, they return at all. The futility of this role is thereby made manifest, as are the sadness and implied anger at the speeding up of the process. The traditional image of the patiently enduring Penelope, as presented in *The Odyssey,* thus proves inadequate.

Circe in "Circe/Mud Poems" characterizes Penelope differently—this time as a middle-class manipulator, a matron with pretensions and a strong sense of decorum:

> Meanwhile she sits in her chair
> waxing and waning
> like an inner tube or a mother
> breathing out, breathing in,
>
> surrounded by bowls, bowls, bowls,
> tributes from the suitors
> who are having a good time in the kitchen
>
> waiting for her to decide
> on the dialogue for this evening
> which will be in perfect taste
> and will include tea and sex
> dispensed graciously both at once. (p. 218)

In this slanted view of Penelope, understandable in the light of Circe's own feelings and ambitions, we can see a structure that reflects the image of Homer's sirens on their island, surrounded by bleached bones, and attracting further victims (Homer, p. 210). Penelope's lure, in Circe's harsh description, is "dialogue," a verbality that establishes her kinship with both Circe and the Siren. In making her part of the same paradigm, Circe, from her position as victim, can define Penelope as a victimizer analogous to the Siren.

That there is indeed a kinship between Penelope and her oppositional figures is demonstrable. In Homer's poem Penelope endlessly weaves a shroud for aged Laertes, Odysseus's father, undoing at night what she accomplishes by day. This is another version of the duplicitous signifier: the production of an artifact turns out to be a strategy of delay. Circe's description of this process in "When you look at nothing" is reminiscent of the Siren's inviting promise of knowledge:

> She's up to something, she's weaving
> histories, they are never right,

she has to do them over,
she is weaving her version,

the one you will believe in,
the only one you will hear. (p. 218)

The aim of Penelope's strategy in Homer's poem, however, is the obverse of the Siren's: delay instead of haste, distraction rather than attraction, fidelity rather than deceit. In Atwood's poem, its aim is to create an "official" history, authenticated by Odysseus's belief, and is thus seen by Circe as a kind of trap, certainly as a lie.

However, in Atwood the features that differentiate Penelope from the figures of Circe and the Siren are more important and positive than those that identify her with them. If Penelope's poems (the last seven in *Selected Poems*) are read carefully, the sense of history, so central to the figures and perceptions of the Siren and Circe, is seen to be submerged in an awareness of the present moment as unique, irretrievable, and therefore valuable. The very title of the first of this group asserts this awareness: "Is/ Not." In this poem, the subject demands: "Permit me the present tense" (p. 225). There is again a characteristic emphasis on verbalization, but it expresses neither the disappointment of Circe nor the alluring call of the Siren, both condemned to solitary existence. Instead, the poem asserts the value of mundane daily life and its provision of a context that must be engaged with if it is to be endured. This realistic attitude is at odds with the sentimentalism of Circe's envisioned desirable alternative existence and with the Siren's high romance of rescue.

Other poems in this group suggest indirectly that their subject is Penelope. The Homeric model used by Atwood permits the identities of Circe, the Siren, and, by implication, Penelope to function metonymically for other figures in the Homeric text. Thus, Athene and Eurycleia belong to the same paradigm as Penelope in that each desires the return of Odysseus, and, for Atwood's purposes, each is an active figure in the dynamic of gender roles. "Four Auguries" (pp. 230–31), for example, culminates in a benediction strongly reminiscent of the various symbolic epiphanies of Odysseus's protector, Athene, whose sacred bird is the owl, while "Head Against White" (pp. 232–35) includes what may be read as a reminder of the famous incident of the recognition of Odysseus by his old nurse Eurycleia, who in bathing the apparent stranger sees a familiar scar. In "There Is Only One of Everything," there is a possible allusion to the bed test imposed by Penelope upon Odysseus. The secret of Odysseus's bed—that he carved it from a living tree and that the bed could not be moved without destroying the tree—becomes in Atwood's poem a characteristic transformation of the physical object into a verbal equivalent: just as "tree" became "bed" in *The Odyssey,* so "tree" becomes "words" in Atwood's poem:

> Not a tree, but the tree
> we saw, it will never exist, split by the wind
> and bending down
> like that again. What will push out of the earth
>
> later, making it summer, will not be
> grass, leaves, repetition, there will
> have to be other words. . . . (p. 236)

This poem is important in the Penelope group because it takes the step from verbality to phenomenality: "When my / eyes close language vanishes." With the disappearance of language as an attempt to shape or create reality rather than merely to describe it or respond to its events, phenomena return to themselves and undergo a kind of epiphany:

> I look at you and you occur
> in this winter kitchen, random as trees or sentences,
> entering me, fading like them, in time you will disappear. . . .
>
> I can even say it,
> though only once and it won't
>
> last: I want this. I want
> this.

With the repetition of that which she can say "only once," the speaker accepts, as Circe and the Siren cannot, the knowledge of the human condition of isolation and the evanescence of those moments, rendered valuable by their very brevity, of community with another being: "it won't last" (p. 236).

It is in the last poem of *Selected Poems,* "Book of Ancestors" (pp. 238–40), that we can see a resolution of the conflicts explored throughout the collection; and since it is the Penelope-subject who speaks, that resolution is envisaged as momentary, available for renegotiation in the continuous dialectic of human relationships. This resolution is placed in a temporal matrix established in the first section of the poem, which shows a series of human sacrifices distributed through history and space: "these brutal, with curled / beards and bulls' heads" (Archaic Greeks, perhaps) are succeeded by "these, closer to us, / copper hawkman arched on the squat rock / pyramid" (Inca or Aztec?). We learn in the succeeding sections that these sacrificial rituals remain as movements, postures: but their meaning changes as the religious purpose (union with the deity) is substituted by another purpose (human union).

In the second section, accordingly, we are told that "History / is over," and that the classification of the past yield to "a season, an undivided / space . . . ," that is, to individual human dimensions. The speaker and her addressee adopt the hieratic postures of priestess and sacrificial victim:

> . . . I lean behind you, mouth touching
> your spine, my arms around
> you, palm above the heart,
> your blood insistent under
> my hand, quick and mortal

In the final section, the true essential sacrifice is made: not the offering of the physical living heart to an undefined deity, but the transformation of the partners into one another. The speaker becomes male in her approach and response to her addressee, while he in turn becomes female. First comes the traditional "ancient pose" of the sacrificial victim:

> On the floor your body curves
> like that: the ancient pose, neck slackened, arms
> thrown above the head, vital
> throat and belly lying
> undefended.

However, despite the reminder or archaic ritual, "this is not an altar, they are not / acting or watching." Instead, it is a moment when by an act of transubstantiation (a sacrifice and transformation drawn from a different myth and a different model) the tensions of difference and separation are emptied out and a unity of identity is achieved:

You are intact, you turn
towards me, your eyes opening, the eyes
intricate and easily bruised, you open

yourself to me gently, what
they tried, we
tried but could never do
before . without blood, the killed
heart . to take
that risk, to offer life and remain

alive, open yourself like this and become whole.

The poem thus ends, as does the volume, with a pax humana between a man become virginal—"intact"—and passive, and a woman experienced and active. The emphasis is on the moment of mutual transformation and submission, not on a past or future definition of relationship, nor on any demand for a definition of the essential or absolute.

## V

Along with its discourse on gender, *The Odyssey* can be read as concerning itself with another, related discourse, that of fidelity in its several versions—as love, loyalty, and trust, in its positive forms, as well as in its negative transformations as enmity, betrayal, and deceit. Seen this way, the Homeric model permits us to read *Selected Poems* as a text that varies or tropes upon this second discourse. Here, the representative figures of Circe, the Siren, and Penelope not only signify themselves, but are metonyms for other female figures in the Homeric paradigm.

According to the Homeric model, Helen first betrays Menelaus by eloping with Paris and then betrays Paris and the Trojans by aiding Odysseus in his mission of espionage (Homer, p. 60). In Atwood's poems, the Siren's duplicity and her implicit history of a series of betrayals become metonymic of the infidelity in *The Odyssey* represented chiefly by Helen. The Siren comes to signify in *Selected Poems* the negation of fidelity as betrayal and deceit in all its aspects.

Similarly, Circe, who in the Homeric original knows and accepts the fact of Odysseus's departure, is a metonym in Atwood's poetry for Nausicaa. As with Nausicaa, Circe's yearning for

Odysseus must remain unsatisfied, and, like the princess on Phaeacia finally sealed forever from the outside world, Circe in Atwood's poetry remains trapped in a narrative that condemns her to loneliness.

Only Penelope's discourse is free from recrimination and unsatisfied (and unsatisfiable) yearnings. Unlike the Siren and Circe, whose insistence on absoluteness and permanence in the politics of gender produces only frustration and sorrow, Penelope manages circumstance in order to arrive at temporary but nonetheless satisfying resolutions of the conflicts produced by the dynamics of gender politics. In this she acts as a metonym for Athene, whose opportunism and persuasiveness enable her to clear the path for Odysseus's eventual return home. Like the resolutions of conflict in *Selected Poems,* however, this conclusion to Athene's efforts to bring to an end the wanderings of Homer's hero is temporary only: his future departure from Penelope and Ithaca, and his "seaborne death" are predicted by Teiresias in book 11 of *The Odyssey* (Homer, pp. 188–89).

## VI

The presence of the Homeric model is foreshadowed in the opening poem of *Selected Poems,* "This Is a Photograph of Me," which contains the elements of metamorphosis, verbality, confusions of tense, and duplicity of signification. In this text, a visual, iconic object, the photograph, is also a verbal, symbolic one, the poem. The "smeared / print" thus offers a double discourse in which words are part of a picture, and which strives to convey the presence of an absent subject. In addition, the temporal matrix is deliberately reversed or inverted:

> (The photograph was taken
> the day after I drowned. . . .

The reader is made to question the temporal frame that permits the text to be spoken by an already drowned subject, who, invisible, invites the reader to find her in the scene described:

> I am in the lake, in the center
> of the picture, just under the surface

. . . . . . . . . . . . . . . . . . . . . . . . . . . .
if you look long enough
eventually
you will be able to see me.)

Spatial concepts, too, are inverted: the lake, though "in the background," is also "in the center / of the picture," just as the drowned speaker, centered by the poem, is virtually invisible in the described photograph (p. 8).

These paradoxes point to a characteristic element of both the Siren and the Circe poems: the trap constructed by language once it is employed to define time and space in absolute fashion. Caught in a temporal irony that makes a fact of the past (the drowning of the speaker) a fact also of the future ("you will be able to see me"), and therefore virtually indistinguishable from it, the drowned speaker of "This Is A Photograph of Me" encourages the reader to search an icon made of words for a true image of the subject. The voice of an unseen speaker emerging from the water inviting closer inspection is precisely analogous to the voice of the Siren luring her victim with the promise of knowledge, just as the transformation of an object (a photograph) into a sequence of words (the poem) is a metamorphosis in the Circean mode.

We are reminded of this poem in another among those to be identified with Penelope, "Eating Fire" (pp. 227–29). In this poem, the addressee, a phoenix who has returned from the fire, is able to see

everything, as you wished,
each object (lake, tree, woman)

transfigured with your love. . . . (p. 229)

If the voice of the earlier poem can be identified with the Siren, the logic of the Homeric model that unites Siren, Circe, and Penelope in a triad permits us, by virtue of the intratextual reference in the later poem, to read that voice as double, as including also the voice of Penelope. In this way, then, the first poem of *Selected Poems* presents the Homeric model covertly, requiring the reader to discover its explicit presence in the poems selected from *You Are Happy* and to read it back into those selected from *The Circle Game* onwards.

VII

The uncovering in *Selected Poems* of the Homeric model shows that the debate about gender and role is not restricted only to our own time and culture. Clearly, the discrepancy referred to earlier, between the fact of the primacy of female figures in the narrative structure of *The Odyssey* and known historical patriarchal social structures in Homer's society, suggests that the question of gender roles was no less complicated in Homer's time than in our own. Atwood's use of Homer foregrounds those issues relevant to her. We can understand how *Selected Poems* re-constructs Penelope because we are aware of how Homer's text constructs her. We are also thereby enabled to see both the differences and the similarities between Homer's culture and our own, and to perceive, further, a continuity of discourse and debate between these two cultures.

The presence in *Selected Poems* of a Homeric model functions to consolidate a theme, the nature of culturally defined sexual roles, that operates also at other levels in the poems. In terms of the "story" that is told, Atwood's poetry arrives at the conclusion that gender relationships are most fruitfully defined as existing in the present moment and that it is necessary always to confirm their existence and structure through negotiation between partners.

The Homeric model is only one of many potential models functioning in and across the entire collection, intersecting with each other, or remaining parallel to and distinct from one another.[4] These models are not each necessarily to be found in every poem, nor indeed in each volume of Atwood's poetry; neither are they to be recognized always by an overt intertextual allusion. Rather, they exist as a repertoire of structures, patterns, and linguistic features to be drawn on at need. Atwood, like her Penelope, uses these models to weave her own version, which rearranges their elements into suggestive new configurations and installs her work as part of an old yet always new discourse.

*Notes*

1. Atwood, *Selected Poems* (Toronto: Oxford Univ. Press, 1976). Page references in the text are to this edition.

2. I am indebted both for this notion of the literary model and for materials other than "Polysystem Theory," to Professor Even-Zohar's semi-

nar on polysystem theory, given as part of the International Summer Institute for Semiotic and Structuralist Studies, 26 May–22 June 1985 at Indiana University, Bloomington, Indiana.

3. Even-Zohar, in his paper "Aspects of the Hebrew Yiddish Polysystem" (1979), argues that this is the actual relation between polysystems, rather than a simple fusing of both into a single system.

4. In *Selected Poems* these include the Gothic, as in "The Wereman" (p. 85; see Judith McCombs, "Atwood's Haunted Sequences: *The Circle Game, The Journals of Susanna Moodie,* and *Power Politics*"); pioneer writing—journals, letters, prose accounts, and poetry—chiefly in *The Journals of Susanna Moodie;* and other classical models, for instance, that of Narcissus, as represented in "Looking in a Mirror" (pp. 90–91) or "Tricks with Mirrors" (pp. 183–86). Models that operate in the background of *Selected Poems* include the poetic models of Yeats, Donne, and Marvell. For example, the entire collection may be read as a reworking of "To His Coy Mistress," asserting finally the lady's equality with the lover. No single model, therefore, will suffice to explain each poem in *Selected Poems:* for instance, in "The Wereman," cited above, we can discern not only the Gothic model, but also such classical models as that provided by Ovid's *Metamorphoses,* as well, of course, as the Homeric model of Circean transformation.

# 11 *Politics, Structure, and Poetic Development in Atwood's Canadian-American Sequences*

## *From an Apprentice Pair to "The Circle Game" to "Two-Headed Poems"*

*Judith McCombs*

I

There exist in the Atwood papers at the University of Toronto two remarkable poem drafts, "The Idea of Canada" and "America as the aging demon lover," that precede and in part prefigure Atwood's published Canadian-American sequences, "The Circle Game" and "Two-Headed Poems." As this essay's first section will show, "Canada" and "America" have the characteristics of Atwood's apprentice period: the two personified nations are allegories, not characters; their multiplicities are statically cataloged, rather than metaphorically evoked; their Gothic elements are mainly grotesques and horrors; the muse of the Canadian poet James Reaney is audible in many lines.

As explication and structural analysis of the published Canadian-American sequences will show, the 1964–1966 "Circle Game" clearly belongs to what I term Atwood's Stage I, the closed world of mirroring, female Gothic elements, where apprentice allegories become skillfully evoked characters, the metaphors become simultaneous and metamorphic, the Gothic grotesques change to implied horrors and interior female terror, and Atwood's muse has, almost always, incorporated or transformed her sources. Finally, as the third part of this essay will show, the political and Jaynesian "Two-Headed Poems" sequence of 1977–1978—which critics up to now have avoided, or but quickly and partially explicated—attempts both to go back to the apprentice grotesques and forward into Atwood's just-then-beginning Stage II, the open world, where mirroring and female Gothic elements are subordinated to realistic, transnational, human ends.[1]

"Canada" and "America" were written around 1962–spring 1963, at Harvard, when Atwood first left Canada for America, to earn a Radcliffe A.M.[2] Their cumulative "who does this, who is that" rhetoric and their sprawling horizontal lines, which at times exceed the page, are obviously a response to Allen Ginsberg's 1956 "Howl," that howl of American national identity. Their politics, mechanical allegories, and varying, overly long lines are also obviously a response to James Reaney's 1960 "Message to Winnipeg," concerning Canadian national identity (*Poems,* pp. 132–40).

Their "packed" and "dispersed" iambic pentameter—to use Atwood's terms, taken from her [c. November 1962] notes and a 20 November 1962 letter—suggests that they were written circa November 1962, when Atwood was deliberately breaking up her hitherto regular iambic pentameter lines. Their atypically long lines run counter to Atwood's 29 October 1962 statement "My Poetic Principles," which advocates short, "vertical" lines; but, as the [c. November 1962] notes indicate, one other way to revive the "dead" pentameter is to absolutely pack it full.[3]

Both "Canada" and "America" cover their pages and are obviously finishable poems, not fragments; in quality they rank with, or above, many, many of the hundreds of apprentice poems that Atwood revised through several drafts and finished. But apparently neither poem was redrafted or finished; only one holograph of each exists. Perhaps the horizontal form, borrowed partly from Reaney and more especially from the American male Ginsberg, who borrowed it from the American male Whitman, was too much borrowed, or too foreign. Or perhaps the Canadian nationalism, which is the only unusual aspect of the two poems' content, was somehow the problem; perhaps they exposed, too early or too crudely, Atwood's ideas of Canada and America? In each title, "Canada" or "America" is coyly semihidden, with asterisks replacing all the vowels.

"The Idea of Canada" begins and ends in Reaneyesque images of an empty, passive, pathetically colonial, or grotesquely violent Canada. It begins with the empty hand an old woman holds in lieu of a flag—Canada had no flag of its own until 1965—while she waits for a royal procession to come to her village. Like Reaney's Stratford, Ontario, folk waiting for a royal visit ("The Royal Visit," *Poems,* p. 53) and like the narrator in his "Upper Canadian" (*Poems,* pp. 56–57) waiting for nothing, Atwood's old woman has no country of her own; where she is, is nowhere.

In the middle stanzas, where the "idea" of Canada becomes the old woman herself, she is recognizably Atwood's Canada, clearly prefiguring Stage I and Stage II versions. This Canada has laced her mouth tight; she is righteous, girdled, cold—an Auntie Muriel of Stage II's *Life Before Man.* She is, however, much poorer: she scrounges chewed food from her (American) neighbor's garbage cans.

As the Stage I *Survival* puts it, this is Canada as Crone, a "nasty, chilly old woman" trapped in the Canadian Rapunzel Syndrome, where "*Rapunzel and the tower are the same*" (pp. 199, 202, 209; Atwood's italics): Canada is her own prison, her own jailer. Or, as "The Idea of Canada" puts it, she keeps busy knitting comforters while stupifying in cages that are her own. The apprentice years are full of poems of frozen, freezing, caged, bottled, towered, lifeless women, poems that were published steadily in Canadian journals—which suggests that Canadian editors could recognize a character relevant to Canada. But "The Idea of Canada" may be the first where the self-caged woman is overtly identified as Canada, the self-caged country.

In the poem's third stanza Atwood's "Canada" becomes a mirror searcher, unable to see herself, seeing nothing, because her eyes (I's) are diseased and her mirror cracked. Here Atwood's Canada follows A. M. Klein's crazed Canadian poet (in "Portrait of the Poet as Landscape"), who "stares at a mirror all day long, as if / to recognize himself"; these lines are quoted in *Survival*'s introductory argument that Canadian literature's many mirror images are a symptom of a nation trying vainly to see itself (p. 16).

But what if Canada were to turn not to her mirror but to her landscape to see herself? Neither Klein's mad, isolated Canadian poet nor Atwood's self-caged Canada turn to their land; the latter prefers her stuffy cages and her pathetically colonial teacups, which bear another country's arms and crowns.[4] But Atwood's narrator does, in the poem's fourth stanza, turn to the land, and for those few lines the poem comes alive with prophetic power: Canada's real polarities are snow, wood, river, trees. Here, for a moment, one can glimpse the Stage I *Journals of Susanna Moodie,* in which the pioneer hero turns away from failed mirror images and confining parlors to claim, enter, and literally become a part of her land.

"Canada"'s last stanza, however, retreats indoors to a tableau of macabre violence: Canada has two heads; Canada thrills with Biblical horror when the orphan-child viciously slits the dog's throat, in the parlor. The orphan's violence here may be a grotesque domestic allegory of English-French violence. Such morbid grotesques are characteristic of much of Atwood's apprentice poetry; here as elsewhere they follow James Reaney's ugly women, repellent orphans, and impacted parlor horrors. The two heads, French and English, will reappear in the Stage II sequence; the orphan child, with milder games, will reappear in the Stage I "Circle" sequence.

"America" may have been written before "Canada" and later revised to make it a companion of sorts. The title of the earlier, pencil holograph is the *un*asterisked "America as the demon"; the revised title, from a pen that seems to be the same as that used for "Canada," is the asterisked "America as the aging demon lover."

The pencil holograph, of about six stanzas, begins and ends with old-fashioned Gothic horror: the demon surrounds you—the poem is cast in the second person—but you can't see him (as America's presence surrounds Canada); at the end, you turn from a mirror to feel the demon's paw, your nightmare.

The middle, penciled stanzas are a catalog of grotesques, drawn from modern and older horrors—from science fiction, demon myths, comic books, and Reaney's anatomized and mechanical personifications of Winnipeg (p. 133). This America, of the mechanical pulse and steel-totem spine nubbed with a smiling steel family, is Atwood's Metal Man, overt and literal in the apprentice years, covert and metaphorical in the mature work (for example, "Man with a Hook" in *The Circle Game* [p. 26] and the "friendly metal killers" of *Surfacing* [p. 130]).

In the next stanza the demon is a wooden Indian, scarred, defaced with a bloody lipstick word. In the next the demon has no skin and is therefore a god. The multiplicities that are here statically asserted, not metamorphically created, prefigure the protean comic-book hero of *Power Politics* and of "Encounters with the Element Man." In the next stanza, the demon is total man, containing many animals, as the progressively insane Canadian pioneer of *The Animals in That Country* (pp. 36–39) will fail to do. An oddly natural organic line, perhaps taken from comic books, has him spider-brained in a web of senses. Whatever he is, comic or mythic, he isn't human.

The ink holograph develops and intensifies both the classic and the comic-book horrors: it, for example, scalps the Indian, adds what may be a Superman with motley costumes (as in *Power Politics* and the "Element Man"), and adds the horror-film ending of Canada's desiring, yet locking the door against, America the demon lover—who like Mr. Hyde is already in the room.

"The Idea of Canada" and "America as the aging demon lover," then, are recognizably Atwood's work; though form, image, and statically asserted multiplicities show only apprentice craft, still the central Atwood figures, of Canada as self-imprisoned Rapunzel Crone and America as Metal Man, are there. This "Canada" comes from Canadian literature and landscape, and will in time become the Susanna Moodie of the *Journals,* Atwood's poetic masterpiece. This "America" comes from science fiction, myth, Reaney's anatomized Winnipegs, and the comic books imported from America—and will in time become the many-motley-costumed hero of *Power Politics,* which is Atwood's poetic masterpiece of female-male relations.[5]

## II

"The Circle Game" sequence is often read, by Americans, as a miniature *Power Politics,* outlining, as it does, a power politics of female versus male. But for Atwood, one power game is like another. As explication and analysis of "Circle"'s concentric structure will show, this sequence enacts not only gender but also national power scenarios: its mirror and window sections dramatize Canadian versus American games; its children's-fortress sections replay Canada's garrison history; and, at its climactic center, as in the apprentice "America" poem, national power games are revealed through a male-female horror scenario.[6]

"The Circle Game" is one of the earliest of Atwood's Stage I poems; it existed by 23 September 1964, when Atwood sent it to Charles Pachter, who hand-printed fifteen copies with his lithographs that December (Atwood Papers, Box 1). Almost all the other major poems of *The Circle Game* were written by the first half of 1965; and in 1966 Contact Press of Toronto published the book, which is Atwood's first real book and the beginning of her Stage I, the closed and mirroring world.

The seven-part, concentric "Circle Game" is built of paired, encircling sections: the unclaimed, solitary circling children of the outer sections, sections i and vii; the mirror-window couple of sections ii and vi; the garrison children of sections iii and vi; and, at the climactic center, section iv, the walled-in, childless, staring, eye-fixed couple.

"Circle" first becomes a national as well as a gender parable in the paired mirror and window sections, sections ii and vi. Being with the *you* is like groping through a gelatinous melted mirror, thinks the *I* in section ii:

> You refuse to be
> and I [eye]
> an exact reflection, yet
> will not walk from the glass,
> be separate. (p. 36)

She looks to him, and he to others, in a travesty of Victorian sex roles—he for images alone, she for images in him:

> You look past me, listening
> to them, perhaps, or
> watching your own reflection somewhere
> . . . . . . . . . . . . . . . . . . . . . . . . . . . . . . .
> There is always
>
> (your face
> remote, listening)
>
> someone in the next room. (p. 37)

His refusal to be enacts what *Survival* calls Canada's colonial mentality, which looks to others, British or American or French. Her refusal to be separate from him enacts gender entrapment—and also enacts the French-Canadian entrapment of a colony within a colony, a country within a country.

In the paired section vi, the glass is other people's windows, outside which the *you* plays orphan, the safe, hungry, "ragged winter game / that says, I am alone." It is "a game of envy" and contempt: he despises the cheap, Victorian Christmas-card suburban laughter of "father and mother / playing father and mother"; he'd rather be left by himself, "hugging himself" in the cold. "You do it too," he accuses: the *I* partly admits and partly denies: "I tend to pose / in other seasons / outside other windows" (pp. 41–42).

These mirror and window games are a national as well as a gender ritual: for Canadians, as for women, the problem is using the wrong mirrors/windows: trying to see oneself as English or American (for English Canadians), or as French (for French Canadians); trying to see oneself as male, for women. Atwood argues in *Survival* that Canadian literature's "large number of mirror and reflection images . . . suggest a society engaged in a vain search for an image, . . . like A. M. Klein's mad poet who 'stares at a mirror all day long, as if / to recognize himself' " (p. 16). Atwood's retrospective essay on "Canadian-American Relations" discusses the Canadians' "amnesia" regarding their Canadian identity in "Circle"'s time: "They'd forgotten. They'd had their ears pressed to the wall for so long, listening in on the neighbours, who *were* rather loud, that they'd forgotten how to speak and what to say. They'd become addicted to the one-way mirror of the Canadian-American border—we can see you, you can't see us—and had neglected that other mirror, their own culture" (*Second Words,* p. 385).

The orphan game of section vi goes back to Reaney's supperless window-gazer: "I had not had mine yet and loved / The match girl orphan loneliness / Of watching other people eating theirs" (p. 137). In Atwood's "Circle" as in Reaney's "Winnipeg," these orphan gazers mimic Canadian history: "Both French and English Canada," the novelist Brian Moore explains in the "Through the Looking Glass" chapter of his 1963 Time-Life *Canada,* "have grown up feeling neglected [by the mother countries, who abandoned them]. 'Canadians,' says Professor A. R. M. Lower, 'are the children of divorced parents and they know the bitterness that comes of a broken home . . .' " (pp. 60–61). Or, as Northrop Frye puts it, the nation, with its history of being treated as a colony, "developed with the bewilderment of a neglected child, preoccupied with trying to define its own identity" (*Bush Garden,* p. 221).

After the couple's mirror games, and before their window-orphan games, come the paired sections iii and v, in which "Circle"'s real and unclaimed children reenact what Northrop Frye terms the Canadian "garrison mentality" (*Bush Garden,* pp. 225–26). In section iii the couple tell the children (who aren't theirs) romantic legends imported from Europe; the children's typically Canadian response is to disbelieve the heroics, but silently believe the danger. The next night, the couple find the children's fortified trenches and "lake-enclosed island / with no bridges," where the children have tried to make a human refuge against whatever "sword hearted" danger walks these night beaches (p. 38). Their sand play thus reenacts Canada's historic garrisons—which were European imports that walled their fearful inhabitants away from whatever was really there.

In section v the couple take the children to a real, adult fort; the children like the archaic guns, armour, explosions. But the fort illustrates what happens to the garrison mentality in the twentieth century: its imperial earthworks crumble, its weapons left in glass cases turn fragile, it becomes a museum whose "elaborate defenses keep / things that are no longer / (much) / worth defending" (p. 41).

At "Circle"'s center, section iv, is the couple's climactic map game, in which imperial and horror scenarios underlie the gender domination:

> So now you trace me
> like a country's boundary
> . . . . . . . . . . . . . . . . . . . . .
> and I am fixed, stuck
> down on the outspread map
> of this room, of your mind's continent
> (here and yet not here, like
> the wardrobe and the mirrors
> the voices through the wall
> your body ignored on the bed),
>
> transfixed
> by your eyes'
> cold blue thumbtacks (pp. 39–40)

This mapped impalement follows both the Anglo-American Prufrock's fear of "the eyes that fix you in a formulated phrase" (Eliot, p. 5) and A. M. Klein's Canadian idea of poet as landscape. The "cold blue thumbtacks" may recall Klein's other isolated Canadian poets, who are "pins on a map of a colour similar to his" ("Portraits", p. 131); they may also recall James Reaney's 1963 editorial on Canada as the unseeing "country that sees itself [in a national flag contest] as either a huge thumbtack or a series of small ones" (Editorial, p. 3).

In "Circle Game" the Prufrock-poet is female as well as Canadian: doubly exposed, doubly colonized. And doubly silenced, without Klein's omniscient narrator to declare her the "nth Adam taking a green inventory" and mapping "his own body's chart" ("Portrait," p. 133). Being mapped—the female Canadian position—is different.

This mapped impalement implies also a Gothic scenario, of the hapless maiden readied for rape and/or torture in the chamber of the ruthless villain: "I am fixed, stuck / down on the outspread map / of this room . . . / transfixed" (p. 40). But the *you* is no "America the demon lover," no foreign conqueror; rather, as in his mirror and orphan games, he is Canadian, a staring, passive, frigid imitator of his imperial models.

"The Circle Game," then, is a series of concentric children's and adult mirror, orphan, garrison, and map games that correspond to Canadian national and intranational games, as well as to Gothic and gender scenarios. In her retrospective appreciation, "Eleven Years of *Alphabet,*" Atwood quotes James Reaney's 1961 explanation of how simply juxtaposing myth to everyday reality can let the reader see the mythic correspondences *in* the real: this is just what happens when a circle is placed by face cards, and the eye sees circles; a triangle, and the eye sees corners and angles (*Second Words,* p. 92). Similarly, if one juxtaposes imperial, intranational, gender, or horror patterns to "Circle"'s games, as this essay has done, just such correspondences appear. Atwood had, by 1964, learned to write for multiple juxtapositions and multiple correspondences: the mature Stage I work, from "The Circle Game" on, lays out real games, and lets the reader juxtapose and see what truths or myths appear.

III

"Two-Headed Poems" is the title sequence of the book that in 1978 began Atwood's Stage II, the open world, in which Stage I mirroring, female Gothic elements are subordinated to a wider social realism and a greater concern for human ethics. Written after several years away from poetry and first published in the October 1977 *This Magazine,* the "Two-Headed Poems" sequence is perhaps best read as an embryonic (or misborn) Stage II work: in a book of poems that celebrate the particular child, the maternal generations, and the universal bicameral human consciousness, this sequence is a political sideshow of the two Canadas, French and English, as quarreling left-brain Siamese twins—who yet, with their Jaynesian right brains, utter supranational oracles on human language.

As this explication and structural analysis will show, the sequence is a difficult composite of three elements: a Siamese-twin monster carried over from Atwood's apprentice years;[7] the French- versus English-Canadian language wars, which by 1977 seemed close to splitting Canada; and Julian Jaynes's mystic *Origins of Consciousness in the Breakdown of the Bicameral Mind,* which inspired both the sequence and the book and apparently induced Atwood's Stage II return to poetry.

That Atwood still considers "Two-Headed Poems" essential is suggested by its inclusion, uncut and prominently centered, in the first section of the 1986 *Selected Poems II* (pp. 27–36). Critics, however, have mostly avoided the sequence, except for Jerome H. Rosenberg's germinal 1979–80 discussion of certain of its Jaynesian elements and Sherrill E. Grace's illuminating 1981 guide to certain of its now-topical political allusions.[8]

The 1977 two-headed monster comes, Atwood's preface indicates, from a Canadian National Exhibition of twenty-some years past of Siamese twins " '*Joined Head to Head, and still alive!*' " Atwood's preface explains that one head speaks French (translated), the other English; they speak the eleven poems singly, together, or alternating within a poem. At readings in the States, Atwood used hand signals to indicate which head, or heads, was speaking; in print, however, Atwood has steadfastly refused to identify the heads, though Dennis Lee, the *This Magazine* editors, and Oxford all felt the need.[9] Perhaps some speeches are interchangeable?

Because, as *This Magazine*'s editors noted in 1977, "Two-Headed Poems" was written after, and in the light of, the previous years' Quebec events, a brief summary may be useful here: by 1976 the two solitudes (as Hugh MacLennan termed them) of French and English Canada had grown increasingly hostile over language and secession; though the Front de libération du Qúebec (FLQ) bombings had stopped, and Prime Minister Trudeau had made the country officially bilingual, René Lévesque's separatist Parti qúebéçois had been gaining power—and so had an English-Canadian backlash. In June 1976 the federal government in Ottawa had apparently supported the Anglophone pilots' and air controllers' protests against Francophone pilots' and air controllers' speaking French over Quebec airspace. On 15 November 1976, Lévesque and his separatist Parti were elected; they quickly mandated French throughout Quebec—in the then-English-dominated businesses, the government, the schools, even on street signs. From summer 1977 on, Lévesque's separatist referendum on Quebec seemed imminent—and winnable.[10]

That, briefly, is where "Two-Headed Poems" begins: poem i opens with the two Canadas almost getting somewhere but not really, as usual, when suddenly America crumbles in a great quake or rift and everything falls south "into the dark pit left by Cincinnati" (p. 60). Only rubble and slogans remain; "What will happen to the children," the two heads ask, "not to mention the words / we've been stockpiling for ten years now," defining and freezing and storing them? (p. 61). Whether the words are pure French for the elite of each Canada, or Quebec's native *joual,* or the endangered English signs in French Canada, they are now useless, outdated tokens of identity, unviable, like the small English family businesses forced out of Montreal.

The first poem ends with disintegration: "the death of shoes [as in the FLQ 1966 shoe factory bombing], fingers / dissolving from our hands, / atrophy of the tongue / the empty mirror"; without America, the Canadas are sublimated "from ice [I's] to thin air" (p. 61). Though this disintegration strongly suggests a nuclear catastrophe, in the next ten poems the heads go on talking, alive and uninjured. What has happened in the first poem, then, must either be a flash forward ("This rubble is the future" [p. 60]), or a nuclear-imaged crumbling of the American economy, as in the midseventies recession, or perhaps, as Cincinnati suggests, a crumbling of the original American ideals.

Though the heads speak 1977 Canadian at each other, however, the underlying strata come from Jaynes: in poem i the catastrophic rift and collapse of America, the stockpiling of useless words, and the ensuing collapse of the two heads' identities, all echo Jaynes's description of the ancient Aegean land's collapse that destroyed Atlantis, its civilization, and gods: whole peoples then became refugees, "strange language bellowed at uncomprehending ears," and "the storings up and distillings of admonitory experience gained in the peaceful authoritarian ordering of a bicameral nation" became unworkable, useless. The ancient bicameral, literally god-hearing mind collapsed into modern godless, *I*-conscious, left-hemisphere man (pp. 212–13).

The entire poetic sequence is structured like its first poem: the 1977 two-headed Canadian overburden rests on Jaynesian bicameral strata, especially as they are explained in his "Causes of Consciousness," which attempts "a paleontology of consciousness, in which we can discern stratum by stratum how this metaphored world we call subjective consciousness was built up and under what particular social pressures" (pp. 204–22, 216). Careful analysis, Jaynes in hand and 1977 Canada in mind, will show that "Two-Headed Poems" is concentrically structured, stratum by stratum, as Atwood's analogous paleontology of Canada's two left-brained national consciousnesses and of the metaphors and pressures that formed them.

"Two-Headed Poems" is internally centered, with three Jaynesian oracles: the first, sun-invocation oracle comes sixth and center in the eleven poems. Poem ix is the second oracle, the right-brain revelation of the way out; the final poem, poem xi, offers a third, briefly dreamt oracle of freedom. On either side of poem vi's central oracle, the poems correspond as they recapitulate certain stages of Jaynes's evolution of language and consciousness: poem i corresponds to poem xi; poems ii and iii somewhat to poem viii (which was added later) and to what are now poems ix and x; poem iv to poems viii and ix; poem v to poems vii and x. These Jaynesian correspondences are not so simple as "The Circle Game"'s centered correspondences; instead they are converse, changed, and magnified, like reflections in a funhouse mirror.

Thus, the first poem's catastrophic disintegrations of America and of the two Canada's identities, and its voluntarily stockpiled words that have been stored like foods in the cellar, recapitulate Jaynes on the Atlantis collapse and on humanity's first use of written language, on the way to consciousness, for inventory of goods (pp. 212–13, 218). The corresponding end poem, poem xi, has the same Jaynesian stages of disintegration and stockpiled language, but conversely developed: poem xi begins with the negative and involuntary use of nouns as foods. English, sneer the French, is good only for groceries, not for song or soul; under Trudeau's federal bilingualism and Quebec's unilingualism, the Canadas—especially the hitherto-privileged English Canadians of Montreal—have become the grocers' prisoners, caged like geese and force fed nouns. The corresponding disintegration of the two Canadas' left-brain identities in the oracular end of poem xi is, conversely, positive, a freedom that transcends borders in a dreamt return to the Jaynesian right brain where language is flowing verbs and song.

Poems ii and iii follow two other Jaynesian causes of consciousness, the perception of others and the development of long-term, treacherous deceit. After Atlantis, Jaynes suggests, the "*observation of difference may be the origin of the analog space of consciousness*"; the individual who posited an interior self in strange others could infer, by analogy, his own (p. 217, Jaynes's italics). "Deceit may also be a cause of consciousness," Jaynes suggests; treachery, impossible for bicameral man, creates a mask self to survive invading strangers (pp. 219–20).

In poem ii the Canadas define themselves by first defining the strange others, the Americans: "They scatter [their words], we / hoard" (p. 62). Economically and culturally invaded, the Canadas grow masks of English propriety and French sneering at those who own and tour their Canada. In poem iii the Canadas posit, stupidly, each other's selves: "We think of you as one / big happy family, sitting around / an old pine table," say the English to the French, patronizingly. "We make too much noise, / you know nothing about us, / you would like us to move away," the sullen French respond (p. 63). Defining others first and oneself after, by negative contrast, is a Canadian reflex and a symptom of the lack of an independent identity (even *Survival* defines other literatures first, and Canadian second or third, in almost every chapter). In poems ii and iii the two Canadas are using Jaynes's stages of the origins of consciousness as excuses and delays: like the couple in "Circle"'s mirror-window games, they focus on others, external and internal, and on masks and complaints.

These two Jaynesian stages of consciousness—the perception of strange others and the development of deceit—will reappear in the corresponding poems after poem vi, progressing to honesty and transformation in poems viii and ix, regressing to violent treachery in the alternate version of poem x.

In poem iv, the "investigator is here," to command and rule by fear: "Stop this heart! / Cut this word from this mouth. / Cut this mouth" (p. 64). The Canadian references are multiple: to the federal Commissioner of Official Languages, who enforced bilingualism; to French attempts to purify French; to the Parti qúebécois purging of English from Quebec, especially from Montreal; to the Anglophone pilots' and controllers' attempt to purge French from the skies of Quebec. For Atwood, whoever enforces and purges words, kills language, hearts, mouths.

The Jaynesian references in poem iv are also multiple: the investigator reenacts the invading strangers who issue commands, "perhaps in a strange language" (p. 220); and "cruelty as an attempt to rule by fear is," Jaynes suggests, "at the brink of subjective consciousness" (p. 214).[11] Thus, in poem iv, the investigator's commands are followed by the Canadas' first consciousness of themselves as a subjected people, lacking names and flag: "For so much time, our history / was written in bones only. / Our flag has been silence, / which was mistaken for no flag" (p. 64).

For Jaynes, commands precede nouns and nouns precede names in the evolution of language (pp. 133–36). In poem iv, the investigator's commands lead to a consciousness of the nameless bones; in the corresponding poem ix, which was originally poem viii, the words that will be named and claimed are those of the dead. (The present poem viii, added later, recapitulates consciousness and cutting.)

Poems v and vii, on either side of the central poem vi, are the modern politicized consciousness that produces false followers and a false leader. Poem v refers particularly to the newly articulate, noisily politicized qúebécois intelligentsia: "Is this what we wanted, / this politics . . . ? . . . Our hearts are flags now, / they wave at the end of each / machine we can stick them on" (pp.

64–65). The intelligentsia have attempted to capture the snow "in a language so precise / and secret . . . / there could be no translation" (p. 65). They have crusaded to "save this language," be it the vulgar native *joual* or the elite French, by pushing back the coarse English and American words "spreading themselves everywhere / like thighs or starlings" (p. 65). For Atwood, this is antilanguage and antilife; as in *Power Politics,* the snow cannot be captured (p. 37).

The way out of such politics, revealed at the sequence's center in poem vi, is a Jaynesian return to the oracular right hemisphere of the mind, which can utter truths transcending the two left hemispheres' hostile nationalisms. Poem vi begins ironically, with left-brain, scientific reasons for humility: "Despite us / there is only one universe, the sun / burns itself slowly out no matter / what you say, is that / so?" (p. 66). This cosmic English rebuke to Quebec's struggle for a place in the sun (see, for example, Trofimenkoff, p. 313) is followed by a French rhetorical retort. Then comes the inset invocation to the sun:

> Close your eyes [I's] now, see:
> red sun, black sun, ordinary
> sun, sunshine, sun-
> king . . .
> ice [eyes] on the sun. (p. 66)

Though poem vi's opening can be misread as mere English versus French irony, and its sun-spelling as mere semantics, what matters is the humility and the invocation. This sun-spelling is what Jaynes calls induced possession: under rationalism, the right-brain god-voices are no longer heard spontaneously; the oracles are vestigal and must be induced, as by the youth Aedesius, who would " 'look at the sun' " to produce oracles (pp. 344–45). The sequence from poems iv and v to vi, from cruelty and flag waving to sun-god, may have followed Jaynes's consciousness-paralleling history (pp. 215–16); clearly the stages in poems iv, v, and vi, which go from commands to namelessness to these sun-spell metaphors that allow new perceptions, recapitulate Jaynes's evolution of language (pp. 133–38).

In the center poem, sun-spelling brings forth the first, right-brain oracle. Language is a birth, "wet & living" and, simultaneously, degenerate and devouring, a Jungian Great Mother tongue: "each / word is wrinkled / with age, swollen / with other words, with blood" (p. 67). The oracular right brain, which may be shared by the two heads, can say to each nationalist left brain:

> Your language hangs around your neck,
> a noose, a heavy necklace;
> each word is empire,
> each word is vampire and mother. (p. 67)

But poem vi ends in left-brain sophistry: is it true or false that "there are as many / suns as" sun words? (p. 67) The mocking questions that precede and follow the central oracle, plus the false politics of poems v and vii, before and after the oracle, indicate that in the two-headed, left-brained Canada of 1977, the oracle falls on jabbering mouths and deaf ears.

"Our leader" in poem vii, then prime minister Pierre Eliot Trudeau, is no oracle, but a deceitful double man of two voices, two heads, two sets of genitals—an allusion to his activities with both sexes. He is a spider who traps and sucks out the life of words. He is a monster of deceit: "Who does our leader speak for? / How can you use two languages / and mean what you say in both?" The rhetoric is neutral, but the caricature is suspiciously English Canadian. Poem vii ends with the passive bitterness of a divided country: "He is ours and us, / we made him" (p. 69).

Poem viii, added after the original sequence ran in *This Magazine* and in response to Dennis Lee's questions (Atwood Papers, Box 14), resumes where poems ii and iii left off, with politeness, the Americans, and mutual recrimination. If I were really a foreigner, each head says to the other, "you would be more polite." In 1977 Canada, America is not the problem—foreigners come and go, "invisible / except for their cameras" and strange fragrances. The problem is the two heads, who "are not foreigners / to each other" but rather "the pressure / on the inside of the skull, . . . the grudging love, / the old hatreds." Are they two left brains, joined only in their deficient right side? The grotesque pun is possible. After all, why fear separation, unless the severing knife "would cut not skin but brain?" (p. 70). However grotesque, this is a new stage of consciousness: political honesty.

As in Jaynes (p. 93), fear precedes prophecy: the sustained and beautiful oracle of poem ix resumes where the originally parallel poem iv left off, with the names of the dead, who must be learned and claimed. The dead belong to particular Canadian history, French *and* English *and* native: "This word [that] was shut / in the mouth of a small man / choked off by the rope and gold / / red drumroll" (p. 70) is the word for Riel, the French Metis hero hung by the MacDonald Conservative government in 1887; is the word for each of the French *and* English hung by the British in the 1837–38 Rebellions of Lower (French) and Upper (English) Canada. The word that was deported is from one of the fifty-eight people deported to Australia from the Rebellion in Lower Canada (Trofimenkoff, p. 78; Atwood, *Days of the Rebels,* pp. 108, 112; Interview, p. 190). The gutteral word that was buried "wrapped in a wolfskin" is native *and* trapper, French *and* English, historic and pre-historic. The word under the lake "with a coral bead and a kettle" is native *and voyageur.* The scrawny self-denying word is a poor settler, probably Protestant; the word that "died of bad water" (p. 71) is anyone.

This eerie, beautiful litany of the dead incorporates and transforms the two nations' language wars, their recitals of ancient wrongs (compare Moore, p. 93; Atwood, Interview, p. 190), and Jaynes's evolution of language from nouns to names and graves (pp. 219–20). Here, transformed, the particular becomes the human species, all the ancestors that must be claimed. The Stage I English-oriented *Survival* had argued that Canadians must claim their own literature and identity, not imported ones, or remain incomplete, colonials. This Stage II oracle says that the two Canadas must transcend their separate histories to learn and claim each other's ancestors, and the first peoples', as they claim their own:

> These words are yours,
> though you never said them,
> you never heard them, history
> breeds death but if you kill
> it you kill yourself. (p. 71)

Whether the heads speak in unison or alternately, their right-brain oracle is speaking, to both left brains.

Poem x shows what has and will occur if the oracle goes unheard: the civil deceits of poems ii and iii, and the politicized hearts of poem vi, will turn to treacherous violence (compare

Jaynes, p. 220). The party "hearts we sent you / in the mail," say the French or the politicized, hold snipers, as your hearts do, "glass-eyed fanatic[s], / waiting to be given life" (p. 72); the image recalls the FLQ's mailbox bombs in Montreal's English Westmount, in the early sixties. Meanwhile, the English and the not yet violent refuse to believe that their hearts too hold violent secrets. Meanwhile, English and French let violence seep in on the evening news "from foreign countries, / those places with unsafe water. / We listen to the war, the wars, / any old war" (p. 73). On both sides, Canadian left-brain hypocrisy and apathy are drifting, stupidly, into civil war.

The sequence ends at poem xi, with Trudeau's sneer at English, and with the Canadas, or the English ones, caged like geese and force fed nouns. A third and final oracle from the right brain envisions what language should be:

> Our dreams though
> are of freedom, a hunger
> for verbs, a song
> which rises liquid and effortless,
> our double, gliding beside us
> over all these rivers, borders,
> over ice or clouds. (p. 75)

This is a third language, gliding over the frozen I's; neither French nor English, but bicameral song and dream. It is also an Indian language, belonging to these rivers and borders and sky, as the imported, fixating, separating, noun-seeing European languages do not. "In one of the languages there are no nouns, only verbs held for a longer moment," the Stage I *Surfacing* vision reveals (p. 181). In the *Meanjin* interview of 6 March 1978 (p. 196), and again in the Hammond interview that accompanies "Two-Headed Poems" in the *American Poetry Review* of 1979 (p. 28), Atwood stresses the need for the third, native language, which does not separate things into fixed objects, but lets them flow within their matrix: the concept, Atwood says, is not even translatable into English, because English scarcely allows such thoughts. For Atwood, "language is everything you do" (*Surfacing*, p. 129); as in Jaynes (p. 292), changing the two nations' languages would change their concepts and behavior.

The last oracle of poem xi is only a vision of what could be; the reality, where poem xi ends, is that for two hostile left brains, dreams "settle nothing. / This is not a debate / but a duet / with two deaf singers" (p. 75). The final sarcasm undercuts what had seemed at least a rude dialogue, of the heads speaking with and at each other.[12]

"Two-Headed Poems," then, clearly belongs to Atwood's Stage II Canadian and human politics. The two Canadas are in the center foreground, causing their own problems with their hostile, ignorant, false, and dangerous left-brain nationalisms, and ignoring the right-brain oracles. The United States is relegated to background and partial cause: poem i shows the collapsed nation as the first victim of its out-of-control technology; Canada gets the trickle-up. Atwood's apprentice poems of the United States as demon lover and Canada as poor frozen Rapunzel, and the Stage I "Circle Game" poems of Canada as passive victim, mirror-starer, and orphan-outsider, seem, in contrast, immature victim games—as in *Survival*'s Victim Position Two, which is blaming one's problems on some overpowering other (p. 37).

In "Two-Headed Poems" the oracles rebuke both of Canada's feuding nations and call for a human, supranational claiming of all the ancestors who have entered the land: French, English, native, nameless. As in the apprentice "Idea of Canada" and the Stage I *Journals of Susanna Moodie,* Canada is the land itself—not the politicians whose slogans divide and desecrate the land. And for Atwood, after Jaynes, language is the wider human territory, the Great Mother tongue that should be learned and claimed, with love—not force, investigators, laws—if we are to become fully human.

One predicts that, from this two-headed sequence of misborn grotesques and Canada's now-topical 1977 language crises, it is the oracles that will survive.

## *Notes*

1. All references to Atwood's novels and books of poetry are to the Canadian editions. The Atwood Papers are in the Fisher Rare Book Library at the University of Toronto; "The Idea of Canada" and "America as the aging demon lover" are in Boxes 7 and 6 of the papers.) Stage I and Stage II are drawn from my book in progress, "Margaret Atwood: Metamorphoses, Evidence, and Archetypes." I am grateful to the National Endowment for the Humanities for a 1982–83 Fellowship for College Teachers to research this book; and to the Canadian Embassy Faculty Re-

search Programme 1984–85 and Senior Fellowship 1985–86 Grants, which supported this paper.

An earlier version of the first two sections of this paper was given at a special session on "Margaret Atwood: Poetics and Politics," Modern Language Association annual convention, Washington, D.C., 28 December 1984. A fuller discussion of Atwood's Gothic elements is provided in my 1981 "Atwood's Haunted Sequences."

2. Margaret Atwood, personal interview, 28 May 1985.

3. [C. November 1962] notes, Box 6; Margaret Atwood, letter to James Carscallen, 20 November [1962], and "Principles," Box 1.

4. Compare the old woman and her teacups in *The Circle Game*'s more subtle poem of Canadian identity, "A Place: Fragments" (pp. 73–74), and, of course, Susanna Moodie in her stuffed, tea-set parlor (p. 47).

5. The Canadian-American politics of these two apprentice poems feed into a number of *The Animals in That Country* poems, particularly "At the tourist centre in Boston," "Roominghouse, winter," and, as Atwood pointed out in the 28 May 1985 interview, "Backdrop addresses cowboy" (pp. 18–19, 28–29, 50–51). The latter two (and perhaps the first) were once part of a series called "American Poems."

6. This essay builds on Sherrill Grace's suggestive remarks on "Circle"'s paired, reflecting structure (*Violent Duality,* pp. 20–22); and on Sullivan's key 1977 discussion of "Circle"'s garrison mentality (p. 31).

7. In the apprentice period, the two heads appeared at the end of the holograph "Idea of Canada," in the holograph "Sideshow" (Box 5), and in the fourth, center poem of the published 1964 "Fall and All" sequence. In "Fall" the Siamese twins are Adam and Eve, caged in a double body, doomed to barren mourning for their unborn children; a stepfather and a cruel mother, serpent-virtued, has imprisoned the two thus in each other's skin and blood. Whether or not these Siamese twins were intended, like the 1977 pair, as figures of French and English Canada, deformed by their parent countries, their allegory was already overloaded, their "Fall" static and contorted.

8. Rosenberg, pp. 134–36, reprinted in his 1984 *Atwood,* pp. 87–88; Grace, "Atwood and Duplicity," pp. 66–68. Irvine's fine 1981 essay on the rest of the book barely mentions this sequence. Of the five essays in Grace and Weir that deal with Atwood's poetry, only Grace (p. 7) and Weir (p. 149) give it brief space; Blakeley, Mandel, and Woodcock barely mention it. Davey (*Margaret Atwood)* and Mallinson ignore the sequence.

9. Margaret Atwood, letter to Bill Toye of Oxford, 27 April 1978, Box 14.

10. "Two-Headed Poems," *This Magazine,* p. 18; Trofimenkoff, pp. 317–32; Milner, pp. 235–53; Jacobs, pp. 78–79.

11. Cf. also Jaynes: "Militarism, police, rule by fear are all the desperate measures used to control a subjective conscious populace restless with identity crises and divided off into their multitudinous privacies of hopes and hates" (p. 205).

12. Song, according to Jaynes, is primarily right-brain (pp. 365–67). Except in the three oracles, this sequence is obviously left-brain argument,

and not "a song / which rises liquid and effortless" (p. 75). Like the idea of two quite articulate Siamese twins unable to hear each other's speech, even by vibrations, the idea of the two heads as singers is a grotesque sarcasm.

# 12 *Real and Imaginary Animals in the Poetry of Margaret Atwood*

*Kathleen Vogt*

Reporting on her visits to the Toronto zoo, in an article entitled "Don't Expect the Bears to Dance," Margaret Atwood describes the modern institution, designed to provide the animals within it with something approaching their natural habitats, as a considerable advance over earlier zoos. Of the latter she writes:

> The traditional zoo was a cross between a circus freak show and a museum with the animal "exhibits" arranged side by side in little cubicles. This kind of zoo was essentially a Victorian institution and the Victorians were great collectors and classifiers; so they put all the cats together in the cat house, all the monkeys in the monkey house, all the birds in the bird house and so forth. Unfortunately, the animals might as well have been stuffed and kept in glass cases; all you could see was what they looked like, as they rarely had the chance to display any form of natural behavior. The arrangement was convenient for people—with all the animals crowded together, not much walking was involved—but hell on the animals.[1]

In the new Metro zoo, Atwood finds herself "walking among the animals rather than being separated from them," unless she visits at an inopportune time (in the afternoon, for example) when many are asleep in their lairs or unless she attempts to approach the very shy, who take to hiding out in long grasses, with at best only their ears showing. "Zoos make me nervous," Atwood declares at the beginning *and* end of her report. But environments that allow animals to ignore or reject encounters with human would-be observers obviously make Atwood less nervous than cages, Victorian or other, in which living creatures, contained in a manner suited to inanimate objects, frequently go mad or die in order to satisfy human curiosity.

Atwood's interest in animals is not confined to expression in an occasional essay on the Toronto zoo. Her essays on pervading themes in Canadian literature, collectively entitled *Survival,* revolve around a thesis concerning animals and the ways they are presented in Canadian writing. And her own poetry and fiction present a multitude of animals of diverse generic and aesthetic kinds: herons and loons, bulls and pigs, pickerel and eels, wolves and cats. Some of these are, as one would guess, situated in the bush, or at least the country; others are found in metropolitan zoos (zoos are very much apart of the worlds Atwood creates as well as the one she observes). Some of Atwood's animals can be found only in museums, where human hands construct imitation animals, following the hints and traces of fossils, out of bones and bits of fur. (Such a museum, filled with dinosaurs, provides the central image of Atwood's novel *Life Before Man.*) Frequently, in fact, bones and bits of fur appear in Atwood's works in their unredeemed, fragmented forms. And there are other breathless animals as well, some built out of wood or carved in it, some painted on boards or rocks. Some of these crafted animals have the heightened aura of the sacred or mythical about them, while others seem sad imitations of living things, or parodies of them, such as the dead minnow encased in plastic, designed as fisherman's bait, in the novel *Surfacing.* Now and then Atwood includes an animal from the everyday domestic world, a cat, for example.

All in all, taken together, the animals of Atwood's art constitute a veritable Noah's ark in several respects: (1) They represent a large assortment of living animal kinds. (2) More interestingly, they represent life on different levels of being—from, for example, the most mundane or physical level to the most spiritual or abstract, in timeless aesthetic forms or in materials and shapes that stress the vulnerability of all mortal things. (3) Some of these animal images function to say something about themselves or nature; others serve primarily as figures of speech through which Atwood reveals the nature of humankind. The best animal images remind us of the integrity of both animals and humans and the necessary interdependence of the two.

Of Atwood's works, *Surfacing,* which George Galt has called "a huge thin novel" (p. 54), harbors the most animals of the most different kinds. Of Atwood's six other published novels, *Life Before Man* comes next in number of references to animals, but these animals are predominantly of but one kind—the prehistoric replicas in the museum of natural history. Though there are many similarities or parallels between these two novels, their overall auras or atmospheres ultimately may be as different as the animals that inhabit them. Within the canon of Atwood's ten volumes of poetry on the other hand, there are animals of all the kinds I have mentioned; in this essay I shall focus upon them.

A cat appears in a transitional poem, "There Is Only One of Everything" (*You Are Happy,* 1974). And if Gayle Wood is right, this cat, right out of somebody's kitchen, represents a shift in a body of poetry that starts out but vaguely indicating the factual bases of emotional landscapes or conditions and ends up dealing in particulars.

> Not a tree but the tree
> We saw, it will never exist, split by the wind
> and bending down
> like that again. What will push out of the earth
>
> later, making it summer, will not be
> grass, leaves, repetition, there will
> have to be other words. When my
>
> eyes close language vanishes. The cat
> with the divided face, half black half orange
> nest in my scruffy fur coat, I drink tea,
>
> fingers curved around the cup, impossible
> to duplicate these flavours. . . .[2]

This poem does seem a celebration of the ordinary particular (if there can be such a thing) to a degree rare in Atwood. The concern, however, for the tree, the tea, the cat, and, in the latter half of the poem, for the person outside the self, coming to be known by the self through a medium other than words, is common in the poems—though the sense in this poem of something approaching unity between the self and the other is not.

One of the simplest and most moving expressions of Atwood's concern for lives outside the single, human self is in poems depicting the victimization of animals. As Atwood—in *Survival*—and other critics have said, this is a favorite subject in Canadian literature, where it is handled from the animal's point of view, indicating human identification with the animal (Atwood, "Animal Victims"; Polk). Here is Atwood's Brian the Still-Hunter in the poem bearing his name, speaking of his occupation:

> I kill because I have to
>
> but every time I aim, I feel
> my skin grow fur
> my head heavy with antlers
> and during the stretched instant
> the bullet glides on its thread of speed
> my soul runs innocent as hooves.
>
> Is God just to his creatures?
>
> I die more often than many.
>
> (*The Journals of Susanna Moodie,* 1970; *SP,* p. 99)

The world is not full of persons with Brian's sensibilities, however, as Atwood knows too well. As she say in the title poem of one of her early volumes, "The Animals in That Country" (1968):

> In that country the animals
> have the faces of people:
>
> the ceremonial
> cats possessing the streets
>
> the fox run
> politely to earth, the huntsmen
> standing around him, fixed
> in their tapestry of manners
>
> the bull, embroidered
> with blood and given
> an elegant death, trumpets, his name
> stamped on him, heraldic brand
> because
>
> (when he rolled
> on the sand, sword in his heart, the teeth
> in his blue mouth were human)
>
> he is really a man

even the wolves, holding resonant
conversations in their
forests thickened with legend.

In this country the animals
have the faces of
animals.

Their eyes
flash once in car headlights
and are gone.

Their deaths are not elegant.

They have the faces of
no-one. (*SP*, pp. 48–49)

In other poems animals are treated as no-ones. "Dreams of the Animals" reveals this in terms reminiscent of the Victorian zoo with which my essay began:

Mostly the animals dream
of other animals each
according to its kind

(though certain mice and small rodents
have nightmares of a huge pink
shape with five claws descending)

: moles dream of darkness and delicate
mole smells

frogs dream of green and golden
frogs
sparkling like wet suns
among the lilies

red and black
striped fish, their eyes open
have red and black striped
dreams defence, attack, meaningful
patterns

birds dream of territories
enclosed by singing.

Sometimes the animals dream of evil
in the form of soap and metal

but mostly the animals dream
Of other animals.

There are exceptions:

the silver fox in the roadside zoo
dreams of digging out
and of baby foxes, their necks bitten

the caged armadillo
near the train
station, which runs
all day in figure eights
its piglet feet pattering
no longer dreams
but is insane when waking;

the iguana
in the petshop window on St. Catherine Street
crested, royal-eyed, ruling
its kingdom of water-dish and sawdust

dreams of sawdust.
(*Procedures for Underground,* 1970; *SP,* pp. 123–24)

When animals are but objects, it seems people are similarly reduced. They become valued according to the limited, separable functions they serve; they are defined or define themselves in terms that are technical and abstract and mock life. Or so Atwood says, mockingly, in the poem that begins:

You want to go back
to where the sky was inside us

animals ran through us, our hands
blessed and killed according to our
wisdom, death
made real blood come out

But face it, we have been
improved, our heads float
several inches above our necks
moored to us by
rubber tubes and filled with
clever bubbles. . . . (*Power Politics,* 1971; *SP,* p. 148)

In a companion poem Atwood writes:

> In view of the fading animals
> the proliferation of sewers and fears
> the sea clogging, the air
> nearing extinction
>
> we should be kind, we should
> take warning, we should forgive each other
>
> Instead we are opposite, we
> touch as though attacking,
>
> The gifts we bring
> even in good faith maybe
> warp in our hands to
> implements, to manoeuvres
>
> ("They are hostile nations," *Power Politics; SP,* p. 161)

In the poems, the abuse of animals, or the loss of contact with them, represents the denial of the significance of anything outside the isolate individual's will or mind.

In some poems, such as those just quoted, animals and attitudes toward animals are not depicted or dramatized in themselves, having instead become reference points for Atwood's description of sterility of human life. In other poems, references to the animal world are obvious metaphors for what humans do to one another. Here, for example, is the tiny epigraph poem from *Power Politics:* "you fit into me / like a hook into an eye / a fish hook / an open eye." And in *You Are Happy* there is a powerful set of poems called "Songs of the Transformed," which are fashioned from the point of view of animals, although these animals frequently sound very much like men, or women, speaking (see, for example, "Pig Song," "Bull Song," "Rat Song.") In this group of poems one is invited to see both animals and humans when responding to the imagery, though within the entirety of the set, the animals range in signifying power from symbolic to allegorical and are seldom, if ever, presented naturalistically.

That the theme of victimization has a certain breadth or scope we have already seen, insofar as it depicts humans both in relation to animals and in relation to each other, including their own selves. The pattern victimization takes is not always one of "power politics," however, or of the imposition of human will on other beings. Indeed, while some persons in Atwood deny any dynamics between self and other by caging armadillos and causing them to go mad, others seem overtaken by animal selves, imagining that they have become deer, foxes, or wolves, and in doing so, revealing their own madness. Brian the Still-Hunter's mental state is close to this, and there seems no doubt about the madness in "Arctic Syndrome: dream fox." (The arctic syndrome is, as Atwood herself explains in an interview with Karla Hammond, "the name of a specific kind of madness, that occurs only north of the arctic circle in which the person becomes a fox or a wolf" [p. 28]). Perhaps the pioneer Susanna Moodie is reporting a narrow escape, when in one of the sequence of poems in which Atwood dramatizes the experiences Moodie recorded in her journals, Susanna says:

> I, who had been erased
> by fire, was crept in
> upon by green
>                         (how
> lucid a season)
>
>                         In time the animals
> arrived to inhabit me. . . .

But by the poem's end, she is making her departure from the bush:

>                 The sleigh was a relief;
> its track lengthened behind,
> pushing me towards the city
>
> and rounding the first hill, I was
> (instantaneous)
> unlived in: they had gone.
>
> There was something they almost taught me
> I cam away not having learned.
>                 (*The Journals of Susanna Moodie; SP,* pp. 92–93)

In an earlier poem, "Progressive Insanities of a Pioneer," the Explorer-settler does not escape:

> Things
> refused to name themselves; refused
> to let him name them.

The wolves hunted
outside.

On his beaches, his clearings,
by the surf of under-
growth breaking
at his feet, he foresaw
disintegration
                    and in the end
through eyes
made ragged by his
effort, the tension
between subject and object,

the green
vision, the unnamed
whale invaded. (*The Animals in That Country; SP,* p. 63)

What has really happened here to Brian, Susanna, and our nameless pioneer? Did a hostile wilderness subdue, or almost subdue, human consciousness? Or was human consciousness flawed from the beginning by an inability to perceive and accept a truly subjective-objective world?

In Atwood's poems the theme of victimization is part of a larger concern with identity. Victimization is one scene in a tapestry showing an individual in relation to a multitude of elements—rocks, mountains, trees, grass, *animals,* and people—sharing the space of existence. Moreover, the tapestry takes into account the temporal as well as spatial dimension of existence, and this complicates things immensely. Although some characters in the poems perceive the world in the form of separate, static objects in a given place,[3] it is clear to Atwood and the reader that both the perceiver and the perceived are constantly moving, changing, and disappearing. Atwood's animals remind us of this world of process and of the artist's efforts to acknowledge and yet transcend that aspect of the process that is death.

In one of the first poems she published, Atwood writes:

Love, you must choose
Between two immortalities:
One of earth, lake, trees
Feathers of a nameless bird
The other of a world of glass,

Hard marble, carven wood.
("Her Song," *Double Persephone,* 1961, p. 13).

But she does not choose, or rather her real choices are not quite so pure or simplistic as this poem implies. As Frank Davey points out in his fine essay, "Atwood's Gorgon Touch," at the center of Atwood's poems is a tension between what Davey describes as "the static, the mythological, or the sculptural and the kinetic, the actual, or the temporal" (p. 172). Moreover, as an artist—as Davey says—the poet is necessarily committed to glass, or at least the word, even though she or he may insist, as Atwood does, on the greater reality and appeal of the tangible, with its inevitable and irremediable resistance to what humans would make of it or have it be.

A "dead dog" helps Atwood express the power of the actual and her relation to it in "The Double Voice," a poem about two ways of seeing and writing:

Two voices
took turns using my eyes:

One had manners,
painted in watercolours,
used hush tones when speaking
of mountains or Niagara Falls,
. . . . . . . . . . . . . . . . . . . . . . . .

The other voice
had other knowledge:
that men sweat
always and drink often,
that pigs are pigs
but must be eaten
anyway. . . .

One saw through my
bleared and gradually
bleaching eyes, red leaves,
the rituals of seasons and rivers

The other found a dead dog
jubilant with maggots
half-buried among the sweet peas.
(*The Journals of Susanna Moodie; SP,* p. 104).

"Bones and bits of fur" represent her commitment at the end of "Comic Books vs. History," a poem in which she explores pseudo-realities associated with "your country" (the United States) and their collapse for her. The poem ends: "I turn back, search / for the actual, collect lost / bones, burnt logs / of campfires, pieces of fur" (*Procedures for Underground; SP,* pp. 128–29). And it is no exaggeration to say bones and bits of fur are everywhere in Atwood as talismen of lives terminated or fragmented by time, even as whole animals in cages are present to suggest spatial isolation.

But there are other kinds of dead animals in the poetry too, and some are images of the transcendence of barriers between beings, and between being and nonbeing itself. The faces or bodies on Indian totems or Eskimo animal sculptures are examples subject to Atwood's contemplation in an early poem entitled "Some Objects of Wood and Stone." Here the "carved animals," with which the poem concludes, if not exactly transcendent, do seem mediators between self and other, the physical and spiritual, and the lifeless and living:

> The small carved
> animal is passed from
> hand to hand
> around the circle
> until the stone grows warm
>
> touching, the hands do not know
> the form of animal
> which was made or
> the true form of stone
> uncovered
>
> and the hands, the fingers the
> hidden small bones
> of the hands bend to hold the shape,
> shape themselves, grow
> cold with the stone's cold, grow
> also animal, exchange
> until the skin wonders
> if stone is human
>
> In the darkness later
> and even when the animal

has gone, they keep
the image of that inner shape

hands holding warm
hands holding
the half-formed air

(*The Circle Game,* 1966; *SP,* pp. 33–34)

The carved animals are less conclusive in projecting a state of unity, however, than the totems Atwood describes in "Fishing for Eel Totems":

The string jumped,
I hooked a martian / it poured
fluid silver out of the river

its long body whipped on the grass, reciting
all the letters of its alphabet.

Killed, it was a
grey tongue hanged silent in the smokehouse

which we later ate.

After that I could see
for a time in the green country;

I learned that the earliest language
was not our syntax of chained pebbles

but liquid, made
by the first tribes, the fish
people. (*Procedures for Underground; SP;* p. 137)

In this poem the living body of the eel, rather than an artistic replica, proclaims its reality, and somehow goes on proclaiming it after it is killed and devoured; indeed this act of eating is a sacramental communion.

Not many dead eels are sacramental fodder in Atwood, however. More frequently they remain bodies, signifying life lost. Sometimes, as in the case of the dead dog nourishing maggots, they are shown in the process of decay; more often they are represented at a remove from energy of any sort. They are the bones of "A Night in the Royal Ontario Museum" which appear to the speaker-narrator as apocalyptic reminders of nothingness:

. . . I am dragged to the mind's
deadend, the roar of the bone-
yard, I am lost
among the mastodons
and beyond: a fossil
shell, then

samples of rocks
and minerals, even the thundering
tusks swindling to pin-
points in the stellar
fluorescent-lighted
wastes of geology.

(*The Animals in That Country,* pp. 20–21)

In some poems, this museum piece for one, Atwood portrays animal bones in the arrangements humankind has made of them so as to create replicas of past life. (This activity occurs and recurs in the novels.) In other poems, as we have seen, the reconstruction involves the sculptor's carvings or the poet's words; often those words are found wanting. "Song of the Hen's Head" offers one example; though it is one in the set of poems "Songs of the Transformed," to which I referred earlier, here no transformation has occurred. Indeed, according to this hen, words are murderers rather than creators or perpetuators of life:

After the abrupt collision
with the blade, the Word,
I rest on the wood
block, my eyes
drawn back into their blue transparent
shells like molluscs;
I contemplate the Word

while the rest of me
which was never much under
my control, which was always
inarticulate, still runs
at random through the grass, a plea
for mercy, a single
flopping breast,

muttering about life
in its thickening red voice.
(*You Are Happy; SP,* pp. 197–98)

The whole idea of transformation, transmutation, or metamorphosis, which is central to the movement of many of Atwood's poems and in its positive phases seems to promise a kind of Yeatsian unity of beings, becomes less and less possible, in transcendent forms at least, as her poems progress. In "Digging" (*You Are Happy,* pp. 181–82) Atwood writes of the "archeology of manure," suggesting this is what past life may amount to:

Witness this stained bone: pelvis
of some rodent, thrown or dragged here,

. . . . . . . . . . . . . . . . . . . . . . . . . . . . . . . .

I will wear it on a chain
around my neck: an amulet
to ward off anything that is not a fact,
that is not food, including
symbols, monuments,
forgiveness, treaties, love.

In "Siren Song," the Siren says:

Shall I tell you the secret [the song that will work]
and if I do, will you get me
out of this bird suit?

I don't enjoy it here
squatting on this island
looking picturesque and mythical (*SP,* pp. 195–96).

In another poem from *You Are Happy,* the narrator declares:

Men with the heads of eagles
no longer interest me
or pig-men, or those who can fly
with the aid of wax and feathers

. . . . . . . . . . . . . . . . . . . . . . . .

I search instead for the others,
the ones left over,
the ones who have escaped from these
mythologies with barely their lives;

> they have real faces and hands, they think
> of themselves as
> wrong somehow, they would rather be trees. (*SP,* p. 202)

In these poems metamorphosis is merely disguise; mythology, merely embroidery; "men with the heads of eagles" are one brand of role player and would-be manipulators.

By the volume *Two-Headed Poems* (1978) all the totems that appear true to the lives they symbolize are of the eel kind, rather than the carved kind. The earth in the form man discovers it seems its own potter in "April, Radio, Planting, Easter":

> I do not mean the earth, I mean the
> earth that is here and browns your
> feet, thickens your fingers,
> unfurls in your brain and in
> these onion seedlings
> I set in flats lovingly under
> a spare window.
>
> We do not walk on the earth
> but in it, wading
> in that acid sea
> where flesh is etched from
> molten bone and re-forms.
>
> In this massive tide
> warm as liquid
> sun, all waves are one
> wave; there is no other. (*Two-Headed Poems,* pp. 95–96)

The bread of communion is the bread baked in the kitchen; it is a part of the processes of nature, which include death and life. These processes are a kind of sacrament in "All Bread":

> All bread is made of wood,
> cow dung, packed brown moss,
> the bodies of dead animals, the teeth
> and backbones, what is left
> after the ravens. This dirt
> flows through the stems into the grain,
> into the arm, nine strokes
> of the axe, skin from a tree,
> good water which is the first

gift, four hours.

Live burial under a moist cloth,
a silver dish, the row
of white famine bellies
swollen and taut in the oven,
lungfuls of warm breath stopped
in the heat from an old sun.

Good bread has the salt taste
of your hands after nine
strokes of the axe, the salt
taste of your mouth, it smells
of its own small death, of the deaths
before and after.

Lift these ashes
into your mouth, your blood;
to know what you devour
is to consecrate it,
almost. All bread must be broken
so it can be shared. Together
we eat this earth. (*Two-Headed Poems,* p. 107)

There are animals in these and other *Two-Headed Poems.* Some are in the form of bodies and bones, flesh gone back to earth. One in "April, Radio, Planting, Easter" is but a way of saying something about the battering man takes from the radio:

there's a limit to how much
you can take of this battering
against the ears without imploding
like some land animal drifting down
into the blackout of ocean, its body
an eye crushed by pliers. (*Two-Headed Poems,* p. 95)

But there's a hawk in "Marsh, Hawk" (pp. 87–88), which, as it soars up from the marsh, against the sky, seems in the figure it casts a kind of revelation of what a right relation with the universe might be—free, a part of the whole, one with it. And in "The Puppet of the Wolf" (pp. 99–100) there is the wolf the narrator makes out of her hand to amuse her child in the bathtub. There is no wolf, not even a puppet, yet the wolf is there at the call of the imagination of the mother and child.

In her poetry Atwood seems to grow more suspicious of beauty of the glass or carved kind and more insistent upon acknowledging birds with real feathers on them. She seems by *Two-Headed Poems* to be seeking immortality in the shapes and materials and movements of the things of this world, and the tone of these poems suggests she sometimes finds it. In this volume her animal images are, however, surprisingly less frequent; and when they come they are less charged with symbolic significance than many of the earlier references, which may not be surprising at all. How ideological as opposed to imagistic are some of the earlier images, I find myself wondering? Although all of them are bound up with Atwood's insistence that our space is a shared space in which trees, sky, hawks, and humankind exist at once, do some of the words signifying animals, for example, have little or nothing to do with calling those animals before our eyes and into our presence? Is the very nature of art, including Atwood's, as Davey suggests, such as to substitute glass or carved animals for real ones, even though to be glass or under glass is to be dead, a part of a Victorian zoo?

Annis Pratt, in a 1972 essay in *Contemporary Literature* entitled "Women and Nature in Modern Fiction," does not deal with Atwood but makes some points about imagery that certainly could be applied to her work. In discussing how images may relate to the concrete objects they name, Pratt compares and contrasts Sarah Orne Jewett's presentation of natural objects with Joyce's, or Joyce's via Stephen Dedalus in *A Portrait of the Artist as a Young Man.* Pratt discovers, for example, that when Stephen sees the vision of a girl who at one moment appears to him in "the likeness of a strange and beautiful seabird," he is regarding both the girl and the bird as signs, portents, symbols of inner essences or states. She contrasts this with the way Sylvia, Jewett's protagonist in "A White Heron," sees birds. Sylvia "experiences her epiphany, a dazzling dawn vision of hawks, sun, heron, and ocean, when she climbs an enormous pine tree to look for the heron's nest." This epiphany leads her to deflect a young male hunter friend from his would-be prey, for in Sylvia's vision "a heron is a heron, valuable for its heronness, a vehicle only of its own particularity and what she perceives as the freedom of the self in nature in contrast to canine servitude." Pratt concludes: "Where Sylvia's naturistic epiphany led her to a heightened perception of existence, Stephen perceives natural objects as vehicles for conceiving an essence."

"If a symbol is a metaphor," Pratt states, "one half of which is concrete and the other half of which indicates something abstract, Stephen's hawk is nearly all symbol while Sylvia's is nearly all hawk" (pp. 478–80).

I suspect that Atwood has more than a little of Stephen in her but that she prefers Sylvia.[4] As I look back on the animal images of the poems, in any case, I see similes and metaphors in which animals function only to establish something about how humans are functioning (the land animal from "April, Radio" is one example.) I see images of animals that express the relations peculiar to human lovers. One poem, for example, in which the speaker warns her mate that her hunger for him threatens to consume him utterly, ends: "There is no reason for this, only / a starved dog's logic about bones." ("More and More," *The Animals in That Country; SP,* p. 74). Another poem, in which lovers touch but do not love, reads in part:

> What is it, it does not
> move like love, it does
> not want to know, it
> does not want to stroke, unfold
>
> it does not even want to
> touch, it is more like
> an animal (not
> loving) a
> thing trapped, you move
> wounded, you are hurt, you hurt,
> you want to get out, you want
> to tear yourself out, I am
>
> the outside. (*Power Politics; SP,* p. 166)

The "dead dog / jubilant with maggots," which I've previously cited, probably serves primarily as a warning that we are flesh and that life and death are one, but we see the dog's body before responding to the concept. And while the birds who dream of "territories / enclosed by singing" may seem a little too romantic to be compelling, "the iguana in the petshop window on St. Catherine Street / crested, / royal-eyed, / ruling its kingdom of waterdish and sawdust" certainly draws us there, full of the desire to free it.

Early and late there are animal animals in Atwood's poems as well as animals who serve metaphorically for humans. And sometimes the most compelling animals are of the carved variety—in a sense, of course, all of the beings who appear in the poems are, as art, carved by human hands—just as sometimes the poems declare that having a fox or iguana in front of the naked eye is no guarantee the beholder will acknowledge the animal's existence in any way that goes beyond sheer sight. Some animals are wooden in that they do not call us to the givens of the earth but to human contrivances instead; other times wooden animals evoke or give rise to the real.

As a poet, finally, Atwood is, I think, a bit like the protagonist of *Surfacing,* who at a climactic moment in the novel observes:

> From the lake a fish jumps
>
> An idea of a fish jumps
>
> A fish jumps, carved wooden fish with dots painted on the sides, no, antlered fish thing drawn in red on cliffstone, protecting spirit, It hangs in the air suspended, flesh turned to icon, he has changed again, returned to the water. How many shapes can he take.
>
> I watch it for an hour or so; then it drops and softens, the circles wide, it becomes an ordinary fish again. (p. 219)

In the nameless protagonist's awareness—represented in her changing vision of the fish—that life includes all levels of being and all ways of knowing them, there is an affirmation both of the reality and significance of the human self as perceiver and creator and of the other, as well as of the inextricable relationship between the two.

In her own art Atwood may be going a step beyond the zoo keepers she refers to in the conclusion of her report on the Toronto zoo, with which I began:

> Why do we do it? Why does mankind construct zoos at all, why do human beings lavish enormous amounts of money, time, and expertise on preserving and peering at creatures that other human beings are just as busy hunting, killing, skinning, stuffing for trophies and eating? Perhaps, it's the insatiable curiosity of homo sapiens, a generic curiosity that's reflected by his cousins staring back at him from the primate enclosures. Or perhaps, the zoo is finally a work of art, a symbol, an attempt to create a healing vision of an Eden-like Peaceable Kingdom, to preserve in artificial form a time when men and animals lived in a more balanced harmony

than they share now, a time before the big-headed monkeys invented agriculture and began to crowd the earth. (p. 71)

Atwood's own zoo suggests that there is no healing or health in a world without animals or where animals are treated like objects,[5] and that there can be joy in the land where animals and humans meet. In some of the later poems as well as in *Surfacing* that land appears.

*Notes*

1. Atwood, "Don't Expect the Bears to Dance," p. 68. Atwood's essay is cited in George Woodcock's "Transformation Mask for Margaret Atwood," in which Woodcock points to Atwood's deep and pervasive interest in animals.

2. *Selected Poems* (New York: Simon and Schuster, 1976), p. 236. Except for poems from *Double Persephone* and *Two-Headed Poems* and "A Night in the Royal Ontario Museum," I have used the Simon and Schuster *Selected Poems*—here abbreviated as *SP*—for the texts of the poems appearing in this essay. Page references for individual volumes of poetry are to the American editions; references for *Surfacing* are to the Popular Library edition (New York, 1972).

3. The most ironic instance of this comes in the poem "Solipsism While Dying," in *The Journals of Susanna Moodie,* where the dying speaker wonders what all the elements of the world will do now "that I, that all / depending on me disappears" (*SP* p. 110).

4. In an essay on Atwood's poetry, John Wilson Foster compares Atwood's animal imagery with the "heraldic stylism" of Indian totem carvers. He states: "We could even argue that the stylistic metamorphoses with which we are familiar in poetry—metaphor, simile and personification—are in Atwood's poetry derived as much from a totemic awareness as from poetic convention" (p. 17).

5. Donna Gerstenberger offers excellent insights into Atwood's understanding of "the total perversion of all life, including the sexual, made possible by the oppressive vision of the world as object" (p. 146).

# 13 *Shamanism in the Works of Margaret Atwood*

*Kathryn VanSpanckeren*

While agreeing on Atwood's mysterious quality of "otherness," critics have differed widely in describing it. It has been linked with genres such as Gothic (Rosowski; Northey), romance (McLay), the ghost story (Garebian), and the fairy tale (MacLulich). The intense, spiritual quality of Atwood's work has also suggested the spiritual quest (Christ), the rite of passage (Ross), the feminine "rebirth journey" (Pratt, "*Surfacing* and the Rebirth Journey"; Rigney), magic (Rogers; Van Spanckeren), witchcraft (Davey, "Atwood's Gorgon Touch"), and the vocation of the seer (Davidson and Davidson, "Margaret Atwood's *Lady Oracle*"; Brown). It has been called "primitivism" (Hinz) and linked with transformation (Jones) and even extraterrestrial experience (Glickson). Shamanism has been most often used as a loose term, mainly to describe the novel *Surfacing* (Ross). Marie-François Guédon, while defining shamanism carefully, limits herself to analysis of that novel. The present essay, however, suggests that an archaic, shamanic vision runs throughout Atwood's writings in all genres, from her earliest to her most recent work, that it accounts for the sense of "otherness" in her work, and that it is a vital and defining source of her power as a writer. Whether or not Atwood consciously adopts a shamanic stance, how her reading affects her work, and the extent to which the shamanic themes, images, and structures permeating her work may be attributed to a Jungian collective unconscious are subjects for other papers. The present essay merely attempts to establish shamanism as a primary mode in Atwood.

The shamanic mode may be seen as the archaic underpinning of the more elaborated genres tapping the "other," such as, to take one example, the tradition of Canadian Gothic discussed by Margot Northey in *The Haunted Wilderness: The Gothic and Grotesque in Canadian Fiction.* Significantly, Atwood herself defines the Gothic shamanistically, not in terms we recognize from Mrs. Radcliffe's novels or *Jane Eyre.* Despite *Lady Oracle's* governesses, escapes, seductions, mazes, and gloomy old mansions, Atwood has written that the defining feature of Gothic is an overriding awareness of death. Just as an orientation to death is the psychological and ontological cornerstone of shamanism (Eliade, *Shamanism,* pp. 508–11), the centrality of death is also the dominant theme or figure in Atwood's works as a whole.

Considerations of space do not permit a lengthy analysis of shamanism; this essay offers what are admittedly generalizations about an exceedingly complex and varied system. Further, shamanism, by its very nature, resists categorization, because it has no dogma. Unlike organized religions, sometimes called "higher spiritual systems"—in a phrase that should be rejected, as it implies a devaluation of pretechnological and preliterate spiritual systems—shamanism, like Zen, is a practice, not a creed. Shamanic practice is in its very essence a "technique of ecstasy," in Eliade's phrase: despite its mediating function between spirits and community, it is a private, ineffable, spiritual experience. It varies not only between tribes, but between individuals of the same tribe. With these considerations in mind, a general definition of shamanism may be ventured (readers desiring fuller information are referred to the Works Cited section of the present volume).

Like the individual on a quest in other mythological systems , the tribal shaman, who may be male or female, undergoes an initiation that roughly follows the stages that Joseph Campbell has popularized as the monomyth, and that structures the journeys to rebirth we see in Atwood's works. The shaman's vocation consists of a series of recurring monomyths, or quests into the spirit realm. The initiation and subsequent spirit journeys generally follow the familiar pattern of the call, withdrawal and preparation, the meeting with helpers (tutelary spirits or animals, ghosts of dead ancestors or dead shamans), a movement across the threshold, a dramatic descent to the underworld or a magic flight, a direct confrontation with the spirits, a gaining of effective spiritual power and knowledge, and a return to the living. This initiation often is modeled on funerary rites (Eliade, *Shamanism,* p. 309). The most frequent condition the shaman is called upon to treat is the loss of the soul, often caused by a broken tabu. Bad fortune and sickness are imagined not as physical diseases, but as psycho-spiritual conditions. As Lévi-Strauss, Kirby, LaBarre, and others point out, shamans are psychiatrists as much as they are doctors or priests.

Vivid, personal experience of the spiritual realm is the center of the shamanic vocation. Though shamans may make their spiritual journeys differently—asleep or in waking trance, intentionally or spontaneously, for profit or for free, with or without certain props or rituals—depending on the culture and the individual, they always make contact with the spirit world. As Jaynes (pp. 201–3), Eliade, and others make clear, the spirit realm is in fact and origin the realm of the dead. Eliade reveals the logical correlative: shamans must be, in some sense, dead themselves in order to receive the teachings of the spirits, who are imagined as knowing everything. Shamans attain a state transcending ordinary life and death, in which they can interact with spirits only the dead (ghosts, ancestors) themselves can give shamans the gift of becoming seers (Eliade, *Shamanism,* p. 84–88).

The poetic narration of quests to the spirit realm of death is a defining feature of shamanism (Kirby, Schechner). Ritual songs and chants, usually accompanied by percussion (a drum in Amerindian tradition and Siberian Asia, gongs in South Asia) suggest the collision of two planes and their release into invisible sonic spirit energy (Lansing; Eliade, *Shamanism,* p. 173). The poem-songs of shamanism are magically efficacious in the journey: they *are* the journey as the shaman narrates it, dramatizing it to an audience. Some songs may be learned in the course of the psychic journey. The evocation of the Great Goddess as archaic embodiment of nature is also a dominant shamanistic element (Graves, *White Goddess;* Schafer) that has entered into our Gnostic and Kabbalistic traditions (Scholem; Pagels).

Despite the wide provenance of shamanism from the Siberian stretches of Europe and Asia to the American Arctic and from tropical Indonesia and New Guinea to aboriginal peoples of South America, a stable set of images appears. These images go back at least twenty-five thousand years in Europe, as seen in Paleolithic cave paintings. This set, or "alphabet," of shamanism is based on primal physical realities available to all humans, whatever their stage of technology or culture. In fact, the image alphabet of shamanism is clearest, because most often experienced, to aboriginal, pretechnological peoples, for whom animals, graves, bones, teeth, plants and trees, rocks, and the elements of fire, air, earth, and water—primary letters of the shamanic alphabet—are everyday parts of life. Especially frequent are mirrors and (reflecting) bodies of water, which suggest a range of reflexive notions such as identity, death, and rebirth by baptism into a new self.

Shamanism is, in Eliade's phrase, "pastoral spirituality," a natural religion or spiritual expression of oneness with nature. As technological societies become increasingly alienated from the animistic pastoral spirituality that has sustained human cultures for millenia, their artists have compensated by restoring the archaic to its centrality. Poets and artists have been quickest to respond to the leaching away of primary experiences—the loss of trees, animals, fire, water—in our direct experience and our emotional lives. Modernism as a whole was deeply influenced by the discovery of primitive art: Tzara, for example, relates how it animated surrealism (pp. 301–2); Stravinsky's *Rite of Spring* and Picasso's *Demoiselles d'Avignon* are other familiar examples. As Gary Snyder writes:

> Poetry must sing from authentic experience. Of all the streams of civilized tradition with roots in the Paleolithic, poetry is one of the few that can realistically claim an unchanged function and a relevance which will outlast most of the activities that surround us today. Poets, as few others, must live close to the world that primitive men are in: the world, in its nakedness, which is fundamental for us all—birth, love, death; the sheer fact of being alive. (pp. 117–18)

For at least twenty years shamanism has been a watchword and touchstone for poets and artists from the Americas and Europe, who often aspire to the condition of shaman in order to heal a contemporary society seen as suffering as "loss of soul." Individual American poets like David Antin, Jackson MacLow, Jerome Rothenberg, Nathaniel Tarn, Armand Schwerner, Clayton Eshleman, Gary Snyder, and Michael McClure have adapted and performed shamanic pieces or written new works inspired by the shamanic tradition; Lucy Lippard notes the same return to the archaic in contemporary visual arts. Contemporary surrealism uses the shamanic alphabet of bones, water, and fire and a range of verbs suggesting the workings of the elements—"dissolve," "fly," "float," "burn," and so on—as can be seen in the works of Robert Merwin, Charles Simic, James Wright, and Robert Bly, whose masks forcibly convey a shamanic presence in his readings. Anthologies such as Jerome Rothenberg's *Technicians of the Sacred* and *Symposium of the Whole* and magazines like *Alcheringa, Io, Caterpillar, New Wilderness Letter,* and *Sulfur* are expressions of the intense recent interest in shamanism and archaic poetic traditions. In the scholarly arena, of course, the great theoreticians have been Mircea Eliade, whose book *Shamanism: Archaic Techniques of Ecstasy* remains the bible of comparative scholarship, and Lévi-Strauss, who goes beyond Eliade in his *Tristes Tropiques* to suggest that a new poetic wisdom based on archaic values can restore psychic unity to fragmented technological Western cultures. The anthropologist most closely associated with upholding "primitive" (or primary, archaic) values is Stanley Diamond. The main assumptions of my discussion follow the work of Eliade, Lévi-Strauss, and Diamond.

In the remainder of this essay I focus especially on themes and images found particularly among Native American, especially North Canadian, peoples. Judging from her work, and my own talks with her, Atwood is familiar with the rich and complex forms of shamanism found among Amerindian tribes in Canada. Themes such as the journey into death by descent to the spirit world, magical vision, the Canadian version of the Great Goddess (the Lady of Beasts), the world underwater, and pools and mirrors recur in her writing, as does the shamanic alphabet of natural images. Scholars such as Astrov, Rasmussen, and Eliade have often noted the especial richness of Eskimo or Inuit shamanic tradition, the great prestige of the shamans, and the unusual fact that they engage in shamanic journeys for their own creative and spiritual enlightenment—a paradigm of the artist's quest—as well as to heal the sick or reestablish the spiritual equilibrium of the tribe. Shamanism, in fact, is allegedly of arctic origin. It would be strange if the sensitive, nature-oriented Atwood were not deeply affected by the rich indigenous spiritual traditions of Amerindian Canada.

It is not difficult to find Eliade's departure, confrontation with the spirit world and return with new power in Atwood's work. The most familiar example is her poem "Procedures for Underground," taken from a Bella Coola legend (Atwood notes that it comes from the Northwest Coast):

> The country beneath
> the earth has a green sun
> and the rivers flow backwards;
>
> the trees and rocks are the same
> as they are here, but shifted.
> Those who live there are always hungry;
>
> from them you can learn
> wisdom and great power,
> if you can descend and return safely.
>
> You must look for tunnels, animal
> burrows or the cave in the sea
> guarded by the stone man;
>
> when you are down you will find
> those who were once your friends
> but they will be changed and dangerous.
>
> Resist them, be careful
> Never to eat their food.
> Afterwards, if you live, you will be able
>
> to see them when they prowl as winds,
> as thin sounds in our village. You will
> tell us their names, what they want, who
>
> has made them angry by forgetting them.
> For this gift, as for all gifts, you must
> suffer: those from the underland
>
> will be always with you, whispering their
> complaints, beckoning you
> back down; while among us here
>
> you will walk wrapped in an invisible
> cloak. Few will seek your help
> with love, none without fear.
>
> (*Procedures For Underground,* pp. 24–25)

In this poem the descent to the realm of dead spirits, now changed and dangerous, is clear. The dead, like the protagonist's father with his wolf's reflecting eyes in *Surfacing,* penetrate the world of the living; they inspirit the body of nature, with its cycles of life and death. We also see the theme of magical vision: the speaker can *see* spirits as winds, "thin sounds in our village," without being seen in her invisible cloak. Magical words appear: the speaker will learn the names of the spirits and be able to hear their whispered complaints. Natural images from the shamanic alphabet, such as rivers, trees, rocks, tunnels, animal burrows, winds, and caves, locate the poem in an archaic landscape that is also transformed, different: the sun is green, the rivers flow backwards, the trees and rocks are "shifted." In the underworld of the Inuit, according to Rasmussen, the seasons are opposites of ours (*Netsilik Eskimos,* p. 315). Atwood's poem not only voices a dreamlike shamanic descent, it identifies it with the creative process, with its powers and dangers, particularly the danger that despite the return, the descent into the creative subterranean realm of the unconscious permanently changes the shaman (Eskimo: *angakut,* "one who dives" [Rasmussen, *Iglulik Eskimos,* p. 124]). For this gift, the shaman suffers and must henceforth move in the world above as an isolated individual: "few will seek your help / with love, none without fear."

Journeys or quests involving sinking into an unconscious realm run throughout Atwood's poetry, from her earliest books to her most recent, as does death as a wellspring of creativity. "Persephone Departing," from *Double Persephone,* published in 1961, begins "from her all springs arose / to her all falls return / The articulate flesh, the singing bone / Root flower and fern," combining themes of death, departure, the magical word, an analogue of the Lady of Beasts (Persephone), and animistic natural imagery. Death is an irreducible hermaphrodite in "Chthonic Love" and a hieroglyphic field of "words cruel as thorns" in "Double Persephone."

The guiding image of *The Circle Game* is a closed space, the circle game; the title poem concludes: "I want the circle broken" (p. 55). Circular dances are the classic form of the ghost dance or dance of the dead in Arctic shamanism and Amerindian tradition generally (Eliade, *Shamanism,* p. 311). The book includes numerous orphic poems—like "Descent

Through the Carpet," "Eventual Proteus" (which uses the shapeshifter theme), "Spring in the Igloo," and "After the Flood, We"—that seem to be written from the perspective of a timeless watery realm specifically imaged as the land of spirits in Inuit shamanism. "After the Flood, We" is typical of Atwood's shamanic poems in that she seems to suggest that the really alive are the already dead, that death is the first step to spiritual life. The speaker must be a spirit to be able to "gather the sunken / bones of the drowned mothers" and hear "the first stumbling / footsteps of the almost-born." She says, "We must be the only ones / left" out of an intenser awareness than ordinary life provides (pp. 18–20). *The Circle Game* also includes numerous poems of departure or journey, like "Evening Train Station, Before Departure, "Migration: C.P.R.," "Journey to the Interior," "The Explorers," and "The Settlers" (these titles of the last two poems in the book are also prominent themes, and chapter titles, in *Survival*). "The Explorers" and "The Settlers" are voiced by the speaker's own skeleton: the speaker imagines explorers "surprised" at "these / gnawed bones . . . at the two skeletons" (p. 93). The settlers' homes and lives, like their lands, are formed from the speaker's archaic skeleton:

> Now horses graze
> inside this fence of ribs, and
>
> children run with green
> smiles, (not knowing
> where) across
> the fields of our open hands. (p. 95)

Rasmussen writes that Eskimo shamanic initiation invariably consists of "a mystical experience of death and resurrection induced by contemplating one's own skeleton" (*Iglulik Eskimos*, p. 118; see also Eliade, *Shamanism*, pp. 58–64).

Descents occur throughout *Two-Headed Poems*—in, for example, "Two Miles Away," in portions of "Daybooks" and "Five Poems for Grandmothers," and in "Nasturtium," which seems to describe Atwood's writing room:

The room does nothing
but like a cave it magnifies. . . .

This is the room where I live
most truly, or cease to live. (pp. 78–79)

Spirits from underwater rise in "Night Poem" and in departure poems like "The Bus to Alliston, Ontario," where "the dead ride with us" (p. 76), echoing the powerful ending of *The Journals of Susanna Moodie.*

In the poem "Nasturtium," Atwood says that her writing is like a nasturtium, the "flower of prophecy." Her writing takes place in a cave room, an underground space like a grave or oracular cavern, recalling Paleolithic cave art ("on the floor, caked mud, ashes"). "Like a cave it magnifies," says Atwood. Caves of course do not magnify images, but sounds, that is, words. The line implies the cave's sacred powers. In the cave, "I live / most truly, or cease to live." In writing Atwood is most alive because most involved in the unconscious or shamanic, most like a dead spirit.

*Interlunar,* Atwood's latest volume of poetry, is filled with descents, as in "Orpheus (1)," "Euridice," "Letter to Persephone" (which sees women in a patriarchy as living in an underworld hell), "Doorway" (which imagines the speaker as a channel for underground voices), and "Orpheus (2)." Orpheus, like the martyred Chilean singer Victor Jara, sings "in the stadium" of actual and metaphorical oppression:

He was down there
among the mouthless ones, among
those with no fingers, those
whose names are forbidden,
those washed up eaten into
among the grey stones
of the shore where nobody goes
through fear. Those with silence. (p. 78)

Despite his dismemberment, Orpheus continues to sing: "praise is defiance" (p. 78). The descent appears as imagery ("my eyes are pure archaeology / through which you can see straight down / past all those bones and broken / kitchen utensils and slaughters" ["Three Denizen Songs," p. 65]) throughout the book, and descents carry feminist as well as political meaning.

To Euridice, who exists, like the Inuit Mother of Sea Beasts, in the deathly underworld ("the stagnant place of the deepest sea," p. 61), Orpheus is not savior but intruder who futilely pulls her toward a life defined exclusively in his terms. Increasingly Atwood identifies woman with the transforming, spiritual power acquired through descent into death and the female underworld: one thinks of Erishkigal, the underworld aspect of Ishtar/Inanna; Eurydice and Persephone; the Great Goddess of the Nag Hammadi Library, whom Judeo-Christian patriarchy has forced underground. The "Snake Poems" that open this volume celebrate the snake/python sacred to the Great Goddess embodied in the Delphic oracle or Pythia, for example; the poems evoke the intuitive, body-oriented and natural religion of the archaic matriarchy. As snake, Atwood writes, "you slide down your body as into hot mud . . . you / must learn to see in darkness . . . / it's the death you carry in you . . . / that makes the world shine . . ." ("Quattrocento," p. 19).

Throughout Atwood's poetry—and her work as a whole—we can see a deepening of awareness of the sources of the descent. The earliest references to Classical myths such as that of Persephone in *Double Persephone* give place to the idea of the European explorers in Canada in poems like "The Explorers" and "The Settlers," which conclude *The Circle Game,* and finally to the explicit image of the shaman in poems like "Procedures for Underground." This progression evidences Atwood's rejection of received material deriving from the colonial heritage in favor first of Canadian, and then indigenous Amerindian archaic material.

At the same time, Atwood's attitude toward death becomes perhaps more life-affirming, as it is in the shamanic tradition, which cures the sick through contact with the dead. In her essay on "Canadian Monsters," Atwood traces a similar move in Canadian fiction from the supernatural "other" as monster in (outer) nature to the supernatural or monstrous within the self. As death or the "other" is identified with the self, the self appropriates its transformative power. *You Are Happy,* a turning-point volume, begins with death in "Newsreel: Man and Firing Squad." Atwood establishes the grim actuality of a man executed: the "torso jumps as the bullets hit / his nerves," in part 1 (p. 8). Part 2 begins "Destruction shines with such beauty" and shifts to a statement of the "debris of the still alive / Your left eye, green and lethal" (p. 8).

Part 3 insists there be "no more of these closeups, this agony / taken just for the record anyway" (p. 9) by inaccurate cameras. Death is not a permanent condition, but a transition within the natural cycle: "The scenery is rising behind us / into focus, the walls / and hills are also important" (p. 9). The poem, which is the book in microcosm, concludes with a vision beyond life and death and categories such as happiness or despair:

> Our shattered faces retreat, we might be
> happy, who can interpret
> the semaphore of our bending
> bodies, from a distance we could be dancing. (p. 9)

In "First Prayer," from the same volume, Atwood writes of bodies, "With their good help we will rise from the dead" (p. 73). There is, however, no easy escape in this volume: "Our way / not out but through" (p. 76). The book is a celebration of transformative death, an eternal following after the spirit seen as a ghostly psychopomp; "these twilight caverns are endless / you are ahead / flicker of white, you guide" ("Useless," p. 10). This poem, like many of Atwood's, uses the idea of magical sight that can see through solid objects and see into the future (in prophesy) and far away places. This magical sight is a shamanic ability; Rasmussen has recorded accounts by Eskimo shamans of such divine illumination ("I could see right through the house, in through the earth and up into the sky" [*Iglulik Eskimos,* p. 113]).

The second part of *You Are Happy,* "Songs of the Transformed," continues the celebration of death as transition. It also exemplifies Atwood's use of animal tutelary spirits found in Inuit shamanism. It is written from the point of view not only of animals, but of dead (transformed) animals—animals, that is, who have become totems of themselves or tutelary spirits. The bull, rat, owl, fox, hen's head, and corpse recall their particular deaths. Like shamans' animal guides, they teach humans truth found only through death. Inuit shamanistic initiation involves an imagined sparagmos (dismemberment) by animals followed by new flesh growing around the shaman's bones; often the tormenting animals are future tutelary spirits (Eliade, *Shamanism,* p. 44, quoting Lehtisalo). The rat hears his mate "trapped in your throat / . . . he is hiding / between your syllables / I can hear him singing" (p. 32). The owl says, "I am the heart of a murdered woman," a murdered woman who, to find out why she was murdered, will turn herself into her own murderer: "my claws / will grow through his hands / and become claws, he will not be caught" (p. 37). The exception is the worm, or death itself, who has an only gradually heard song: "when we say attack / you will hear nothing / at first" (p. 35). The worm and the corpse affirm that death is triumph and the condition of being doubly alive. The corpse, like the shaman, shares in this double existence: "I exist in two places / here and where you are. / / Pray for me / not as I am but as I am" (p. 44).

*You Are Happy*'s concluding section, "Circe/Mud Poems," is spoken by a shamanlike Circe. Atwood's Circe has affinities with the Inuit Lady of Beasts. Animals like "wrecked words" litter the ground around her. She wears an amulet, has many faces, and presses her face to the earth, perhaps a reference to the common practice of divination by the feeling of heaviness in the head practices by northern Amerindian women (Rasmussen, *Iglulik Eskimos,* p. 141ff). She is familiar with ghosts and vampires demanding blood: "fresh monsters are already breeding in my head" (p. 63). As a prophetess she clearly has the last word: "To know the future / there must be a death / Hand me the axe" (p. 66).

To appreciate the "Circe/Mud Poems" and other of Atwood's works, and especially to appreciate the emotionally or physically disabled women of the novels, it is helpful to recall a specific body of ethnographic materials documenting the shamanic descent to the "Mother of Sea Beasts" among coastal northern tribes (Eliade, *Shamanism,* pp. 293–97, 311). Though there are several versions of this descent, certain distinctive features predominate. Perhaps due to the importance of water and fishing, the main element of the shamanic descent here is through water. The infernal shamanistic descent to the underworld or undersea realm has been linked with female cults, as opposed to the predominately male form of celestial magical flights (Eliade, *Shamanism,* p. 34), and Inuit tradition almost entirely lacks a celestial great (male) god (Eliade, *Shamanism,* p. 12). At the bottom of the sea is the Mother of Sea Beasts, Takánakapsâluk, Great Goddess of the Animals, a Circe-like archetypal figure, in Eliade's words, "source and matrix of all life upon whose good will the existence of the tribe depends" (*Shamanism,* p. 294). The shaman must periodically reestablish contact with this goddess in order to ensure plentiful game, good weather, and human fertility. She is, significantly, highly offended by abortions or induced miscarriages (Eliade, *Shamanism,* p. 289), a fact of some interest in thinking about *Surfacing.*

The shaman's underseas descent to Takánakapsâluk is often undertaken to overcome a threat of famine and is made with the help of the spirits of dead shamans or other dead persons, whose voices are heard during the seance that accompanies the descent, coming as if from "far underwater, as if they were sea beasts" (Eliade, *Shamanism,* pp. 294–96). At the bottom of the ocean, the shaman faces various dangers based on initiatory ordeals: clashing rocks reminiscent of the Symplegades in the Odyssey, a ferocious dog like Cerberus, a father figure who mistakes the shaman's spirit for that of someone dead and seizes it, and a wall that may rise to block the Mother's house if she is angry at the actions of humans. In the case of famine, many kinds of marine animals are gathered in a pool by the Mother's fire; these animals' cries can be heard by the audience at the seance.

The goddess is filthy and unkempt, and her hair hangs over her face: humanity's sins have made her crippled and sick. The shaman must comb her hair, as she has no fingers or hands to do this. As the shaman combs her hair and tells her the problem occasioning this visit, the goddess will tell the shaman which tabus have been broken. The shaman struggles to appease her; at length she releases the animals from the pool. The audience hears them moving in the sea, and the shaman's gaspings as if he or she were coming up from the sea floor. The shaman recounts the broken tabus to the audience gathered to witness the descent, they confess their sins, and cosmological order is restored. Edmund Carpenter, discussing the related legend of Sedna or Nuliajuk ("young girl"), who rules all animals from the bottom of the sea, fingerless and abducted by a cruel dog disguised as a man, writes, "Every Eskimo knew it and had his own version, all equally true, for this myth was too complex for any simple telling" ("Eskimo Artist," pp. 109–12). There are numerous parallels: in shamanic legends from islands in Japan, for example, the woman shaman or animal unhappily marries a human (Schafer).Atwood's Circe combines many strands of the tradition.

The Circe in part 3 of *You Are Happy* is a type of Mother of Sea Beasts, with power to grant various wishes (for food and sex, for example) of the visitor, who like a shaman has the power to leave her, to return to his home. The first poem ends "You move within range of my words / you land on the dry shore // you find what there is," indicating that her realm is one of supernormal truth or authenticity. The second poem tests the visitor. Circe rejects gods, "men with the heads of eagles" and "those who can fly," and asks for authenticity in return for her own: for real men who have "escaped from these / mythologies with barely their lives." The third poem evidences the destructive powers of false myths, old stories or ideas about the self that are no longer true. They are old words (on one reading, Atwood's previous works) and dead animals "littering the ground," indicating a spiritual or emotional famine. The fourth piece, a prose poem, explicitly imagines the vocation of a shaman: that of curing the sick through supernatural wisdom:

> People come from all over to consult me, bringing their limbs which have unaccountably fallen off, they don't know why, my front porch is waist deep in hands, bringing their blood. . . . They offer me their pain, hoping in return for a word . . . from those they have assaulted daily, with shovels, axes . . . the silent ones. . . . Around me everything is worn down, the grass the roots, the soil, nothing is left but the bared rock. (p. 49)

The image is of the Mother of Beasts in a wasteland caused by humanity's sins. The cycle continues to describe an ill-fated love, in which Circe, like Sedna, yields, albeit unwillingly, passionately falling in love, offering all, losing and receiving little in return except pain. Unlike Sedna's, Circe's pain initiates her into human feeling; she experiences the cycle of rejection, anger, and finally acceptance.

The cycle shows an original and sophisticated use of the mythic shamanic material to enforce an antimythic meaning—that an earned, emotionally lived life is more powerful than myth's escapes and illusions. Through suffering and spiritual death, Circe gains the shamanic power to heal herself. This Mother of Beasts, who is made ill by the man's treatment, like the female protagonist of so many of Atwood's novels learns that salvation comes not with a relationship with a man, but only from self-sufficient ability to live, to "be right" on only one of two islands. Atwood provides a fine example of women embodying not a static reward for men but the active heroic life demanded by Carolyn Heilbrun, Annis Pratt, and other feminist critics concerned with the creation of imaginatively viable heroines.

Atwood's self-reliant female heroines and pervasive water and animal imagery take on new significance when set against the figure of the Mother of Beasts. *Surfacing*'s protagonist, for example, gains wisdom and sees spirit ancestors (her real father, petroglyphs) in the lake; after she sees the final wolflike vision of what her dead father had become, a totemic fish jumps from the lake. The fish suggests the Ojibwa water monster Mis-shi-pi-zhiw, as Guédon notes. *Lady Oracle*'s Joan Foster stages her death by drowning in another of the lakes that recur in each of the novels; this fake death ironically leads to the beginnings of self-knowledge. The novel is in one reading a search (descent) for reconciliation with a deadly mother (Sedna) and her vindictive spirit: the descent is made through the "pool" of the mirror and trance.

Rennie in *Bodily Harm* also follows the pattern of the shamanic descent. Like Circe, the protagonist of *Surfacing,* and Joan, Rennie is both the ill person seeking cure and her own shaman—a configuration Barbara Hill Rigney notes, in different terms, as the need for feminine heroines to "become" their own mothers. Rennie descends into depression caused by breast cancer, seeks a doctor, and goes to an area of sea and islands, where she meets a helper named Dr. Minnow—perhaps a reference to the totemic fish as much as to Christ. She meets her animus in the form of Paul. Lora, who yearns for a child and whose innocent boyfriend is killed, may be compared to the Mother of Sea Beasts, who is crippled, made filthy and sick by the ill-doings of men. Rennie's sense of self is restored by Paul and Lora, whose hair she combs in prison, a realm of actual and metaphoric death. Her return and cure is not merely personal but serves the entire community in that she resolves in the end to write the true stories Dr. Minnow and Lora had asked for, revealing the political crimes she has witnessed. In writing the true story, she will be confessing and testifying, purifying the large community. Unwitting and initially unwilling, she undergoes an enforced initiation and brings enlightenment back from her encounter with the realm of death. It may be worth noting, in this context, that the shamanic call cannot be denied: an attempt to evade it inevitably leads to sickness and even psychosis, as Eliade documents from various cultures.

In *Bodily Harm* Rennie learns that "she is not exempt," that "nobody is exempt from anything," as she realizes the brutal fact that she and Lora may be killed (p. 290). Grasping that fact, Rennie comes to feel compassion for Lora despite her mutilated body, passionately trying to pull her spirit back from death, to cure her. This compassion, which Rennie could not previously feel, recalls the treatment of the grandmother as ancestor in many of Atwood's novels. The Grandmother is a debased form of the Great Goddess, in Inuit myth imaged as lacking hands and existing at the ocean floor. In *Bodily Harm* this grandmother keeps misplacing her hands, forgetting where they are. Rennie is repelled by this, though her mother shows her how to comfort the old lady—by grasping the hands with warm human touch, and by reassurance—telling her her hands are there, at the end of her arms, where she left them. This sort of compassion and human touch is part of the wisdom and power that Rennie learns from her descent, as we see in her compassion for Lora. Similarly, Rennie is disembodied—dies and is transformed—when she makes love with Paul and regains touch with herself and her body: "she stroked the back of his neck and thought of the soul leaving the body in the form of words, on little scrolls like the ones in medieval paintings" (p. 206). Infatuated with the physician Daniel, she remembers medieval pictures of souls leaving their bodies (p. 198). At Rennie's most alive movements, she automatically imagines death.

*Life Before Man* even more explicitly invokes death. The tutelary animal spirits and dead ancestors of shamanism have analogues in taxidermy and in the dinosaurs, who are extinct, and thus doubly dead. The subject of suicide in that novel similarly intensifies the death theme: in committing suicide Chris kills an important part of Elizabeth's soul, casts her in the role of guilty killer, and demands reparation in the form of her psychological breakdown or descent. Staring at her ceiling as if it were her tomb, Elizabeth must become her own shaman to cure herself of this loss of soul and guilt. Death, descent, tutelary animals, magical vision and words, prophesy, and spirits (for example, the Lady of Animals) as used in Inuit shamanism inform Atwood's work in all genres.

The alphabet of shamanism's primitive imagery of bones, teeth, skin, vegetation, food, eating, eliminating, birth and death, and the elements similarly appears throughout Atwood's work as a whole. Space does not permit enumeration, though close readers of Atwood will be able to provide numerous examples. The "Spring Poem" from part 1 of *You Are Happy* illustrates the combination of the descent and shamanic imagery:

> I plunge
> my hands and arms into the dirt,
> swim among the stones and cutworms,
> come up rank as a fox,
>
> restless. Nights, while seedlings
> dig near my head
> I dream of reconciliations. (pp. 22–23)

The most sustained and successful use of this imagery is perhaps found in *The Journals of Susanna Moodie,* the protagonist of which has "sunk down into the sea" ("First Neighbors," p. 14) of the Canadian wilderness:

> I need wolf's eyes to see
> the truth.
>
> I refuse to look in a mirror
>
> Whether the wilderness is
> real or not
> depends on who live there. ("Further Arrivals," pp. 12–13)

Susanna Moodie imagines her life after death in "Alternative Thoughts from Underground" as literally buried:

> Down. Shovelled. Can hear
> faintly laughter, footsteps;
> the shrill of glass and steel (p. 57)

and she feels what the dinosaurs felt,

> scorn but also pity: what
> the bones of the giant reptiles . . .
>
> felt when scuttled
> across, nested in by the velvet immoral
> uncalloused and armourless mammals. (p. 57)

Her wisdom is, again, that of death: "god is the whirlwind / at the last judgement we will all be trees" ("Resurrection," p. 58). In the final poem, "A Bus along St. Clair: December," Moodie takes the shape of "the old woman / sitting across from you on the bus," who mutters a prediction: "Turn, look down: / there is no city; / this is the centre of a forest // your place is empty" (p. 61). As often happens in shamanic poetic style, and as Margot Astrov notes in Amerindian poetry as well, the declarative command form of the sentences endows the prediction with the force of a magical charm or spell. The poetry becomes the magical song of shamanism.

One of the most arresting of Atwood's recurring images is the mirror, an important article in shamanic ritual. Spirits are thought to be visible in mirrors, and shamans gaze into them to fall into a trance. Mirrors are found worldwide in shamanic practices. They adorn shamans' costumes and archeologists have unearthed statues of powerful female shamans (*miko*) with mirrors in Japan dating back to 400 A.D. (Blacker, p. 104). Anyone familiar with Atwood will have noticed her frequent use of mirrors to suggest a host of meanings, most of them centering on a split-off deathly or spirit self. In the ending of "Tricks with Mirrors," the mirror says, "You are suspended in me // beautiful and frozen, I / preserve you, in me you are safe" (*You Are Happy,* p. 26). The speaker, in a rejection reminiscent of the desire to break the circle in *The Circle Game,* objects:

> I wanted to stop this,
> this life flattened against the wall
>
> mute and devoid of colour,
> built of pure light,
>
> this life of vision only, split
> and remote, a lucid impasse. (p. 27)

The ending, "Perhaps I am not a mirror. / Perhaps I am a pool. // Think about pools" (p. 27) in the context of shamanic underwater descent suggests a possible way out of static mirrors: the way of a descent into the transforming element of the unconscious, and a confrontation with the spirit forces and ancestors, the analogous buried complexes within the self.

Atwood's recurring use of the natural alphabet of shamanic images, journey structures (especially descents to the spirit world), and supernatural themes link her with the shamanic tradition, as does her stress on the cure of the soul. An understanding of shamanism clarifies Atwood's works and helps locate the source of her mysterious tone of otherness and her appeal to contemporary readers deprived of spiritual values in a secular world. It can also suggest a way of reading contemporary literature (and experience) in a spiritual and ethical manner without reference to any given religious dogma.

Death orientation is central not only to shamanism but to archetypal psychology, which has clarified the vital importance of death in the life of the soul. James Hillman, the most provocative writer on the subject, argues in *Re-Visioning Psychology* that Hades is the "God of the hidden, the underworld meaning in things, their deeper obscurities" (p. 205). Loss of Hades, also known as Pluto, "Riches," or "Wealth-Giver," has, in Hillman's phrase, turned our imaginings of soul too "maidenly pure," "woodwashed and bare" (p. 205). Hillman theorizes that Hades is the god of the historical Renaissance and of "all psychological renascences" and that he is "the archetypal principle of the deepest aspect of the soul and of rebirth" (p. 206). In order to repossess Hades we must "see through" the one-sided Aristotelian and analytical approaches in favor of a deeper concern with the relation of soul to death, rebirth, and the eternal. Hillman writes that we need the Hades perspective, "the wealth that is discovered through recognizing the interior deeps of the imagination. For the underworld was mythologically conceived as a place where there are only psychic images. From the Hades perspective *we are our images*" (p. 207).

The great need of contemporary persons, Hillman says, is to admit that "we are not real," that is, to admit that our idea of ourselves and of the world is illusion, a concept familiar to Buddhist and Hindu thought. We are spirits to the extent that we exist in the deathless creative reality of our emotions and images; to realize this we must struggle against limiting materialistic and empirical tendencies of our technological Western culture. Like Henry Adams, Hillman finds the ancient female spiritual principle, the Great Mother (potent in the Renaissance figures of Persephone, Laura, and Mary), to be lacking in current expression. The Great Mother (as Mother of Beasts, Circe, Persephone) appears in Atwood's shamanic writings, and, for her, death has a function like Hillman's: to draw us away from ordinary human life and closer to the spirit realm or gods, who in Hillman's words "are not human but to whose inhumanity the soul is inherently priorly related" (p. 193).

Rank made a similar point almost thirty years ago in *Beyond Psychology* (p. 18), correctly warning of the necessity for a release of chthonic, Dionysian impulses (historically celebrating the Great Mother and her cults of death and rebirth) lest their repression only lead to an uncontrollable breakout of irrational violence (Hinz). The expression of death and violence clearly issues, in Atwood, in a sense of heightened life and creativity, and in Atwood's recent work we see an explicit engagement with social justice that would bear our Rank's prediction that given our Apollonian culture the Dionysian ultimately leads to balance. Despite the many journeys in her works, Atwood has not had to leave Canada to discover the Great Mother: she travels back in cultural time to reach archaic realities inspiriting her given Canadian territory. Her work regenerates our sacral awareness through indigenous North American spiritual traditions.

Atwood's use of shamanism can bear out a feminist reading as well. Eliade believes that present day shamanism retains earmarks of an earlier matriarchal structure, particularly the variety of shamanism that focuses upon death and descents, as opposed to male-oriented magical flights and a celestial God (*Shamanism,* p. 505). Studies of isolated communities in the circumpolar regions—for example in Japan, Southeast Asia, and South America—indicate a continued tradition of extremely powerful female shamans found alongside legends and artifacts representing the Mother of Beasts and the theme of marriage between humans and nonhumans. The nonhumans are not only gods or spirits of the dead, but animals, especially water dragons or snakes, beasts living underwater perhaps related to the Amerindian water deities in *Surfacing* pictographs (Blacker, pp. 104–26; Schafer). This anthropological and ethnographic evidence of descent shamanism as a largely female mode is born out by numerous theories such as Jung's asserting women's inherent affinity with the earth. If, as Eliade holds, shamanism is humankind's original and innate ecstatic spiritual orientation, that innate orientation may well be female, or at least more female than later organized religions, which envision God as male, would have us believe.

One need not categorize Atwood as a feminist, however, in order to grasp the importance of a shamanic literary mode in embodying a female and at the same time universal perspective. Shamanism, unlike sophisticated or sentimentalized pastoral written by urbanites, presents nature from within, not as refuge but as primary locale, not as peaceful and good but as a holistic unity of life and death, and life in death. It is an expression of an ecological vision, an ancient mode whose wisdom we are only now coming to appreciate.

Because its images are as instinct with death as with life and show the two as intertwined and mutually dependent in transformation, shamanic writing can dramatize feminist themes of breakdowns and madness as well as of healing and rebirth, as seen in Doris Lessing's *Golden Notebook,* Charlotte Brontë's *Jane Eyre,* and Virginia Woolf's *Mrs. Dalloway.* The observations of feminist scholars such as Ellen Moers and Gilbert and Gubar that women writers tend to employ image systems drawing upon the human body, blood, flesh and bone, and cavelike enclosures in rooms and houses may be related to a tendency of women writers to use a shamanic mode, drawing upon the body, the elements, and ecstatic madness leading to cure, such as one finds also in Anne Sexton, Sylvia Plath, and Adrienne Rich.

The shamanic mode may seem a superfluous or unusual phrase but is not more so than the suggestive elemental poetics of Gaston Bachelard, who notes that certain poets embody world views encompassed by such elements as fire and water. Marie von Franz suggests that the artist's stance is that of the creative, irresponsible, eternal child, the Puer Aeternus. The notion of a shamanic stance restores dignity and maturity to the idea of the artist as a spiritual spokesperson for the community. Insofar as the shaman's vocation is not only spiritual ecstasy but also healing, the shamanic mode accommodates the artists' engaged ethical vision that writers like Carolyn Forché have projected. It is one more tribute to Margaret Atwood's importance as a writer that her works may be said to possess a shamanic vision that speaks the language of nature to tell the oldest and most pressing stories.

## *Notes*

1. Page references to Atwood's novels, stories, and books of poetry are to the following: *Bodily Harm* (New York: Bantam, 1983); *The Circle*

*Game* (Toronto: Anansi, 1966); *Dancing Girls* (Toronto: McClelland and Stewart, 1977); *Double Persephone* (Toronto: Hawkshead Press, 1961); *Interlunar* (Toronto: Oxford Univ. Press, 1984); *Life Before Man* (New York: Simon and Schuster, 1979); *Procedure for Underground* (Boston: Atlantic–Little, Brown, 1970); *The Journals of Susanna Moodie* (Toronto: Oxford Univ. Press, 1970); *Two-Headed Poems* (New York: Simon and Schuster, Touchstone, 1978); *You Are Happy* (New York: Harper and Row, 1974).

# 14 *Sexual Politics in Margaret Atwood's Visual Art*

*Sharon R. Wilson*

Since Margaret Atwood's watercolors have never before been published or exhibited to the general public[1] and are either privately owned or in the Atwood Papers at the University of Toronto (Atwood Papers, Art Work), few critics realize the extent to which her visual art not only parallels her literary work but highlights her always provocative presentation of sexual politics.

Like Atwood's fiction, poetry, and essays, many of the archive watercolors, which are sometimes untitled or undated, present gothic images of female-male relationships in fairy tales, myth, legend, the Bible, literature, popular culture, and history. Several watercolors, in fact, were created while she was working on *Power Politics,* the third section of which, as Atwood says, "has lots of references to fairy tales and gothic stories. . . . Those particular kinds of things are close to patterning. Jungians would call them Jungian." Furthermore, the Grimm brothers' tales, which Atwood read when very young, have the "depth for [her] that certain Biblical stories and Greek stories also have." While she doesn't "think that doing visual art has particularly affected literary art," Atwood frequently has painted before, during, or just after doing related poems or novels (she is more likely to paint when writing poetry than when working on a novel). As Atwood says, "sometimes I paint things before I write about them; the thing appears as a visual image. On the other hand, sometimes I don't. Poets and artists . . . [shouldn't] think too much about processes—it interrupts work. The visual art and the rest of it is connected at some level. I don't really have any way of verbalizing it" (taped interview).

This connection is most evident in cases where Atwood's art has been designed, used, or adapted for covers of particular texts: *Double Persephone* (linocut put into a flatbed printing press, 1961, uncredited [Atwood, taped interview]); *The Journals of Susanna Moodie* (photograph, 1970); *Power Politics* (watercolor, 1970; William Kimber cover based on the watercolor, 1971); the Canadian edition of *Two-Headed Poems* (Graeme Gibson photograph of Atwood flour-and-salt Christmas tree ornaments, 1978); *Bodily Harm* (undated watercolor of a cell under a microscope, not used [Atwood, taped interview]); the Canadian edition of *True Stories* (watercolor of a broken heart, 1980; book 1981); *Murder in the Dark* (photograph of a collage composed from caviar, sun block, and wet-look bathing suit ads in *Vogue* [Atwood, taped interview]; book 1983); and *Interlunar* (watercolor of landscape; book 1984). Atwood often works on book covers just after doing the poetry and, in some cases, she has designed and laid out the cover itself: *Double Persephone,* 1961; the Contact Press and Anansi editions of *The Circle Game* (both 1966); the American edition of *Two-Headed Poems* (a magnified cell in process of division, which was not used);[2] and *The Journals of Susanna Moodie.*

While not all of these covers can be discussed here, several are linked to literary images of sexual politics. *The Circle Game* cover design, which is made of sticker dots (Atwood, taped interview), is not a closed circle but a spiral that "suggests possibility of breakthrough."[3] Also, Atwood's use of her own photographs as a component in two book covers, *Murder in the Dark* and *The Journals of Susanna Moodie,* is significant in interpreting her recurrent literary images of camera and photograph. Contrary to popular impression, Atwood is not only widely photographed; she is also an occasional photographer who feels "some [of her photographs] are actually quite good." Atwood is interested in a photograph's ability to freeze time (Atwood, taped interview); a photograph also seems to freeze characters in roles that are socially conditioned, desired, or feared. Thus, her literary works often feature couples turning reality or one another into photographs (Wilson, "Camera Images," p. 31). Similarly, eating imagery is recurrent in both her literary and visual art; it is linked to fairy tales as well as power politics in "Speeches for Doctor Frankenstein," *Power Poli-*

*Plate 1. Untitled Watercolor, Archive-Labeled "Death as Bride," 1970, Signed*

*Plate 2. Untitled Watercolor, Archive-Labeled "Lady and Sinister Figure," 1969, Signed*

*Plate 3. Untitled Watercolor, Archive-Labeled "Lady and Executioner with Axe," 1969, Signed*

*Plate 4. Untitled Watercolor, Archive-Labeled "Man Holding Woman's Body," 1970, Signed*

*Plate 5. Untitled Watercolor, Archive-Labeled "Mourners at Woman's Bier," 1970, Signed*

*Plate 6. Untitled Watercolor, Archive-Labeled "Hanged Man," 1970, Signed*

*Plate 7. Untitled Watercolor, Archive-Labeled "Insect in Red Gown with Bouquet," Undated, Unsigned*

*Plate 8. Untitled Watercolor, Archive-Labeled "Atwoods as Birds," 1974, Signed*

*tics, The Edible Woman, Lady Oracle,* and an untitled watercolor. While the photographed flour-and-salt Christmas decorations on the cover of *Two-Headed Poems* only appear edible, they illustrate Atwood's skill in culinary art. Atwood was and still is a good cake decorator, and this interest in edible art was "part of the impetus for the cake in *The Edible Woman,* an anthropomorphic *objet* made of foodstuffs, such as candy brides and grooms and Donald Duck cakes in Woolworth's" (Atwood, taped interview).

When asked about a relationship between her recurrent and negative literary images of packaging and surfaces and either her experiences with commercial publishers or her decision to do cover art, Atwood says the negative images of packaging don't come from negative experiences with publishers, "although you might fit them in." In fact, Atwood has "been interested in packaging for a very, very long time." Like *Surfacing*'s narrator, when she was eight or nine Atwood made a scrapbook that included numerous pictures cut from ads. Later, "when [Marshall] McLuhan brought out *Mechanical Bride,* [she] got it immediately and was very interested." She doesn't, however, "consider [her] cover designs to be packaging." *Murder in the Dark*'s cover, which is not a parody, is "neither art [n]or merchandizing. It is a cover design appropriate to the book" (Atwood, taped interview).

In other cases Atwood has done artwork, not as illustration of literary texts, but as a "parallel activity that had to do with the same body of material" (Atwood, taped interview): the "Termite Queen" poetry series (unpublished), "Dreams of the Animals" (broadside, 197–), *The Journals of Susanna Moodie,* and particular poems in *Procedures for Underground, The Animals in That Country,* and *Power Politics.* Most of the archive watercolors are of this type. She has also done comic strips and illustrations for children's books.

Despite the extraordinary power of some of her visual art, however, Atwood, like many women artists (including her own narrator of *Surfacing*), seems to undercut the value of her visual work: "I paint images but am not a painter, if you understand the difference" (Atwood, taped interview). Often working in styles or media outside the mainstream, women artists may be denied formal recognition and thus lack confidence in their work. Finding it necessary to insist that some paintings are "done for fun" and that some details in the archive watercolors are accidental, she maintains that others occur "just because [she] do[es]n't paint very well" (Atwood, letter; taped interview). Thus, she doesn't take artistic influence very seriously but mentions Hieronymus Bosch and Bruegel. The atmosphere of these two painters' work certainly resembles Atwood's literary as well as visual landscape, which might be variously considered gothic, super real, or distorted in the direction of surrealism. Like Atwood's poetry and fiction, the watercolors present recurrent, archetypal images of power politics, in which women and men may not only oppose but also represent aspects of one another, playing roles evoking fairy tales, gothic stories, myths, television, comic books, and nursery rhymes.

1. Untitled watercolor, archive-labeled "Death as Bride," 1970, signed. This watercolor (see plate 1), which in many ways typifies the mood of the archive art, is based on the Grimms' fairy tale "Fitcher's Bird," one of many Bluebeard stories. This fairy tale is about a disguised wizard whose touch forces pretty girls to leap into his basket. When they are taken to his castle, they are given an egg, which they must carry everywhere, and keys to every room but one, which they are forbidden to enter. Most versions of the tale deal with three sisters: the first two are curious and open the door, discovering the chopped-up bodies of former brides. Fitcher/Bluebeard, seeing the egg's indelible blood stains, recognizes their disobedience. The third sister, who cleverly leaves the egg outside, passes the test, thus gaining power over the wizard. She escapes by disguising herself as a marvelous bird and, more important, she is able to rejoin the severed pieces of her sisters, recreating rather than destroying life (*Complete Grimm's,* pp. 216–20). "Fitcher's Bird" is a paradigm of the sexual politics underlying Atwood's work, and it is the basis for the menace of the room (or unopened door to the room) from *The Circle Game* to *The Handmaid's Tale* (Wilson, "Bluebeard," p. 390).

The watercolor shows the ornamented skull that the groom and his friends mistake for the bride. But the female figure is, as well, the death previous sisters and brides encounter in the room and, ironically, the death the man ultimately marries because of his expectations. The red flowers seem to bleed down the front of the figure's gown, anticipating the bleeding flowers in *The Handmaid's Tale* (1985) as well as the consequences of "loving"

"Bluebeards" in that and other Atwood works, including "Hesitation Outside the Door" (*Power Politics,* 1970) and *Bluebeard's Egg* (1983), in which the "Fitcher's Bird" fairy tale is embedded. The closely related Grimms' fairy tale "The Robber Bridegroom," in which the groom actually eats prospective brides, is alluded to in *Bodily Harm* (1982), whose original title was "The Robber Bridegroom," and in a poem of the same name in *Interlunar* (1984). Atwood's watercolor "The Robber Bridegroom" pictures a man holding both an axe and a blond head. The head emits light (Atwood, telephone conversation with author). As in "Fitcher's Bird," the female protagonist in the Grimms' "The Robber Bridegroom" survives the sexual battle, in the first case by using her wits and in the second, by speaking.

2. Untitled watercolor, archive-labeled "Lady and Sinister Figure," 1969, signed. Atwood says this female figure, shown in plate 2, is Mary, Queen of Scots, Ann Boleyn, or "someone like that" (taped interview). In addition to "Fitcher's Bird," the figures suggest the dynamics of Mme. de Villeneuve's "Beauty and the Beast" or the Grimms' "Little Red-Cap." There is a visual contrast and tension between the apparent male, who seems primitive and menacing, and the somewhat prim female, whose dress is both formal and red, the color of blood, death, birth, and passion and the color Marian in *The Edible Woman* associates with being a target, a hunted rabbit. As the beheaded Anne Boleyn, one of Henry VIII's six wives who failed to produce a male heir, the figure is again one of the interchangeable wives of Bluebeard and a victim of patriarchal politics. As Mary Stuart, the figure can suggest betrayed innocence, the absurd consequences of religious intolerance, or the no less deadly or abstract power politics between women. Much admired for her intelligence and poise in the moments before execution, Mary was beheaded, dressed in red, on orders from her cousin, Elizabeth I (Anne Boleyn and Henry VIII's daughter), who probably never met her.

Already missing her right hand, which was, perhaps, too close to the bestial other, the female figure resembles the narrator of *Bodily Harm* and numerous other Atwood personae recalling "The Girl Without Hands" (*Complete Grimm's,* pp. 160–65). Among other amputated pieces, both figures seem to be missing their hands—their ability to touch and keep in touch. Whether Anne or Mary, the woman, an inhabitant of Bluebeard's castle and a figure of legend, is finally a pawn in a series of relentlessly unfolding events. Her powerlessness is dramatized in her being beheaded, a condition many Atwood personae fear and a fate suffered even by female characters in male novels (Atwood, "Women's Novels," pp. 34–36).

3. Untitled watercolor, archive-labeled "Lady and Executioner with Axe," 1969, signed. Atwood pairs this watercolor (reproduced as plate 3), which again pictures Mary Stuart or Ann Boleyn, with "Lady and Sinister Figure" above (Atwood, taped interview). I am reminded of "Marrying the Hangman" (*Two-Headed Poems* [1978]), which is based on a true story of a couple's escaping death, in his case by becoming the executioner and in hers by marrying the executioner. In Atwood's poem, the woman must not only create the hangman; she must also convince him to exchange his face for the "impersonal mask of death, of official death which has eyes but no mouth." We are reminded that "there is more than one hangman." As the female narrator asks, "Who else is there to marry?" (p. 49). Despite Atwood's preference for stories in which women are more than victims (Atwood, telephone conversation with author), the woman in the painting is victimized. Significantly, her head seems already detached from her body, the axe is marked with red, and her dress, like both figures' eyes, is the color of blood. Like many of the watercolor figures, these appear to be mouthless, voiceless; his barlike eyes make him appear an automaton, like the Frankenstein below.

4. Untitled watercolor, archive-labeled "Man Holding Woman's Body," 1970, signed. According to Atwood, this watercolor and "Mourners at Woman's Bier" (see plates 4 and 5) deal with the Frankenstein story (Atwood, taped interview), to which Atwood alluded in "Speeches of Doctor Frankenstein," originally published with Charles Pachter's woodcuts (1966) and later in *The Animals in That Country* (1968). Again the figures make a striking contrast. He, like the "sinister figure" and executioner, is partly black and, in this case, blocklike, powerful, robotic. Although he is "holding" the inert, pink body of the woman, who, unlike the man, is fluid, he appears armless, as incapable of touch as she is of action. Both are faceless. Viewed through Shelley's *Frankenstein* and Atwood's "Speeches," the watercolor has a number of other dimensions. As Atwood says, Shelley's novel is "a creation parable, where God forsakes Adam . . . because he can't face the gro-

tesque creature that he's produced. But the monster's not *evil*. . . . He's totally innocent." In her poem, however, "the monster is the narrator's other self, and the process of writing that poem involved separating the two selves." In this case, "it's the monster who deserts his maker" (Sandler, p. 15). Thus, while the watercolor may depict the monster holding the lifeless body of Elizabeth, Dr. Frankenstein's fiancée, or more generally, the passive female victim in a battle of sexual politics, it may also show the monster holding his female creator or, to put it another way, the female being held by the monster she has created.

5. Untitled watercolor, archive-labeled "Mourners at Woman's Bier," 1970, signed. The subject of the watercolor reproduced as plate 5 again is Frankenstein, and a number of questions arise. Is the dark figure framed in the doorway Dr. Frankenstein, who is viewing the results of his Faustian attempt to play God? If the dead woman is Shelley's Elizabeth, does the bouquet again serve a double purpose, so that marriage to an artist is simultaneously a funeral? Does the rootlike hair suggest a possibility of rebirth? Does the dead woman, like the monster, represent a part of Dr. Frankenstein, who appears to be either male or female creator? Or, in this case, has the female creator been murdered by her creation? Does creation always involve "murder"? More generally, again a female has been victimized by a hidden part of her financé's personality. But what if she, like the persona in "Speeches for Doctor Frankenstein," has sliced loose a reflection that refuses to stay framed in the mirror?

6. Untitled watercolor, archive-labeled "Hanged Man," 1970, signed. Based on the hanged man card of the Tarot, this watercolor (though not so credited in the book) is the original for the cover of *Power Politics* (Atwood, tape interview) and a pattern for the theme of sexual politics that underlies most of the archive watercolors (see plate 6). The right figure, the male, wears medals recalling *Power Politics*'s wooden general with the statue concubine as well as that volume's other matched sets, with both projected and defensive false skins or disguises. As one of my students observed, if the work were turned upside down, it would be the man, not the woman, who would be powerless. Speaking of the actual cover, which adds mummy wrapping to the woman and a suit of armour to the man, Judith McCombs asks, "Is he there at all? If so, is he a prisoner in his rigid iron role?" (Review of *Power Politics*,

p. 55). Some question also exists about the complacent expression and possibly voluntary arm and leg position of the cover's female figure, which would seem to allow struggle. In any case, the woman's arms in the watercolor remind us of "Lady and Sinister Figure," and the ritualistic position seems timeless. The man and woman are tied to or are extensions of one another, both victims/victors of prescribed or projected roles that, because of each figure's aura or halo, seem to be either intrinsic or divine.

7. Untitled watercolor, archive-labeled "Insect in Red Gown with Bouquet," undated, unsigned. Atwood says this watercolor (reproduced as plate 7) is a termite queen, an illustration for the unpublished "Termite Queen" poem series (Atwood, telephone conversation with author). Pictured with a crescent moon, she evokes not only Diana, Venus, Persephone, and Hecate as life-love-fertility-death and creator-destroyer aspects of the mother goddess,[4] but also the red-clad Handmaid breeders of *The Handmaid's Tale,* the Grimms' "Little Red-Cap" (to which *The Handmaid's Tale* alludes), American TV's "Queen for a Day," prom queens, and winners of beauty pageants. Again she is targeted in blood red, with a tiny head and huge, pregnant body reminiscent of Venus of Willendorf and other fertility figures. She is what Adrienne Rich calls "the eternal fucking machine" (p. 285), one of the reflected or conditioned images Marian, Joan, Rennie, and Offred (the protagonists, respectively, of *The Edible Woman, Lady Oracle, Bodily Harm,* and *The Handmaid's Tale*) want to repudiate. Like the termite queen in *Power Politics*'s "She Considers Evading Him" and Joan Foster in *Lady Oracle,* the figure in the watercolor is also satirically linked with the reduction of women's ancient images to quick-change costumes for the escape artist.

8. Untitled watercolor, archive-labeled "Atwoods as Birds," 1974, signed. Identifying these figures (see plate 8) as a mother harpy and chicks rather than one or several Atwoods, Atwood is interested in the idea of women (chicks) as birds (Atwood, taped interview). The societal inconsistency of viewing women as bitch-harpies as well as chic chicks is made ludicrous here. Atwood has also done a watercolor of a mermaid with eggs (Atwood, letter) and comic ones of a male harpy (archive-labeled "Red Bird," 1976) and a Dracula (archive-labeled "Portrait of Graeme Gibson," 1974).

Thus, both tragic and comic, the images of sexual politics in Atwood's visual art parallel those of her fiction, poetry, and criticism. Whether alluding to the literal consummation of "mates" by the Robber Bridegroom or the wolf; a Bluebeard's deadly sexual test, which culminates in his own death; or the female Frankenstein's creation of a monster who shadows her, Atwood's images reflect, parody, and transform the timeless roles to which we have been married. According to *True Stories*'s "Variations on the Word 'Love,' "

> This word is not enough but it will
> have to do. It's a single
> silence, a mouth that says
> O again and again in wonder
> and pain, a breath, a finger-
> grip on a cliffside. You can
> hold on or let go. (p. 83)

## *Notes*

I appreciate the assistance of Margaret Atwood, of Katharine Martyn and James Ingram of the Thomas Fisher Rare Book Library at the University of Toronto, of Dr. Norman London and the Canadian Embassy, and of the University of Northern Colorado. All photographs are by Thomas Moore Photography, Inc., Toronto.

1. The first published print (color) of Atwood's untitled watercolor archive-labeled "Death as Bride" (1970) recently appeared in my article "Bluebeard's Forbidden Room: Gender Images in Margaret Atwood's Visual and Literary Art." That essay discusses "Death as Bride" in greater detail. Page numbers to Atwood's *True Stories* and *Two-Headed Poems* are to the Simon and Schuster editions.

2. Margaret Atwood, letter to Bill, 18 May 1978, *Two-Headed Poems* Correspondence, Atwood Papers.

3. See Margaret Atwood Correspondence, 1961–1967, Charles Pachter file, letter from Atwood to Charles Pachter, 3 December (year omitted, but presumably 1965), the Atwood Papers. Pachter, Atwood's friend, "whose visual imagination is quite different from [hers]" (Atwood, taped interview), did the original covers of *The Circle Game, The Edible Woman,* and *Second Words,* as well as the art work for the rare editions of *Speeches for Doctor Frankenstein, Expeditions, Kaleidoscope Baroque,* and *What Was in the Garden?* Despite Pachter's suggestion that she use his last illustration, a "sort of cameo- womb- circle- what have you" (Pachter to Atwood, "close to Hallowe'en," (1965), Atwood did her own Contact edition cover. She is quite aware that many of her images, in this and other works, are visual. See, for example, her 3 February 1965, letter to Pachter.

4. Cf., e.g., J. E. Cirlot, *A Dictionary of Symbols.* According to Mary Daly, the Triple Goddess has been associated with Athena, Neith, Hera-Demeter-Kore, Eire-Fodhla-Banbha, Thetis-Amphitrite-Nereis, and Hecate-Artemis-Diana (pp. 75–78), all variants of the Maiden, Mother, and Moon or Maiden, Nymph, and Crone to which Atwood also refers in *Survival* (pp. 199–200).

# 15 *An Interview with Margaret Atwood 20 April 1983*

## *Jan Garden Castro*

JAN GARDEN CASTRO: Your early reading of American comic books, Canadian animal stories, and Grimm's fairy tales surface in most of your novels. What makes these sources so enduring as inspiration, motifs, and metaphors?

MARGARET ATWOOD: You left out Beatrix Potter. I read a lot as a child. There are probably a lot more sources. Grimm's fairy tales are important. I think Greek mythology is important, which I read in the beginning, in the Charles Lamb *Greek Mythology for Children* and then went on to read more extensively, and of course I studied Latin in high school, which took us right into the *Aeneid*.

CASTRO: So you read the *Aeneid* in Latin?

ATWOOD: Some of it, sure. Obviously not the whole thing. And Ovid, of course; we did *Metamorphoses.* When I was in university, it was part of the honors English course at the University of Toronto that you had to take a course that touched on Greek—actually I took Greek history at one point, too. But I guess what I'm getting around to is that there is a lot of source material. When people ask me that question, What was your early influence? I usually drag out Grimm's fairy tales, but it's by no means the only thing.

CASTRO: Did you continue to study mythology to any extent at Harvard?

ATWOOD: Only as part of studying English. You can't study English literature without knowing something about the Bible, and Greek and Roman Mythology, and you have to know it, because it comes up in so much literature that was written in English. That was what people studied, of course, when they went to university. They took classics, and, therefore, all of that got into English literature.

Castro: Do you think you overlay the theme of metamorphosis on other themes, for instance, in *The Journals of Susanna Moodie*?

Atwood: I never have done academic criticism of my own work, and I never will. The reason I never have and never will is that once authors start making pronouncements about how people should read their work, in a dogmatic kind of way, it eliminates other readings.

Castro: It just seemed to me that you had given Susanna Moodie more dimensions than the real Susanna Moodie.

Atwood: The real Susanna Moodie is different from the Susanna Moodie that we find by reading her work. Because the real Susanna Moodie by no means told all. So let us say there are four elements operative here. There is Susanna Moodie we get by reading her texts, which never go into things like what she thought about her husband; she just never mentions it. The prime example is the story she tells about the boy who drowned, who wasn't related to her at all. Then there's the throwaway line at the end of the story when she says, "I also had a child who drowned in this way," and that's all you hear about it. She doesn't go on to say how that affected her, how upset she was, anything. The whole thing is contained in the metaphor that she has given previously of this other child who drowned. So there's a lot she doesn't tell. There's a gap between the Susanna Moodie of the texts and what we can speculate was the real Susanna Moodie, who thought and felt all kinds of things she never wrote down because decorum did not permit it. Then there's the Susanna Moodie I have created, who is neither of the above. And then there's myself, who is neither of any of them. So there are four things there. What was the question?

Castro: I think you've answered the question.

Atwood: The Susanna Moodie in my book is not the real Susanna Moodie nobody will ever really know. Nor is it the Susanna Moodie of the text, although a lot of the incidents are similar; in fact, they're identical. Nor is it myself, since my attitude toward the forests that she found so horrible is very positive.

CASTRO: I thought the collages for *The Journals of Susanna Moodie* were very beautiful and compelling, and they added another dimension to the book. Have you done other art?

ATWOOD: I was once poster designer when I was at college. It was a little business I ran in my cellar. I have always taken an interest in the covers of my books, some of which I have no control over whatsoever, namely the American paperbacks, but the hardbacks and the Canadian books, I'm quite closely connected with and in some cases, I've actually done the covers. I did the cover to Susanna Moodie except that they fooled around with the design by putting that red on it, which I don't like. It should have been black writing at the top and white against the black. It should have been black and white completely. And they did that without consulting me.

CASTRO: Have you ever literally sketched the plots or characters for other writings?

ATWOOD: Sketched, you mean drawn? Oh, yes. A number of my watercolor paintings are, in fact, illustrations for other things.

CASTRO: Have these been exhibited?

ATWOOD: Oh, no. I do it completely privately. The University of Toronto has them. I just gave them all to them.

CASTRO: Do you also make diagrams, maps, charts of the characters?

ATWOOD: No, I don't do that.

CASTRO: Is there some kind of shape, structure that comes to you when, for example, you're starting to work on a novel?

ATWOOD: No. That's how people teach things. That's how people draw things on the blackboard. I do that myself. When I used to teach, I would draw a diagram of *Great Expectations,* or *Hamlet.* But that's a teaching method, not a writing method.

CASTRO: That's very interesting. So the growth is much more organic.

ATWOOD: It's very organic.

CASTRO: Did you read H. Rider Haggard's *She* when you were writing *The Edible Woman?*

ATWOOD: I had read it by that time. What does *She* have to do with *The Edible Woman?*

CASTRO: Well, there's a mummy metaphor in *She,* in which a white African queen has been sleeping with a mummy for two thousand years.

ATWOOD: She hasn't actually been sleeping with it. Oh, you mean the Royal Ontario Museum. There really are mummies in the Royal Ontario Museum. It's one of their best exhibits. Sorry, I do take a lot of things from real life. Everything in *The Edible Woman* in the museum is exactly as described. They may have rearranged it a bit since I wrote the book; in fact, they've redone the museum, but I'm sure they have the same mummies, and they do have the little thing of the sand burial. They've got that, and they've got the mummy and the mummy case that's closed. It's all there. Same with the dinosaurs and *Life Before Man.* They're just exactly as described.

CASTRO: Did you have researchers also working with you on *Life Before Man?*

ATWOOD: To do the Ukrainian stuff. My right-hand person, who is, in fact, from Macedonia, went around and talked to some Ukrainian women because at that time I was in Scotland. I couldn't get at the stuff. I also sent a young man back at Christmas, who was going anyway, and I had him check out some of the physical things that I'd already written about. My research is always done after the fact. I write the book. Then I research the details to see if I've got them right. Usually I have.

CASTRO: That's a great process. Did you write *Surfacing* when you were in Europe?

ATWOOD: I wrote it in England.

CASTRO: Was your separation from Canada and the wilderness a factor in creating the language and tone of *Surfacing?*

ATWOOD: No. I had made the first notes for *Surfacing* in 1965, at the same time I was writing *Edible Woman.* It goes back that far. I had the time in England to actually write the book. And, remember, at that time in my life I was holding down jobs a lot, so I couldn't write novels and teach at the same time. I could write poetry and teach at the same time, but I couldn't write novels. The year in Scotland was a free year so I was able to write the book. You can find a practice run of the style of *Surfacing* in a couple of short stories that I also wrote in England. "Under Glass" is one of them.

CASTRO: The narrator is nameless and she distances herself from some of her—

ATWOOD: That's because she's nuts. I often have people come up to me after I've written novels and tell me that this is their experience. And with *Surfacing* the winner was somebody who came up to me after a reading when it had just been published and said, "Hi. I'm schizophrenic. I want you to know *Surfacing* almost put me right back in." My narrator isn't really schizophrenic; it's just that this schizophrenic girl found it very familiar.

CASTRO: One of the most-often-quoted feminist statements in *Surfacing* comes at the beginning of the last chapter, which opens, "This above all, to refuse to be a victim." I was trying to figure out if this phrase is consistent with the narrator's consciousness, if it is the author's advice to the narrator similar to the advice of father to son in *Hamlet,* or if it is a fusing of the author and narrator?

ATWOOD: It's the narrator. It's all very well to say I refuse to be a victim, but then you have to look at the context in which one is or isn't a victim. You can't simply refuse. You can refuse to define yourself that way, but it's not quite so simple as that. And the whole book isn't so simple as that. But it's good advice.

CASTRO: In that same chapter, the narrator says that her love for Joe is as useless as a third eye. So again this seems to contradict her understanding when she says, "We can no longer live by avoiding each other." That's part of her character.

ATWOOD: This seems to be material for people to write their theses on. Again, you can't really ask me for an answer. I wrote the book, you know, thousands of years ago. The stuff is there. Everything is there in relation to everything else. That's other people's business, if they're interested in those things. And since when was anybody ever totally consistent?

CASTRO: I think that's a good point. I have a question that nobody has ever brought up about *Surfacing* and that is, and this is possibly naïve, I'm trying to figure out if the younger brother exists or if he is another double on whom the narrator blames childish acts she doesn't want to admit.

ATWOOD: Well, you can have it either way. I would be in favor of saying that he exists, but if you want to fool around, you can say that nobody exists. In fact, the interesting thing about *Surfacing* was that we switched to Simon and Schuster with it because of a junior editor at Atlantic Monthly Press. The senior editor went away on vacation and left this guy in charge, and it was his opinion that we should take out all the characters except the narrator.

Castro: I can tell from *Lady Oracle* that it is a struggle to get the editors and publishers to leave your work intact.

Atwood: It's not a struggle for me. It's a struggle for her and for a lot of people, but it never has been for me. I've just said no and switched publishers.

Castro: That's a good move. That's a good way to handle it.

Atwood: It's the only move.

Castro: Since I've mentioned the third eye—is the poem "The Third Eye" based on Buddhist or another Eastern religious concept that you've secularized?

Atwood: Most religions believe in something similar, but so does physiology. There actually is a physical third eye. Did you know that? Well, it exists. A number of old amphibians, extinct amphibians, did have an actual third eye, and there is the remnant of it right about there in your forehead. People have been experimenting with it to see what it's for, if anything. It's there. I mean, it's an actual physical area of the body.

Castro: I agree with the poem; being conscious of it helps create a whole other circle of vision.

Atwood: If you want to do the academic thing, I can refer you to a poem by Jay MacPherson called "The Third Eye," which is in *The Boatmen,* but a number of people talk about the third eye. In fact, one of the areas of the body that you meditate on when you're doing yoga is where the third eye is, and one meditation technique is to put something there, like a drop of water, or I recommend Tiger Balm, on the third eye to help you concentrate on it. You can concentrate on that or on the solar plexus.

Castro: As another extension of this topic, in "On Being a Woman Writer," you state writers are eyewitnesses, eyewitnesses. Let me ask about the endings of your novels. I mean, you intend them to be ambiguous, and you kind of toss the ball of yarn into the reader's lap . . .

Atwood: Where it should be. Are you familiar with Charlotte Brontë at all? The first really ambiguous ending is in *Villette,* where the reader is given a choice of two endings, one happy, one unhappy.

Castro: I think it's one of the things that's characteristic of metafiction.

Atwood: Well . . . A lot of things that are trotted out now as new are really quite old. Even metafiction has its eighteenth-century antecedents, not to mention things like Apuleius. So no technique is really that new. It's just that things have vogues, things have fashions. And double endings. Anybody who reads nineteenth-century literature in any depth knows about those, and indeed about authors who wrote several endings to their books, only one of which would appear. *Great Expectations* has two endings, one in which Pip doesn't get together with Estella, and one in which he does. Dickens printed the second one, finally. That was the one he chose to be the ending. But the first one he wrote was the one in which Pip didn't get together with Estella and that is probably the more appropriate ending to the book.

Castro: It seems to me in *Bodily Harm,* which has more social realism, that that device also ends up casting doubt on whether or not Rennie ever did get out or get involved . . .

Atwood: Oh, she got involved. She was involved already. Whether she got out or not is open to question, because as soon as you start using the future tense at the end of a book then of course it's open as to whether this actually happened or whether this is just what she's postulated is happening.

Castro: Have you even been to Grenada or any of the other islands in the Caribbean?

Atwood: How could I have written that book without . . .

Castro: Going to that particular country?

Atwood: That particular country. Not Grenada. The history of revolution in Grenada was quite different. Would you like to hear it? Grenada happened in the following way: The CIA discovered that there were vats of vegetable oil in New York destined for Grenada that contained guns. So they contacted the government of Grenada and told them this, and said they'd better have a look around Grenada and see if they could find any similar vats that had already arrived and they did and they did find them, but they were empty. So the head left orders for the extermination of all his opponents and flew to New York to see if he could track down who was sending the guns in. He left orders with the police force, some of whom were sympathetic to the revolutionaries and told them. They then seized the radio station and a couple of officials, put the officials on the radio to say the revolution had been successful, and that was the revolution. Not a shot was fired, practically. No deaths. There you go. That was quite different. The one I'm talking about was on a different island, and it did not succeed and it was a very confused attempt. But the government did seize the opportunity to round up all its political opponents and put them into the bottom of this fortress. It's currently used as a women's prison.

CASTRO: What island is this?

ATWOOD: Am I going to tell? It's three islands condensed into two, but you can pinpoint it pretty well by looking at a map. It said in the book you can see Grenada on a clear day from the headland of one of these islands. All you have to do is go to the appropriate island, go out to the point, and if you can see Grenada from it on a clear day, then that's the island. *Treasure Island* is one of my favorite books. I love maps.

CASTRO: Could you comment on the telescopic ending of *Surfacing*?

ATWOOD: The ending of *Surfacing* . . . you mean the swiftness with which everything happens? There are a number of events packed into the ending but they are all events that you could not spend a lot of pages of prose on without weakening the impact considerably. Anybody who has studied, for instance, the structure of tragedy knows that the denouement is always swift. It would be fairly intolerable if it weren't, if that stretched out as long as the part that led up to it. So I think it would have been a structural mistake to have made it a lot longer. You'll notice that the ending of *Bodily Harm* is fairly rapid as well. Things condense. But I think real life tends to be that way too. You have a long buildup, and then whatever happens, happens, really quite suddenly, the momentous moment when so and so . . .

CASTRO: I think of *Moby-Dick*.

ATWOOD: All of a sudden the ship sinks! But you see, you couldn't make that ending of *Moby-Dick* really long. You couldn't do it. It's an event. It's swift. There's only so much description you can put into that without weakening it.

CASTRO: And I think of *One Hundred Years of Solitude*, also.

ATWOOD: It has a lot of people being polished off all the way through. Endings are endings. They're not middles.

CASTRO: In terms of nationalism, do you see nationalism as a universal problem?

ATWOOD: Do you mean everywhere? It's usually only defined as a problem by imperialistic countries, for whom it is a problem because it means the colonies are acting up. For the colonies, it's not nationalism that's the problem. It's imperialism. It's like the woman problem. Well, women are a problem, for men, when they start acting up.

CASTRO: Is there another aspect of nationalism—the problem of unifying the various provinces?

ATWOOD: You mean in Canada? OK. I was talking in world terms.

CASTRO: In any country there are always several different parties or cultures . . .

ATWOOD: Canada is very divided. Definitely. Quebec, as you know, is in a constant state of deciding whether or not to remain in Canada. It's very fashionable to be regionally inclined these days and for Newfoundland to say, we are being trodden upon and so on. It has not always been helped by the attitude of the federal government. But it comes and goes. Canada has always been a conglomerate and so was the United States, originally, and as you may recall, you had a few problems that way, yourself, about 1860.

CASTRO: Sherrill Grace has noted that you reverse the male pattern of making cities metaphorically female, and make cities male. Why and when do males dominate city spaces?

ATWOOD: When don't they? I guess the answer would be in maternity shops they don't, in women's clothing stores they don't, in certain kinds of restaurants where you get tea they don't, in women's clubs they don't. What else is left? That's about it, I think.

CASTRO: So are there parallels between the colonization, the victimization, and vulnerability of both women and the land?

ATWOOD: This has been often noted. But any of those paradigms can be applied to other paradigms. In *Surfacing,* I think there are probably seven layers of that. There's humans vs. the land; there's Quebec Hydro vs. the lakes; there's the English vs. the French; there's the whites vs. the Indians; there's men vs. women; there's Canada vs. the United States. They're all paradigms of dominance/subservience. Was that seven? I think it was about seven.

CASTRO: Picking up on one small aspect of your answer, the Indian myths in *Surfacing*—are they real? Again, a critic has speculated that they're Ojibwa myths of the Great Lynx of Misshipeshu as a guiding force, so is this one of the sources?

Atwood: The sources for the Indian stuff in *Surfacing,* apart from the sort of general knowledge, was a very specific book called *Indian Rock Paintings,* by Selwin Dewdney. In there you can find many, many pictures of rock paintings, photographs, diagrams, plus speculations as to what the paintings were of, which nobody really knows. Nobody has really come up with the final answer for who made these paintings, what they meant, what they were of, why they were where they were. Indians still leave offerings at these sites. You will still find from time to time something somebody has left there. But they've forgotten why they do it. There are various stories. They'll tell you why, or whatever, but the stories conflict.

Castro: Often it has to do with a journey. Or you're going to the rock and drawing a sign that you're going off someplace.

Atwood: Nobody knows that. It's simply not known. If you're drawing a sign that you're going off someplace, why do you draw a water monster? Which is a sacred being. They had other ways of signaling that they were going off someplace, and what direction they were going in. They didn't have to go through this elaborate—and it is elaborate—routine of making these paintings, which are often in quite inaccessible places. You would have had to go to a lot of trouble to get there, to mix the pigments. It's not like, you know, putting a piece of chalk on a wall to say I'm going to the drugstore or whatever. They were very elaborate and a lot of time was spent on some of them. There again it's like the cave paintings in Europe. I mean, if you're going to leave a sign you're going somewhere, why go into this inaccessible cave?

Castro: Have you been to the one in the Pyrenees?

Atwood: No. But I have a lot of pictures of it.

Castro: Which caves have you been to?

Atwood: I haven't been to any in Europe. Just the rock paintings in Canada, which aren't in caves.

Castro: Missouri has a lot of caves and has one petroglyph site that I'm fond of. It's in a forest setting and it just struck me that it reminds me very much of the rock paintings in Peterborough in terms of the kind of location, very remote.

Atwood: There are two different kinds of sites. One kind has actual petroglyphs, which are carvings, and the other has paintings that are made with a pigment and painted onto the rock.

Castro: I've seen mostly the petroglyphs.

Atwood: The petroglyphs would have taken a long time to make and for sure had nothing to do with saying I'm going to the drugstore.

Castro: But the ritual significance is definitely there.

Atwood: There's a ritual significance, but nobody knows what it was.

Castro: Two shamanist themes the critics have noted are the interrelation of human and animal behavior, and again the appearance of the spirit, such as the water monster. How did you decide to develop this theme? How did you get interested in the Indian rock paintings?

Atwood: They were there. It you're going to put a book in that setting, you're then limited to what occurs in that setting, what you can find in that setting. That automatically limits and dictates a lot of choices. If I were going to set a novel in the South, I mean automatically there would be certain things in that book. You couldn't avoid it, because that's what's there. And if you're going to make a novel with only four characters in it, set in a remote area of bush, and you want a place of significance to be in that novel, well, you don't have a lot of choice.

Castro: Do you have quest stories that are your favorites, by other people?

Atwood: Quest stories abound. They are very central to both Greek mythology and the Bible. Moses in the wilderness is a quest story. And in the Western literary tradition as it developed through people like Dante, the descent into Hell is a quest. Where don't we find it? Well, we didn't find it until recently in a lot of women's literature, because the quest, when it occurred, was very internalized. *Pride and Prejudice* is a quest story, and Mr. Darcy is the object of it, but that's stretching things a bit because Elizabeth doesn't actually go anywhere. She just stays in the same location, but it's an internal uncovering or discovery.

Castro: One of my favorite quest stories by a nineteenth-century woman is George Sand's *Consuelo,* or *The Countess of Rudelstadt.* That has a wonderful cave, like you've never before experienced. You have to go through this elaborate underground passage to get there; amazing things take place in the cave.

ATWOOD: As in *The Magic Flute*?

CASTRO: Yes. It's got some parallels there, and it's got some biographical parallels. There's a lot of music in the book also. I think that language itself is a theme of your quests. Do you see this as an unending search / process?

ATWOOD: It's particularly pertinent in Canada because of the linguistic tensions. But for any writer, language is always both a tool, a medium, and something that limits. It's always both things.

CASTRO: Do you make conscious choices to keep the language within a certain range? In other words, everyone has a different vocabulary and writing style and actual use of language, and so a lot of your use of language seems to be very symbolic so that, by repetition, there build up multiple layers of meanings.

ATWOOD: The language is limited by what you're describing and by the words that are available in it, and by the fact that if you look at the shorter Oxford dictionary, a lot of the words in there are words nobody ever uses. There's a wonderful game that you can play with it called Dictionary. Have you ever played that? Everybody sits around and they look in the Oxford Dictionary or the equivalent and they find the most obscure, unknown word they can, like for instance *volar,* and they tell what the word is and the other players then have to write a dictionary definition of the word. The intention is to deceive all the other players as to its authenticity. So you put in Middle English derivations and then usages to make it sound like an actual entry. Then all the entries are read out and people vote on them, and the one that gets the most votes, if it isn't the real definition, you get points for that. The real definition is read out along with the others. I forget how the points are allotted. I think if people guess the real one, the person picking it gets points off because they haven't picked a deceptive enough word. It's a wonderful game, and it leads you to understand how very, very many words there are in a dictionary that nobody's ever heard of. The actual vocabulary of any writer, including Shakespeare, is limited to words people understand, by and large.

CASTRO: Talking about Shakespeare—this is going back a couple of minutes—how would the narrator of *Surfacing* come up with a paraphrase of Shakespeare? "This above all, to refuse to be a victim." Don't you think it's a paraphrase of "This above all, to thine own self be true"?

Atwood: Who doesn't study Shakespeare in high school? We took five plays—one a year. In fact, the most prevalent problem among young poets, when you take groups of them, is that they slide into iambic pentameter without having the least idea they're doing it. They do it on purpose. The young kids don't realize what they're doing. They just write iambic pentameter lines because they've had Shakespeare in high school. It's very pervasive. You know, once you've studied iambic pentameter, it's hard to get that line rhythm out.

Castro: I think American high-school education is usually not that rigorous, unless you're going to a small private school.

Atwood: Well, we took that. We took *The Mill and the Floss*. We took *Tess of the D'Urbervilles*. We took *The Mayor of Casterbridge* in grade 10.

Castro: Was this a public high school?

Atwood: Yes. I studied Latin, French, German. This was in Toronto. In Ontario, this was a standard curriculum with set exams at the end of it that were provincewide, so the curriculum was the same for everybody in the province. That's changed. There was a period in the sixties when they weren't doing that, but they brought it back.

Castro: Do you think this might account for the fact there are usually bigger audiences for poetry in Canada than there are in the United States?

Atwood: There is a bigger reading audience for poetry in Canada than there is in the United States, per capita. It's bigger. But the actual sizes of the audience vary according to the city that you're in. I can give a poetry reading in Canada and there'll be 700 people at it, but I can give one here and there'll be 700 people at it. It just depends what city and where and all of that. If you look at book sales, then you can see that, taking the operative size of the English reading audience in Canada at 14 million, book sales are way, way higher per capita. But there are 223 million people in the United Sates, so that actual numbers can be greater in the United States, although the per capita ratio is lower.

Castro: Would you like to talk about your experiences working with Anansi Press and organizing the Writers' Union of Canada?

Atwood: I didn't really do much organizing of the Writers' Union of Canada. Graeme Gibson did it. I was one of the founding members, and I've been a chairman. I don't like organizations. I don't like working in them. I do it out of a sense of duty. Anansi Press—I put some money into it in the beginning. I wasn't in Toronto at the time. I went on as a member of the board in 1971 and edited the poetry list for a few years. I wouldn't say I was a driving force, though. I certainly kept them solvent. *Survival* made the difference to their remaining in existence or not. Basically, given the choice, I would rather not work under those circumstances.

CASTRO: I thought it was very gracious of you to do that because I realize it's such a different process from writing.

ATWOOD: Editing? I didn't mind the actual editing. When you work with a small publisher like that, as you know, they're always on the verge of bankruptcy. Keeping ahead of the bill collector was a bit of a strain. Writers in Canada have more of a sense of owing something back to the community, and they are more willing to take on things like that. There were some attempts being made to organize a writers' union here in the States. Did anything ever come of that?

CASTRO: It's still in the process, but the politicking is fairly . . . intense and I would say, unpleasant.

ATWOOD: My sense of it was that they would have a lot of trouble, partly because it's such a big country, and if you tried to pack all the writers into a meeting, where would you put them? It's just so huge. The other feeling was that those who've made it usually don't want to have anything to do with organizations like that. There is something called the Authors Guild that people belong to. I voiced an opinion in public a while ago that I thought it would be difficult here, and I got this outraged letter from one of the organizers saying I shouldn't say things like that, because it was counterproductive and so on, but it's the truth. It is going to be difficult here. More difficult. Canada is a small country. It has a manageable number of writers. You can put them all in a room, and therefore it can work. But here—where would you put them? It would be like a meeting of Jehovah's Witnesses or something. You'd have to hire a stadium. And then people would immediately feel alienated and not involved because it's too big, and other people are running it, and they don't feel in contact with it and all those kinds of problems.

CASTRO: In Canada, it must be nice to get together with different writers from different places.

Atwood: It's the only time we get to see one another, because the distances are so huge, that the only other times you get to see people is when you're on a reading tour. When we started the union, people met who had ever met, at all. So they liked it for that reason. It was a chance to actually be in contact with people that they otherwise wouldn't have.

Castro: Is the danger of Canada being Americanized diminishing?

Atwood: Oh, no. It's increasing. This big-dish television is just going to obliterate national border of all kinds.

Castro: You mean you get American programs?

Atwood: We get them all the time. We're going to be getting more of them. Soon it will be possible to get something like eighty channels and that's going to change things around a lot down here, too. It's going to be very bad for the networks. They will no longer have the big monopoly they once had. The whole area of communications is something we pay a lot of attention to, and it is pretty much a one-way mirror. We can see everything you do, and you can't see a thing we do. There's no reason for that to change. This is *réal politique.* This is a huge country, and there's no particular reason for people to pay attention to Canada. There would be if we suddenly became Communist and established Russian missile bases pointing at you. That would force attention just as when Cuba did that. Everybody knew where Cuba was, suddenly. But the way things are now, although we are your biggest foreign market, there's no particular reason for you to know those things. Life is life. If there isn't a reason, people don't know them. Whereas there's a very good reason for us to know what you're doing, because it affects us so immediately. So don't feel bad about it.

Castro: When I was in Canada, I traveled from Vancouver to Ontario, and I have great memories of two million acres of land at Algonquin Park with only one road through it—and space! I have memories of beautiful spaces and lakes.

Atwood: Beautiful spaces that are being killed at the moment.

Castro: I haven't seen that, but it's too bad to hear about it. Yet it must be worse to have to experience it.

Atwood: Well, it's the acid rain problem, as you know. It's falling from you. Don't you remember the big uproar about this film on acid rain that was declared to be the product of enemy agents by the United States government? And you have to get a certificate if you're showing it, and it just won an Oscar. And her acceptance speech was, "You folks sure know how to treat an enemy agent."

CASTRO: What are some of your commitments to expressing things that females experience?

ATWOOD: I'm a writer. You automatically express those things because you're a writer. You can't help it. If you write about a woman in this society, this society being what it is, you automatically express those things, unless you're writing Harlequin romances. And even those are an upside-down expression of the same thing. I mean, you're not writing about a society in which things are the same for everybody. They're not the same for everybody. That doesn't mean to say that everything is automatically worse for women than it is for men. It's not. Some things are worse for men. But you don't have to have an a priori commitment in order to express certain things. They're unavoidable. Just as Jane Austen expressed certain things whether she knew it or not, because she was writing about that kind of society. Her books are really how-to books: given the fact of being a woman in that kind of society, here's how you manage it better than otherwise. It's better to be Eleanor than Mary Ann. You get along better.

CASTRO: I'm thinking of this particular image that is in both *True Stories* and *Second Words* of a woman in childbirth who is being tortured because her legs are tied.

ATWOOD: That's right out of Nazi Germany. It's real. That's a real-life event. All of the things in that poem sequence "Notes Towards a Poem That Can Never Be Written," they're all real. You don't have to make stuff like that up, because it exists.

CASTRO: I think it's very powerful that you're dealing with it so directly. One critic has written that in *Sexual Politics*—I mean *Power Politics,* but that's what it's about—the characters are eyewitnesses observing the sexual politics.

ATWOOD: But that's how people live. You can't not observe it unless you're deaf, dumb, and blind. It's just there. Now you can observe it, and there are various interpretations you can put on what you've seen, just as anybody who's ever attended a trial will know that witness A looking at the car crash will have seen the green car crash into the blue car, and witness B will have seen the blue car stop suddenly and then the green car crash, and witness C may have even seen the blue car back up. It depends who's looking. But the events are there. They're there to be seen.

Castro: Do those things you've just listed on what the eyewitnesses are going to report have something to do with who we are as women?

Atwood: Of course. And it also has to do with who we are and how old we are, and what we feel we can say and what we feel we can't say, and what we automatically repress so instantaneously that we don't even see it. You know, that's just gone. Let's go back to Susanna Moodie. There are a lot of things that she didn't say, partly because they weren't choices; they weren't available to be said. She wouldn't even have considered saying them. Writing her memoirs, it wouldn't have even entered her consciousness to put in a chapter on her sex life. That wouldn't have been a choice. It would just be completely blotted out. I think that probably in a century or so people will look back at writing of this period and say, why were they repressing X? We don't know what X is yet. Because we aren't conscious of it. We don't know what they are going to say that we were repressing. But I'm sure there's something. I'm sure there are a lot of things that somebody looking back at us will be able to see that we just don't see because it's not a choice for us to see it. It's not part of our vocabulary at this time. So I think a lot of the energy in women's writing over the past ten years, and there has been a tremendous amount of energy, has come from being able to say things that once you couldn't say. And therefore, being able to see things that once you couldn't see, or that you would have seen but repressed, or that you would have seen and put another interpretation on, and those things are changing all the time and that's part of the interesting thing about writing. One point of view will be established and then somebody else will say yes, but . . . Yes, but what about . . . I think there was a period, for instance, in the early seventies, when one party line was that all men are bad. By nature of being men, they were automatically bad. And there is no point in talking to them or having anything to do with them. As soon as that point of view is expressed, somebody else says yes, but . . . But what about Henry whom I've known for years?

Castro: I think that even the leaders of that particular line of thought were the ones who changed.

Atwood: In some cases, yes. In some cases, no. Or in some cases, they dropped out of sight and didn't go on to express anything else. It's a constant, ongoing process. Does the fact that we are women alter what we see? What we report? It has to, but nobody knows what the neutral stand would be. There's not such thing as a person who's neither a man nor a woman. So we don't know that person in between, what that completely objective Martian would say. We've never had an example of it. I think one thing that the women's movement has pointed out is that the fact of being male alters what men say. Whereas once we thought they were doing just objective truth, and it's obvious now that everything passes through a filter. Doesn't mean it's not true in some sense. It just means that nobody can claim to have the absolute, whole, objective, total, complete truth. The truth is composite, and that's a cheering thought. It mitigates tendencies toward autocracy.

*This interview was professionally recorded by the American Audio Prose Library (Columbia, Missouri); it took place in the Women's Building, Washington University, St. Louis.*

# 16 *A Conversation*
## *Margaret Atwood and Students*
## *Moderated by Francis X. Gillen*

Q: Who are some of your favorite authors?

A: I was trained as a Victorianist; that was my field of study. Some of my favorite authors are the old nineteenth-century chestnuts like George Eliot's midcentury Victorian novel *Middlemarch.* Dickens is one of my favorites. You're wondering about modern day? The American author who has had the most influence on Canadian writing is Faulkner. I read Faulkner at quite an early age, and I thought, "This man has a wonderful imagination; look at all the stuff he has made up." And then I met someone from Oxford, Mississippi, who told me he didn't make anything up. He just changed the names. So I was quite impressed by that. More modern writers—there are a number of women authors that I like a lot apart from the nineteenth-century ones that I was brought up with. There are a number of British ones. I don't know if you know the names: Fay Weldon, Margaret Drabble, Angela Carter. Linda Gregg from the United States is a poet whom some of the writers here may have heard of.

Q: Is there any special process you use when you write? I used to know someone who locked himself in his room with seven bottles of whiskey and wrote.

A: No, I also have a family, and if you have a family and you are involved with your family, you do not lock yourself in a room. I lock myself in my room at certain hours of the day, but I don't lock myself up for days at a time. I come out in the evenings and in the mornings. I write when my child is at school.

Q: Why do you say that writing can be political?

A: When you go to the rest of the world, nobody even thinks

about this question. They assume that a writer writes about everything. In the States there is a tradition of writing that encompasses things like that: Melville, Whitman, Doctorow. Even *The Great Gatsby* is a political novel; it examines the fabric of social life. Any novelist who is not just writing total fantasy is interacting with life. It may be that you can write the life of a person in the United States who never thinks a political thought. I can hardly imagine people so isolated that they have no such thoughts. But somehow its been decided generally that the Freudian subconscious is OK for art, but one's conscious political decisions are not. I don't know why that is. It's not universal. It's just an assumption that you often run into in the minds of people who say it's too political. What they mean is it's too political to be art. There are certain things that have been designated as OK for art, namely trees, sunsets, love, and death.

Q: Who are some Canadian authors to read?

A: Well, there are probably some that you may have read already, without knowing that they are Canadian. Robertson Davies is widely available, particularly the Deptford Trilogy. Alice Munro. You can easily get hold of Canadian writing by writing to the following address: Longhouse Book Store, 626 Yonge Street, Toronto, Ontario M4Y 12B. Alice Munro deals particularly with lives of girls and women. Try Mordecai Richler, Timothy Findley, Marian Engel.

Q: Could you talk about your work for Amnesty International?

A: Amnesty was quite small in Canada a number of years ago. It needed to raise funds, and I was involved in some of that. Amnesty is a very worthy organization. It is apolitical, it doesn't make choices of who to support or whether the country is right-wing or left-wing. It's just dealing with violations of human rights. They're also doing investigations into torture worldwide—on the increase I might add. The reason I did that: there are only a few countries left where you can. This is one of them. Canada is one, Britain is one, some of the Western European countries. In a lot of countries Amnesty is outlawed. You can be put in jail for just belonging to it.

Q: Were you a good English student?

A: One of my high-school teachers said to one of my friends who went back to school to visit, "There was nothing distinctive about her at all that I can remember." I didn't become a good English student until I was in twelfth grade. I was quite good after that. The reason was that I got a good teacher I liked, and when you have a teacher you like, you tend to put more effort into it. I started writing poetry then, and she once made a wonderful comment: "Well, I can't understand it, dear, so it must be good."

Q: Which of your own books do you like the best?

A: The next one. Otherwise why would you keep going? You never feel that anything you have ever done is perfect. If you did, you would stop.

Q: Margaret, can you tell us about the novel you're working on now?

A: That is the one question I cannot answer because I never talk about the writing I'm doing now. It's my second superstition. My first is that I don't like anyone using my typewriter.

Q: You have recently returned from Cuba: What are your perceptions about Cuba? Is it really an evil place?

A: Well, I have something to compare it with because I've been to lots of "evil places." I've been around the world twice. First time I stopped in Iran and Afghanistan. Of all the evil places we have to choose from, those are among the evilest now, I'd say. What the Russians are doing in Afghanistan is pretty evil, and what Iran is doing to itself is pretty evil. Just to give us something to compare Cuba with. Number two, I've also been in other East-bloc countries, so I've got some of those to compare it with as well. This spring I was in Poland and Czechoslovakia. Not at the invitation of the governments, but at the invitation of our Canadian embassies there, which meant that I did not have official sanctions or a guided tour, and I didn't have to go to any knitting factories. But I did get to speak with a lot of people who were not officially sanctioned spokespersons for those countries, and it is obvious to me that those regimes are not loved. The people feel they are conquered people and in the control of a foreign power. The number of party members in those countries is very low.

What I felt about the Cubans was that they feel closer emotionally to Americans than they do to Russians, which is obvious once you think about it. They feel temperamentally more akin to Americans. They have no feelings of animosity towards individual American people. They did not see Castro's takeover primarily in terms of political theories. They saw it in terms of a continuation of something that has been going on since 1850. They started out back then having a colonial revolution against Spain, as the U.S. had a revolt against Britain. They wanted to be independent. They didn't want to be dictated to by Spain. That one revolution didn't work, so they continued it at the end of the nineteenth century. The big hero is a poet, José Martí. That revolt was brutally fought: talk about war atrocities. Then the battleship *Maine* blew up in the Havana harbor; nobody knows to this day who blew it up. The States intervened, settled the war and imposed their own conditions. Cuba was then somewhat run by the United States for the next fifty years, and what that meant in practical terms for them was that there were many gambling casinos and a great deal of prostitution. It's estimated that one of every four Cuban families at that time had a female employed as a prostitute. This was insulting to Cuban men. I think unless you understand that, you don't understand Castro, because Castro is not seen as some kind of Marxist person, but as the person who continued what José Martí had been doing, and when people talk about this stuff they don't talk theory. There weren't any equivalents of the lectures you get in East Germany and those other places. What they talk about is their own history and social conditions before the revolution and after. I would say that there are probably some things that you as Americans would find onerous—gasoline shortages and so on—but the people in general don't seem to find things nearly as onerous as people in Czechoslovakia and Poland do.

The Russians are there in Cuba, and they have a great big embassy which they are still building. How is it referred to by the Cubans? In a joking fashion behind everybody's back they call it the "Control Tower." The Russians don't overtly boss them around, but I'm sure they have some influence on policy. I think it's very unfortunate that the U.S. did not make their peace with Cuba quite early on. If they had, the Russians would not be there. As for whether Cubans like Castro or not, most of them seem to.

Q: How are things for the people—especially the writers—in Cuba?

A: I talked to all kinds of people individually when there was nobody else listening, and they're not dumb. They read the papers from North America all the time. They keep up and watch what's going on. They were quite worried a couple of months ago that the U.S. was going to bomb their airport. They ordered an alert. Note that they gave weapons to their citizens, and everybody is part of the citizens' army—if they felt really insecure about things, they surely wouldn't do that. If the Soviet Union had given weapons to all the Poles, imagine what would have happened! Immediately there would have been a war. Cuba evidently doesn't feel insecure about doing that.

I asked a lot of questions about how things are for writers—what about the fact that they rounded up homosexuals and put them in concentration camps? They said immediately that was a mistake. They reversed that policy; it is not being done any more. I asked about the writing, and I pushed quite hard on this. People started giggling. "What would happen for instance if you wrote a novel which had a nasty portrait of a Russian in it?" They giggled because they thought the idea was funny. They said, "We went through a ten-year period during which things were somewhat 'gray and Asiatic.' " They said that was over now. What they meant was what a writer writes about was interpreted more narrowly back then. They feel that they can write about anything—except that they cannot attack Castro or the official government. By that they mean not that you can't criticize government policies, but you can't say, let's overthrow them. But can you say that here? Can you say, let's overthrow the U.S. government? If you did, you would have a bunch of secret service men on your back quite instantly.

As a member of Amnesty International, I am always on the lookout for who is in jail and why. All I can tell you about Cuba is the trend is towards letting them out. On the PEN (Poets, Essayists, Novelists) list now there are about seventeen names. When I asked about those names, nobody had even heard of any of them. They said, well, it is true that people get put in jail for blowing things up, and then they declare afterwards that they are writers. The Dutch ambassador there is quite a wonderful person—he doesn't act like an ambassador. He rides a bicycle, for example. I asked him what was the real truth, and he said that certainly no major writers were in jail at the moment. We also said to them, What would happen if you did write something like that (anti-Castro), and they said nobody would publish it. So, there is that degree of control.

Q: What do women wear?

A: Women wear high-heeled shoes. They strangely enough do not wear what you would expect them to wear—mainly cotton dresses. Why? Because they export all that. Men are very flirtatious. I asked about rape. The death penalty is for two things. One is for trying to kill Castro the *second* time, the other is for rape. Remember what happened in the fifty years before this. Not only was there a lot of prostitution and dirty nightclub shows, but there was a lot of violence. The old regime was an assassinating regime and also a very violent one. I met somebody there who had grown up at that time. Machine-gun fire at night was a very normal sound; you just expected it. What El Salvador is now, Cuba was then, and that's another thing you have to remember when you're talking about evil places. The other interesting thing about women: there is a high divorce rate. I asked why is that? They said, a young girl growing up is still considered to be under the parental control of her father, but once you get married, that stops and you can do what you like. They get married, and then they get divorced, and then they can do what they like. They also said the high divorce rate had something to do with the crowded living conditions. Divorces are cheap. If you do get a divorce, there is the problem of where to move, because you can't just move into an apartment there. There aren't any available. I asked, "Do men hit their wives?" They said, "What?" Then they said that would not be natural. Hitting is not socially acceptable. Infidelity, flirtation, yes, but hitting, no.

Q: What about Angola?

A: I have a feeling that the Angola situation shows there are no free trips. You must remember that when the U.S. cut off trade with Cuba, Cuba was financially isolated. They were up the creek, and they tried to make it on their own for a number of years. Finally they just couldn't do it.

It's like any other foreign country; the things that are the most different are the things that are the most interesting. You can sit and tell them stories about wild animals and they think it is so interesting.

Any encroachment on freedom of speech, freedom to publish, freedom to say what you think should be stopped immediately because lights are going out all over the world. There are greater and greater encroachments on those freedoms here and there and everywhere. There is also a publication called *Index on Censorship,* which is very informed. So, in your country I would say try to keep things as open as possible. One would hope in a country like this there would be enough people with their little antennas up to notice any closing down, but I would say that any group that tries to tell you that voicing a certain opinion is un-American, or against God, or any of those other hammers that people use to make other people shut up, is to be resisted. I think you should go back to your first principles of the American Revolution, and you should keep to those.

The American Revolution is the revolution that inspired other revolutions all over the world. Go back there and look at your Constitution—keep that firmly in mind and ask yourself, is somebody trying to violate this; is somebody trying to overturn this? Is some kind of monopoly being established? America is traditionally a country where the voice of every individual is supposed to have equal rights, through the vote. I was alarmed to see that only fifty percent of the people voted in the last presidential election, and that was considered a lot. Is that a democracy, is that a functioning democracy? So the other thing you could do is help in voter registration. Now your particular custom of having people declare Democratic or Republican when they are registered as voters to me seems like the Thought Police in George Orwell. But, anyway, it's the system you have, and it's what you've got to work with. But try to convince people that their feelings of helplessness and being adrift needn't be. They ought to register and they ought to vote.

Q: Could you suggest a good topic for a research paper?

A: I'm not a person to ever tell another person what he or she should be writing about. I think that you should key in more to world news. U.S. papers tend to do local coverage. Any fire, any catastrophe, any murder—that hits the papers; they do state stuff, and they do things about states right around them. They do national and U.S. state things. I would say write to your newspaper and say, I want more world news, or tell your television station, I want to know more about what is going on in the world. It's not that I'm not interested in things here, but I would like to know more about things there. Now in Canada, we have the opposite problem. We have lots of world news; it's just that we sometimes skimp on the Canadian news.

Q: Would you consider the exclusion of the media in Grenada dangerous?

A: I would. The exclusion of the media seems more than anything a danger signal to me. They know perfectly well that during the Nicaragua uprising, if the media hadn't been there covering it, they probably could have put in U.S. troops. Because what you don't know about, you can't voice an opinion about, can you? So if you must, subscribe to the *Manchester Guardian.* Get the *Washington Post* along with it. The U.S. is now a world power. It can't go back to being a colony. So, therefore, one must take responsibility. And taking responsibility means learning about the things you're going to be involved in. Do you know about the Philippines? It's coming toward you. I would say, try to inform yourself as much as you can, and ask of your media—demand—that they provide this coverage. They will respond to public pressure. If people say this is what we want, then they'll do it.

Q: In a lot of instances the media's general coverage seems critical of the government. They are being slapped right down. Could you comment?

A: The media also has to be responsible. They can't just say any old thing about anybody. But any reporter knows that. You have to try to get your facts absolutely straight. And if you are going to make a controversial statement, you better have some backup for it. Otherwise you will get slapped. But libel laws are much looser in the United States than they are in Canada. The media in Canada are more pussy-footed as a result. The coverage is wider but we don't have people who are willing to do what the *Washington Post* did with Watergate. They're too timid. So we don't have a lot of hard-hitting investigation journalism about our own politicians. So, I would just say to your media, get out there into the rest of the world and tell us what's going on even though it may not directly affect Americans, because ultimately it will.

Q: What responsibilities do you see for the writers and the artists concerning the nuclear trend?

A: The U.S. is one of the few countries in the world in which, if you ask people in earnest what their responsibilities are, the first answer you'll probably get from most of them is, my responsibility is to be true to myself and to my inner integrity. You'll get that speech. And this is the only country where you will get that speech. In the rest of the world that kind of answer wouldn't make sense to the people; of course they would assume one has inner integrity, but doesn't that include other people? I think what happened here was there was a lot of uproar in the late sixties, and people wrote a lot of that kind of poetry, and the generation that came right after that reacted against it. I have nothing against that. It's essential, but if you contemplate your soul for a certain time, you'll get to the point where you'll realize that your soul is not in a box. It's not sealed off from everybody else, and this particular issue, the nuclear issue, I don't consider "politics" in any limited sense. I consider it something like the Black Death. The Black Death wasn't "politics," but it sure killed a lot of people. I refuse to dictate to people what they should write about, but I will point out to Americans who believe that art is over here and politics is over there, that it's not two boxes. Other writers in other countries don't have that problem. What people are afraid of here is that if they write political poetry, some reviewer is going to say it's not poetry and sure, you take that risk, but what is life without risks? I give unto you Carolyn Forché. Is that poetry or not? It's certainly political. She had trouble getting that book published. Why? Because people she showed it to said, this is too political. All I'm saying is it's an anomaly to say that political things are not artistic. Political engagement can give a writer tremendous energy.

Q: Could you give an example of how art and poetry go together? Or don't?

A: There's a book you should read by Lewis Hyde, *The Gift.* It's not poetry and it's not prose fiction and it's not criticism. It's partly anthropology and partly folklore and partly sociology. Partly economics and partly political theory. Partly literary criticism. It's a study of the gift as a medium of exchange. He makes a distinction between the commodity exchange—the market economy—and the gift exchange. He puts art in the gift-transaction economy, and he examines this through primitive societies, through art, through folktales, through all kinds of things. Still, all ideologies have trouble with writers. No exceptions. Because ideologies have a "should" and writers are an eccentric bunch of people; they don't always like having their feet crammed into those particular ideological shoes, and they often refuse to put their feet *into* those shoes. That's the way it will always be unless we have some kind of dictatorship. So writing is exploration. Exploration is going into a territory without knowing what you may find. It is then recording as accurately as you can what you do find rather than what you think you should find.

Q: I was reading in the paper today how popular you are in Canada, and it struck me as very odd that a poet could be so popular because in America poets have difficulty, say, selling five thousand books. What do you perceive as the difference between Canadian people and American people that makes this possible?

A: When I was growing up, as a young writer in the 1960s in Canada, it was very hard to publish anything. The writing community was very small. What that meant in Canada at that time was that poetry became the dominant literary form for about ten years. Why? Because it was cheap to do. The number of pages in a book was smaller, and you could do it in your cellar. You could have little printing presses, and that's how most poets of my generation started. They were published by themselves in print initially in their cellars. And I did that too. In 1961 there were about four literary magazines and most of those were recent. In 1965 there began to be a cultural explosion that has not stopped, and the increase in the readership was astronomical. It was partly because the school-leaving age of Canadians was going up so they were more educated. Canadians before that read books, but not Canadian books: they had the usual colonial attitude (which corresponded with the United States' in 1820), that things in their own country were of negligible interest and that the important things were elsewhere. The audience has increased geometrically now, but the holdover from that is that poetry was considered a dominant literary form for many years and Canadians still have the highest per capita readership of poetry in the English-speaking world (compared with the U.S., Britain, Australia, and New Zealand).

But I also write novels. My highest selling book, initially, was the book of criticism (*Survival: A Thematic Guide to Canadian Literature*) that I wrote in 1972 and that sold a hundred thousand copies, which surprised me because I expected to sell five. That shows the change. Suddenly the Canadians were interested in their own literature.

Q: Do you think Canada cares more about people and America more about money?

A: Do I think Canada is more people oriented and America is more economically oriented? Canadians have the sense that things have to be spread around, that you can't let one part of the country be very, very rich and another part be very poor. They try to equalize things in that way. There are a lot of differences. It's not that Canadians aren't interested in money, but that they have other interests as well. They did a survey with Canadian college students, and the number one priority was the economy. The number two and three priorities were freedom of speech and equality for women. The big seller in Canada in the late sixties through the seventies was a man called Pierre Berton, and what he writes is popular history of Canada. He did a history of the railroads and the War of 1812. The Canadians eat these up. They don't learn a lot at school about this, not as much as should be taught. I was taught ancient Egyptian history, Greek and Roman history, Renaissance history, European and British history, and American history, but not much Canadian history. It is still not stressed as much as it ought to be.

Q: How do you go about writing something with your own experiences?

A: That's one of the most interesting parts of writing. If you believe that writing is merely self-expression, then you'll forever be trapped in your own persona, or a character very much like yourself. But if you look at novels through the ages you'll see a great many novels that did not do that. If you hang on to the self-expression approach for two or three novels, you'll pretty much be exhausted, unless you live a wild life. I think that's what writing novels is like, that you do not impose yourself on a character all the time. To try to think the way another person would think, or feel the way you think they feel. If I'm doing a character that has a certain job that I don't have, I usually give them a job that I wish I had or would like to have. I usually write first and then research after, I have to admit, and often I find that I guess right. For instance, for the paleontologist in *Life Before Man,* I wrote a book first and then went to the museum and asked if they had a person who had this kind of job. They said yes, and lo and behold, she was a woman. I asked her if she would show me what she did. She did, and afterwards, she read my manuscript and told me, "This is how I feel!" These are the nice payoffs in what I do.

*Honors Conversation held at the University of Tampa, 25 January 1987, taped by Daniel Comiskey, transcribed by Rachel Stein. Program arranged by Kathryn VanSpanckeren.*

*Works Cited*
*Notes on Contributors*
*Index*

# *Works Cited*

PRIMARY


Atwood, Margaret. *The Animals in That Country.* Toronto: Oxford Univ. Press, 1968

______. *Anna's Pet.* Toronto: James Lorimer, 1980.

______. *Bluebeard's Egg.* Toronto: McClelland and Stewart, 1983; Boston: Houghton Mifflin, 1986.

______. *Bodily Harm.* Toronto: McClelland and Stewart; New York: Simon and Schuster, 1982. Reprint. New York: Bantam, 1983.

______. *The Circle Game.* Bloomfield Hills, Mich.: privately printed, 1964. Reprint. Toronto: Contact Press; Anansi, 1966.

______. *Dancing Girls.* Toronto: McClelland and Stewart; New York: Simon and Schuster, 1977.

______. *Days of the Rebels, 1815–1840.* Canada's Illustrated Heritage Series. Toronto: Natural Science of Canada, 1977.

______. "A Disneyland of the Soul." In *The Writer and Human Rights,* edited by The Toronto Arts Group for the Human Race, pp. 129–32. Toronto: Lester and Orpen Dennys, 1983.

______. "Don't Expect the Bears to Dance." *Maclean's,* June 1975, pp. 68–71.

______. *Double Persephone.* Toronto: Hawkshead Press, 1961.

______. *The Edible Woman.* Toronto: McClelland and Stewart; New York: Andre Deutsch, 1969. Reprint. Boston: Atlantic–Little, Brown, 1970; New York: Warner Books, 1983.

______. "Encounters with the Element Man." *Impulse* 1, no. 2 (Winter 1972): 24–31. Reprinted as *Encounters with the Element Man.* Concord, N.H.: William B. Ewert, 1982.

______. "Fall and All: A Sequence." *Fiddlehead,* no. 59 (Winter 1964): 58–63.

______. *The Handmaid's Tale.* Toronto: McClelland and Stewart, 1985; Boston: Houghton Mifflin, 1986.

______. *Interlunar.* Toronto: Oxford Univ. Press, 1984.

______. Interview. *Meanjin* 37, no. 2 (July 1978): 189–205.

______. *The Journals of Susanna Moodie.* Toronto: Oxford Univ. Press, 1970.

______. *Lady Oracle.* Toronto: McClelland and Stewart; New York: Simon and Schuster, 1976. Reprint. New York: Avon, 1976.

———. Letter to Sharon R. Wilson, 29 September 1986.
———. *Life Before Man.* Toronto: McClelland and Stewart; New York: Simon and Schuster, 1979.
———. Margaret Atwood Papers. Thomas Fisher Rare Book Library, University of Toronto.
———. *Murder in the Dark.* Toronto: Coach House Press, 1983.
———. "One Writer's Use of Grimm." Lecture sponsored by Delaware Humanities Forum, 20 November 1985.
———. *Power Politics.* Toronto: Anansi, 1971; New York: Harper and Row, 1973.
———. *Procedures for Underground.* Toronto: Oxford Univ. Press; Boston: Atlantic–Little, Brown, 1970.
———. *Second Words: Selected Critical Prose.* Toronto: Anansi; Boston: Beacon Press, 1982.
———. *Selected Poems.* Toronto: Oxford Univ. Press; New York: Simon and Schuster, 1976. Reprint. New York: Houghton Mifflin, 1987.
———. *Selected Poems II: Poems Selected and New, 1976–1986.* Toronto: Oxford Univ. Press, 1986; New York: Houghton Mifflin, 1987.
———. *Surfacing.* Toronto: McClelland and Stewart; New York: Simon and Schuster, 1972. Reprint. New York: Popular Library, 1972; Markham, Ont.: Paperjacks, 1973.
———. *Survival: A Thematic Guide to Canadian Literature.* Toronto: Anansi, 1972.
———. Taped interview for Sharon R. Wilson, August 1985.
———. Telephone conversation with Sharon R. Wilson, December 1985.
———. *True Stories.* Toronto: Oxford Univ. Press; New York: Simon and Schuster, 1981.
———. "Two-Headed Poems." *This Magazine* 11, no. 5 (October 1977); 18–21. Reprinted in *American Poetry Review* 8, no. 5 (September 1979): 26.
———. *Two-Headed Poems.* Toronto: Oxford Univ. Press; New York: Simon and Schuster, Touchstone, 1978.
———. *Up in the Tree.* Toronto: McClelland and Stewart, 1978.
———. *You Are Happy.* Toronto: Oxford Univ. Press; New York: Harper and Row, 1974. Reprint. New York: Simon and Schuster, 1978.

## SECONDARY

Astrov, Margot. *The Winged Serpent.* New York: John Day, 1946. Reprinted as *American Indian Prose and Poetry.* New York: Capricorn, 1962.
Auerbach, Nina. *Communities of Women: An Idea in Fiction.* Cambridge: Harvard Univ. Press, 1978.
Austen, Jane. *Northanger Abbey.* 1818. Reprint. Baltimore: Penguin, 1975.
Bachelard, Gaston. *The Psychoanalysis of Fire.* Translated by Alan C. M. Ross. Boston: Beacon Press, 1964.
Berger, John. *Ways of Seeing.* Middlesex: Penguin, 1972.

Bettelheim, Bruno. *The Uses of Enchantment.* New York: Vintage Books, 1977.

Blacker, Carmen. *The Catalpa Bow: A Study of Shamanistic Practices in Japan.* London: Allen and Unwin, 1982.

Blakely, Barbara. "The Pronunciation of Flesh: A Feminist Reading of Atwood's Poetry." In Grace and Weir, pp. 33–51.

Brown, Russell M. "Atwood's Sacred Wells." *Essays on Canadian Writing* 17 (1980): 5–43.

Cappon, Paul, ed. *Our House: Social Perspectives on Canadian Literature.* Toronto: McClelland and Stewart, 1978.

Carpenter, Edmund. "The Eskimo Artist." In *Anthropology and Art: Readings in Cross-Cultural Aesthetics,* edited by Charlotte Offen, pp. 163–71. Garden City, N.Y.: Natural History Press, 1971.

———. *Oh, What a Blow That Phantom Gave Me!* New York: Bantam Books, 1974.

Carpenter, Mary Wilson. Letter to the Editor. *The Women's Review of Books* 3, no. 12 (1986): 5.

Christ, Carol P. *Deep Diving and Surfacing: Women Writers on Spiritual Quest.* Boston: Beacon Press, 1980.

Cirlot, J. E. *A Dictionary of Symbols.* New York: Philosophical Library, 1962.

Cixous, Hélène. "The Laugh of the Medusa." *Signs* 1 (1976): 875–93.

Daly, Mary. *Gyn/Ecology: The Metaethics of Radical Feminism.* Boston: Beacon Press, 1978.

Davey, Frank. *Margaret Atwood: A Feminist Poetics.* Vancouver: Talonbooks, 1984.

———. "Atwood Walking Backwards." *Open Letter,* no. 5 (Summer 1973): 74–84.

———. "Atwood's Gorgon Touch." *Studies in Canadian Literature* 2 (1977): 146–63.

———. *From There to Here: A Guide to Canadian Literature Since 1960.* Erin, Ont.: Press Porcepic, 1974.

Davidson, Arnold E., and Cathy N. Davidson. "Margaret Atwood's *Lady Oracle:* The Artist as Escapist and Seer." *Studies in Canadian Literature* 3 (1978): 166–77.

———. "Prospects and Retrospect in *Life Before Man.*" In Davidson and Davidson, pp. 205–21.

———, eds. *The Art of Margaret Atwood: Essays in Criticism.* Toronto: Anansi, 1981.

Davidson, Cathy N. "A Feminist *1984.*" *Ms.,* 17 February 1986, pp. 24–26.

———. Interview with Margaret Atwood. Toronto, 22 July 1985.

Davidson, Cathy N., and E. M. Broner. *The Lost Tradition: Mothers and Daughters in Literature.* New York: Frederick Ungar, 1980.

Diamond, Stanley. *In Search of the Primitive: A Critique of Civilization.* New Brunswick, N.J.: Transaction Books, 1974.

Djwa, Sandra. "The Where of Here: Margaret Atwood and a Canadian Tradition." In Davidson and Davidson, pp. 9–34.

Douglas, Mary. *Purity and Danger: An Analysis of Concepts of Pollution and Taboo.* New York: Frederick A. Praeger, 1966.

DuPlessis, Rachel Blau. *Writing Beyond the Ending: Narrative Strategies of Twentieth-Century Women Writers.* Bloomington: Indiana Univ. Press, 1985.

———. "The Critique of Consciousness and Myth in Levertov, Rich, and Rukeyser." In *Shakespeare's Sisters,* edited by Sandra Gilbert and Susan Gubar, pp. 280–300. Bloomington: Indiana Univ. Press, 1979.

———. "The Feminist Apologues of Lessing, Piercy, and Russ." *Frontiers* 4 (1979): 1–8.

———. "Psyche, or Wholeness." *Massachusetts Review* 19 (1979): 77–96.

Eliade, Mircea. *From Primitives to Zen: A Thematic Sourcebook of the History of Religions.* New York: Harper and Row, 1967.

———. *Shamanism: Archaic Techniques of Ecstasy.* Translated by Willard R. Trask. Bollingen Series, no. 76. New York: Pantheon, 1964.

Eliot, T. S. *The Complete Poems and Plays, 1909–1950.* New York: Harcourt, Brace, 1952.

Even-Zohar, Itamar. "Polysystem Theory." *Poetics Today* 1, no. 1 (1979): 304–5.

———. "Aspects of the Hebrew-Yiddish Polysystem." Paper presented at Conference on Research in Yiddish Language and Literature, Oxford, August 1979.

Fetterley, Judith. *The Resisting Reader: A Feminist Approach to American Fiction.* Bloomington: Indiana Univ. Press, 1977.

Fordham, Frieda. *An Introduction to Jung's Psychology.* Baltimore: Penguin, 1963.

Foster, John William. "The Poetry of Margaret Atwood." *Canadian Literature* 74 (Fall 1977): 5–20.

Freeman, Michelle A. "Marie de France's Poetics of Silence: The Implications for a Feminine *Translatio.*" *PMLA* 99, no. 5 (1984): 860–83.

Friedrich, Paul. *The Meaning of Aphrodite.* Chicago: Univ. of Chicago Press, 1978.

Freud, Sigmund. *The Interpretation of Dreams.* Translated by James Strachey. New York: Basic Books, 1955. Reprint. New York: Avon, 1965.

Frye, Northrop. *The Bush Garden: Essays on the Canadian Imagination.* Toronto: Anansi, 1971.

Gallop, Jane. *The Daughter's Seduction: Feminism and Psychoanalysis.* Ithaca: Cornell Univ. Press, 1982.

Galt, George. "*Surfacing* and the Critics." *Canadian Forum* 54 (1974): 12–14.

Garebian, Keith. "*Surfacing:* Apocalyptic Ghost Story." *Mosaic* 9, no. 3 (1976): 1–9.

Garnett, Angelica. *Deceived with Kindness: A Bloomsbury Childhood.* London: Hogarth Press, 1984.

Gerstenberger, Donna. "Conceptions Literary and Otherwise: Women Writers and the Modern Imagination." *Novel* 9, no. 2 (Winter 1976): 141–50.

Gilbert, Sandra, and Susan Gubar. *The Madwoman in the Attic: The Woman Writer and the Nineteenth-Century Literary Imagination.* New Haven: Yale Univ. Press, 1979.

Ginsberg, Allen. "Howl." In *The Norton Anthology of Modern Poetry,* edited by Richard Ellmann and Robert O'Clair, pp. 1121–26. New York: W. W. Norton, 1973.

Glickson, Susan Wood. "The Martian Point of View." *Extrapolation* 15 (1974): 161–73.

Grace, Sherrill E. "Articulating the 'Space Between': Atwood's Untold Stories and Fresh Beginnings." In Grace and Weir, pp. 1–16.

______. "Margaret Atwood and the Poetics of Duplicity." In Davidson and Davidson, pp. 55–68.

______. "Quest for the Peaceable Kingdom: Urban/Rural Codes in Roy, Laurence, and Atwood." In *Women Writers and the City: Essays in Feminist Literary Criticism,* edited by Susan Merrill Squier, pp. 193–209. Knoxville: Univ. of Tennessee Press, 1984.

______. *Violent Duality: A Study of Margaret Atwood.* Montreal: Véhicule Press, 1980.

Grace, Sherrill E., and Lorraine Weir, eds. *Margaret Atwood: Language, Text, and System.* Vancouver: Univ. of British Columbia Press, 1983.

Graves, Robert. *The Greek Myths.* 1955. Rev. ed. 2 vols. Harmondsworth: Penguin, 1960.

______. *The White Goddess: A Historical Grammar of Poetic Myth.* New York: Vintage Books, 1958.

Grimm, Jacob, and Wilhelm Grimm. *The Complete Grimm's Fairy Tales.* Translated by Margaret Hunt with James Stern. 1944. Reprint. New York: Pantheon Books, 1972.

Gubar, Susan, " 'The Blank Page' and the Issues of Female Creativity." *Critical Inquiry* 2 (1981): 243–63.

Guédon, Marie-Françoise. "*Surfacing:* Amerindian Themes and Shamanism." In Grace and Weir, pp. 91–111.

Hammond, Karla. "An Interview with Margaret Atwood." *American Poetry Review* 8, no. 5 (1979): 27–29.

Hansen, Elaine Tuttle. "Fiction and (Post)Feminism in Atwood's *Bodily Harm.*" *Novel* 19, no. 1 (1985): 5–21.

Hillman, James. *Re-Visioning Psychology.* New York: Harper and Row, 1975.

Hinz, Evelyn J. "Contemporary North American Literary Primitivism: *Deliverance* and *Surfacing.*" In *Other Voices, Other Views,* edited by Robin Winks, pp. 150–71. Westport, Conn.: Greenwood Press, 1978.

Hirsch, Marianne. "Spiritual Bildung: The Beautiful Soul as Paradigm." In *The Voyage In: Fictions of Female Development,* edited by Elizabeth Abel, Marianne Hirsch, and Elizabeth Langland, pp. 23–48. Hanover, N.H.: Univ. Press of New England, 1983.

Holland, Norman N., and Leona F. Sherman. "Gothic Possibilities." In *Gender and Reading,* edited by Elizabeth A. Flynn and Patrocinio P. Schweickart, pp. 215–33. Baltimore: Johns Hopkins Univ. Press, 1986.

Homans, Margaret. " 'Syllables of Velvet': Dickinson, Rossetti, and the Rhetorics of Sexuality." *Feminist Studies* 11 (1985): 569–93.

Homer. *The Odyssey.* Translated by Robert Fitzgerald. Garden City, N.Y.: Anchor-Doubleday, 1963.

Hutcheon, Linda. "From Poetic to Narrative Structures: The Novels of Margaret Atwood." In Grace and Weir, pp. 17–31.

Irigaray, Luce. *This Sex Which Is Not One.* Translated by Catherine Porter with Carolyn Burke. 1977. Reprint. Ithaca: Cornell Univ. Press, 1979.

Irvine, Lorna. "One Woman Leads to Another." In Davidson and Davidson, pp. 95–106.

———. "A Psychological Journey: Mothers and Daughters in English-Canadian Fiction." In Davidson and Broner, pp. 242–52.

———. *Sub/Versions: Canadian Fiction By Women.* Toronto: ECW Press, 1986.

Jacobs, Jane. *The Question of Separatism: Quebec and the Struggle over Sovereignty.* New York: Vintage Books, 1981.

Jaynes, Julian. *The Origin of Consciousness in the Breakdown of the Bicameral Mind.* Boston: Houghton Mifflin, 1976.

Jones, Anne G. "Margaret Atwood: Songs of the Transformer, Songs of the Transformed." *Hollins Critic* 16, no. 3 (1979): 1–15.

Jung, C. G. *Four Archetypes.* Translated by R. F. C. Hull. Princeton: Princeton Univ. Press, 1973.

Kerenyi, Carl. "Koré." In *Essays on a Science of Mythology,* edited by C. G. Jung and Carl Kerenyi, and translated by R. F. C. Hull, pp. 101–55. Princeton: Princeton Univ. Press, 1950. Reprint. New York: Harper Torchbooks, 1963.

Kermode, Frank. "Secrets and Narrative Sequence." *Critical Inquiry,* 1 (1980): 83–101.

Kirby, Ernest Theodore. "Shamanistic Theater: Origins and Evolution." In *Ur-Drama: The Origins of Theater,* pp. 1–31. New York: New York Univ. Press, 1975.

Klein, A. M. "Portrait of the Poet as Landscape." In *The Oxford Book of Canadian Verse in English,* edited by Margaret Atwood, pp. 129–33. Toronto: Oxford Univ. Press, 1982.

Kogawa, Joy. *Obasan.* 1981. Reprint. Boston: David R. Godine, 1982.

Kolodny, Annette. Commentary on paper read before the Modern Language Association Special Session, "Social Comment in the Novels of Margaret Atwood." New York City, 28 December 1986.

Kroetsch, Robert. *Badlands.* Toronto: New Press, 1975.

———. "Unhiding the Hidden: Recent Canadian Fiction." *Journal of Canadian Fiction* 3, no. 3 (1974): 43–45.

LaBarre, Weston. *The Ghost Dance: Origins of Religion.* Garden City, N.Y.: Doubleday, 1970.

Landy, Marcia. "The Silent Woman: Towards a Feminist Critique." In *The Authority of Experiences: Essays in Feminist Criticism,* edited by Arlyn Diamond and Lee R. Edwards, pp. 16–27. Amherst: Univ. of Massachusetts Press, 1977.

Lansing, J. Stephen. "The Sounding of the Text." In *Symposium of the Whole,* edited by Jerome Rothenberg and Diane Rothenberg, pp. 241–57. Berkeley: Univ. of California Press, 1983.

Leach, Maria, ed. *Standard Dictionary of Folklore.* New York: Funk and Wagnall, 1950.

Lecker, Robert. "Janus Through the Looking Glass: Atwood's First Three Novels." In Davidson and Davidson, pp. 177–204.
Lehtisalo, T. "Det Tod und die Wiedergeburt des kunftigen Schamanen." *Journal de la Société Finno-Ougrienne* 47 (1937): 1–34.
Lessing, Doris. *The Golden Notebook,* 1962. Reprint. New York: Bantam, 1973.
______. *Landlocked.* 1965. Reprint. New York: New American Library, 1970.
______. *Martha Quest.* 1952. Reprint. New York: New American Library, 1970.
______. *A Proper Marriage.* 1954. Reprint. New York: New American Library, 1970.
Lévi-Strauss, Claude. *Structural Anthropology.* Translated by Jackobsen and Schoept. New York: Doubleday, Anchor, 1967.
______. "The Effectiveness of Symbols." In *Tristes Tropiques,* pp. 181–202. New York: Atheneum, 1967.
Lippard, Lucy. *Overlay: Contemporary Art and the Art of Prehistory.* New York: Pantheon, 1983.
McCombs, Judith. "Atwood's Haunted Sequences: *The Circle Game, The Journals of Susanna Moodie,* and *Power Politics.*" In Davidson and Davidson, pp. 35–54.
______. Review of *Power Politics,* by Margaret Atwood. *Moving Out* 3, no. 2 (Spring 1973): 54–69.
McGregor, Gaile. *The Wacousta Syndrome: Explorations in the Canadian Landscape.* Toronto: Univ. of Toronto Press, 1985.
McLay, Catherine. "The Dark Voyage: *The Edible Woman* as Romance." In Davidson and Davidson, pp. 123–38.
MacLennan, Hugh. *Two Solitudes.* Toronto: Macmillan of Canada, 1945.
MacLulich, T. D. "Atwood's Adult Fairy Tale: Lévi-Strauss, Bettelheim, and *The Edible Woman.*" *Essays on Canadian Writing* 11 (1978): 111–29.
McMillan, Ann. " 'Fayre Systers Al': *The Flower and the Leaf* and *The Assembly of Ladies.*" *Tulsa Studies in Women's Literature* 1 (1982): 27–42.
McNall, Sally Allen. *Who Is in the House? A Psychological Study of Women's Fiction in America.* New York: Elsevier, 1981.
Mallinson, Jean. "Margaret Atwood." In *Canadian Writers and Their Works, Poetry Series,* edited by Robert Lecker, Jack David, and Ellen Quigley, pp. 17–81. Toronto: ECW Press, 1985.
Mandel, Eli. "Atwood's Poetic Politics." In Grace and Weir, pp. 53–66.
Marks, Elaine, and Isabelle de Courtivon. *New French Feminisms: An Anthology.* New York: Schocken Books, 1981.
Mathews, Robin. "Survival and Struggle in Canadian Literature: A Review of Margaret Atwood's *Survival.*" *This Magazine Is About Schools* 6, no. 4 (Winter 1972): 109–24.
Mendez-Egle, Barbara, ed. *Margaret Atwood: Reflection and Reality.* Living Author Series, no. 6. Edinburg, Tex.: Pan American Univ. Press, 1987.
Merivale, Patricia. "The Search for the Other Woman: Joan Didion and the Female Artist Parable." In *Gender Studies,* edited by Judith Spector, pp. 133–47. Bowling Green, Ohio: Popular Press, 1986.

Milner, Henry. *Politics in the New Quebec.* Toronto: McClelland and Stewart, 1978.

Moers, Ellen. *Literary Women.* Garden City, N.Y.: Anchor Books, 1977.

Moore, Brian, et al. *Canada.* New York: Time, Inc., 1963.

Morley, Patricia. "Survival, Affirmation, and Joy." *Lakehead University Review* 7 (Summer 1974): 21–30.

Moss, John. *The Canadian Novel Here and Now.* Toronto: NC Press, 1978.

Neumann, Erich. *The Great Mother: An Analysis of the Archetype.* Princeton: Princeton Univ. Press, 1972.

Northey, Margot. *The Haunted Wilderness: The Gothic and Grotesque in Canadian Fiction.* Toronto: Univ. of Toronto Press, 1976.

Oates, Joyce Carol. "A Conversation with Margaret Atwood." *Ontario Review* 9 (1978): 5–18.

———. "Margaret Atwood: Poems and Poet." *New York Times Book Review,* 21 May 1978.

Ortner, Sherry. "Is Female to Male as Nature Is to Culture?" In *Woman, Culture, and Society,* edited by Michelle Z. Rosaldo and Louise Lamphere, pp. 67–89. Stanford: Stanford Univ. Press, 1974.

Pagels, Elaine. *The Gnostic Gospels.* New York: Random House, 1979.

Patai, Raphael. *The Hebrew Goddess.* New York: Ktav Publishing House, 1967.

Pearsall, Derek, ed. *The Floure and the Leafe and The Assembly of Ladies.* Oxford: Alden, 1980.

Piercy, Marge. "Margaret Atwood: Beyond Victimhood." *American Poetry Review* 2 (1973): 41–44.

Polk, James. "Lives of the Hunted: The Canadian Animal Story and the National Identity." *Canadian Literature* 53 (Summer 1972): 51–59.

Pratt, Annis. *Archetypal Patterns in Women's Fiction.* Bloomington: Indiana Univ. Press, 1981.

———. "*Surfacing* and the Rebirth Journey." In Davidson and Davidson, pp. 139–57.

———. "Women and Nature in Modern Fiction." *Contemporary Literature* 12, no. 4 (1972): 476–90.

Prescott, Peter S. "No Balm in This Gilead." *Newsweek,* 17 February 1986, p. 70.

Radcliffe, Ann. *The Mysteries of Udolpho.* 1794. Reprint. Oxford: Oxford Univ. Press, 1981.

Radway, Janice A. *Reading the Romance: Women, Patriarchy, and Popular Literature.* Chapel Hill: Univ. of North Carolina Press, 1984.

———. "The Utopian Impulse in Popular Literature: Gothic Romances and 'Feminist' Protest." *American Quarterly* 33, no. 2 (Summer 1981): 140–62.

Rank, Otto. *Beyond Psychology.* New York: Dover, 1958.

Rasmussen, Knud. *The Intellectual Culture of the Iglulik Eskimos.* Copenhagen: Gyldendalske Boghandel, 1929.

———. *The Netsilik Eskimos: Social Life and Spiritual Culture.* Copenhagen: Gyldendalske Boghandel, Nordisk Forlag, 1931.

Reaney, James. Editorial. *Alphabet,* December 1963, p. 3.

______. *Poems.* Edited by Germaine Warkentin. Toronto: New Press, 1972.

Rich, Adrienne. *Of Woman Born: Motherhood as Experience and Institution.* New York: W. W. Norton, 1976. Reprint. New York: Bantam, 1977.

Rigney, Barbara Hill. *Madness and Sexual Politics in the Feminist Novel: Studies in Bronte, Woolf, Lessing and Atwood.* Madison: Univ. of Wisconsin Press, 1978.

Rogers, Linda. "Margaret the Magician." *Canadian Literature* 60 (1974): 83–85.

Rosenberg, Jerome H. *Margaret Atwood.* Boston: Twayne, 1984.

______. " 'Of Such Is the Kingdom . . .': Margaret Atwood's *Two-Headed Poems.*" *Essays on Canadian Writing* 16 (1979–80): 130–39.

Rosowski, Susan J. "Margaret Atwood's *Lady Oracle:* Social Mythology and the Gothic Novel." *Research Studies* 49, no. 2 (1981): 87–98.

Ross, Catherine Sheldrick. "Nancy Drew as Shaman: Atwood's *Surfacing.*" *Canadian Literature* 84 (1980): 7–17.

______. "A Singing Spirit: Female Rites of Passage in *Klee Wyck, Surfacing,* and *The Diviners.*" *Atlantis* 4, no. 1 (1978): 86–94.

Rothenberg, Jerome, ed. *Technicians of the Sacred: A Range of Poetries from Africa, America, Asia and Oceania.* Garden City, N.Y.: Anchor, 1969.

Rothenberg, Jerome, and Diane Rothenberg, eds. *Symposium of the Whole: A Range of Discourse Towards an Ethnopoetics.* Berkeley: Univ. of California Press, 1983.

Rubenstein, Roberta. *Boundaries of the Self: Gender, Culture, Fiction.* Champaign: Univ. of Illinois Press, 1987.

Sale, Roger. *Fairy Tales and Afterward.* Cambridge: Harvard Univ. Press, 1978.

Sandler, Linda. "Interview with Margaret Atwood." *Malahat Review,* no. 41 (January 1977): 7–27.

Scarborough, Margaret N. "Songs of Eleusis: The Quest for Self in the Poetry of Sylvia Plath, Anne Sexton, and Adrienne Rich." Ph.D. diss., Univ. of Washington, 1978.

Schafer, Edward H. *The Divine Woman: Dragon Ladies and Rain Maidens in T'ang Literature.* San Francisco: North Point Press, 1980.

Schechner, Richard. *Essays on Performance Theory, 1970–76.* New York: Drama Book Specialists, 1977.

Scholem, Gershom. *On the Kabbalah and Its Symbolism.* Translated by Ralph Manheim. New York: Schocken Books, 1965.

Schreiber, LeAnne. Interview with Margaret Atwood. *Vogue,* 26 January 1986, pp. 208–10.

Showalter, Elaine. "Feminist Criticism in the Wilderness." In *Writing and Sexual Difference,* edited by Elizabeth Abel, pp. 9–35. Chicago: Univ. of Chicago Press, 1982.

Snitow, Ann Barr. "Mass Market Romance: Pornography for Women Is Different." In *Powers of Desire: The Politics of Sexuality,* edited by Ann Snitow, Christine Stansell, and Sharon Thompson, pp. 295–63. New York: Monthly Review Press, 1983.

Snyder, Gary. *Earth House Hold.* New York: New Directions, 1969.

Spacks, Patricia Meyer. *The Adolescent Idea.* New York: Basic Books, 1981.

Steele, James. "The Literary Criticism of Margaret Atwood." In Cappon, pp. 73–81.

Stiller, Nikki. "Eve's Orphans: Mothers and Daughters in Mediaeval English Literature." In Davidson and Broner, pp. 22–32.

Sullivan, Rosemary. "Breaking the Circle." *Malahat Review,* no. 41 (January 1977): 30–41.

Thomas, Audrey. "Topic of Cancer." *Books in Canada,* October 1981, pp. 9–12.

Thomas, Clara. "*Lady Oracle:* The Narrative of a Fool-Heroine." In Davidson and Davidson, pp. 159–75.

Thrall, William Flint, Addison Hibbard, and C. Hugh Holman. *A Handbook to Literature.* Rev. ed. Indianapolis: Bobbs-Merrill, Odyssey Press, 1960.

Todorov, Tzvetan. *The Poetics of Prose.* Translated by Richard Howard. Ithaca: Cornell Univ. Press, 1977.

Trofimenkoff, Susan Mann. *The Dream of a Nation.* Toronto: Macmillan of Canada, 1982.

Turner, Victor. *The Ritual Process: Structure and Anti-Structure.* Chicago: Aldine, 1969.

Tzara, Tristan. *Oeuvres Complètes.* Vol. 4, 1947–63. Paris: Flammarion, 1975.

VanSpanckeren, Kathryn. "Magic in the Early Novels of Margaret Atwood." In Mendez-Egle, pp. 1–11.

Von Franz, Marie Louise. *Puer Aeternus.* New York: Spring Publications, 1970.

Wagner, Linda W. "The Making of *Selected Poems,* the Process of Surfacing." In Davidson and Davidson, pp. 81–94.

Wasson, R. G., Carl A. P. Ruck, and Albert Hofmann. *The Road to Eleusis: Unveiling the Secret of the Mysteries.* New York: Harcourt Brace Jovanovich, 1978.

Weir, Lorraine. "Atwood in a Landscape." In Grace and Weir, pp. 143–53.

Wilson, Sharon R. "Bluebeard's Forbidden Room: Gender Images in Margaret Atwood's Visual and Literary Art." *American Review of Canadian Studies* 16, no. 4 (Winter 1986): 385–97.

———. "Camera Images in Margaret Atwood's Novels." In Mendez-Egle, pp. 29–57.

Wollstonecraft, Mary. *Maria, or the Wrongs of Woman.* 1798. Reprint. New York: W. W. Norton, 1975.

Wood, Gayle. "On Margaret Atwood's *Selected Poems.*" *American Poetry Review* 8, no. 5 (1979): 30–32.

Woodcock, George. "Metamorphosis and Survival: Notes on the Recent Poetry of Margaret Atwood." In Grace and Weir, pp. 125–42.

———. "Transformation Mask for Margaret Atwood." *Malahat Review,* no. 41 (1977): 54–56.

# *Notes on Contributors*

*Elizabeth R. Baer* is Dean of the College and Professor of English at Washington College, Maryland. She has published on Charlotte Brontë and Jean Rhys and served on a national advisory board for the National Endowment for the Humanities and the American Library Association. Dr. Baer regularly reviews scholarly books for *Choice* and *Booklist* and is currently preparing a book-length manuscript on the diaries of five nineteenth-century Virginia women.

*Pamela Bromberg* is Associate Professor and Chair of the English Department at Simmons College in Boston. Her recent publications include essays on Margaret Drabble, Lillian Hellman, and William Blake. She continues to work on narrative technique in contemporary women's fiction.

*David Buchbinder* teaches English in the School of Communication and Cultural Studies at the Curtin University of Technology, Western Australia. His scholarly interests include contemporary literary theory, with particular reference to poetry, and Renaissance literature, especially drama. He is currently writing a text for students on contemporary theories of reading, applied to poetry.

*Jan Garden Castro* has taught at Southern Illinois University at Edwardsville, Webster University, and Lindenwood College. She has published essays and poetry, and was founding editor of *River Styx* (St. Louis) and founder of the Margaret Atwood Society. Her critical biography *The Art and Life of Georgia O'Keeffe,* published by Crown in 1985, is in its sixth printing.

*Arnold E. Davidson,* Professor of English at Michigan State University, has coedited *The Art of Margaret Atwood: Essays in Criticism* and authored books on Mordecai Richler, Jean Rhys, and Joseph Conrad. A Canadian citizen, he is the author or coauthor of some sixty essays, mostly on contemporary British and Canadian literature. He is past copresident of the Margaret Atwood Society, has previously published five articles on her poetry and fiction, has presented numerous papers on her fiction, and has organized and chaired two MLA annual convention panels on Atwood's work.

*Francis X. Gillen* is Professor of English at the University of Tampa and Director of its Honors Program. His extensive publications on the modern novel and drama include articles on Virginia Woolf, E. M. Forster, Mary McCarthy, Donald Barthelme, Joseph Heller, Henry James, Tennessee Williams, and Harold Pinter. Currently he is coediting the *Pinter Newsletter* and working on a book on Harold Pinter.

*Sherrill E. Grace* is Professor of English at the University of British Columbia. She has published *Violent Duality: A Study of Margaret Atwood* (1980) and *The Voyage That Never Ends: Malcolm Lowry's Fiction* (1982) and coedited the collection of essays *Margaret Atwood: Language, Text, and System* (1983). The author of thirty articles on modern literature and interdisciplinary studies, she has recently finished a book-length study on expressionism in North America.

*Gayle Greene,* Assistant Professor of English at Scripps College in Claremont, California, has published numerous articles on Shakespeare, feminist criticism, and contemporary women writers. She coedited *The Woman's Part: Feminist Criticism of Shakespeare* (1980) and *Making a Difference: Feminist Literary Criticism* (1985). Currently she is working on a book, *Re-Visions: Contemporary Women Writers and the Tradition,* forthcoming from the University of Illinois Press.

*Lorna Irvine,* a Canadian citizen, is Associate Professor of English and American Studies at George Mason University. She is the author of *Sub/Version,* a study of Canadian women writers, and has published and presented papers on Canadian literature throughout Canada, the United States, and Europe. She is currently working on a book-length study of modernity in Canadian fiction entitled "Maternal Metaphors."

*Judith McCombs* is currently working on a book-length manuscript, "Margaret Atwood: Metamorphoses, Evidence, and Archetypes," and coauthoring, with Carole L. Palmer, an Atwood bibliography. A Canadian Embassy Senior Fellow for 1985–86, and Professor on extended leave from the Center for Creative Studies College of Art and Design, Detroit, she has published two books of poetry, *Sisters and Other Selves* and *Against Nature: Wilderness Poems.* Her *Critical Essays on Margaret Atwood* (G. K. Hall) appeared in 1988.

*Ann McMillan* received a doctorate in English from Indiana University and is currently a writer and editor in Richmond, Virginia. Her publications include a modern verse translation of Chaucer's *Legend of Good Women,* with an introduction discussing the tradition of women destroyed by love (Rice University Press, 1987) and articles on medieval women. Currently she is writing on women's responses to erotic texts.

*Roberta Rubenstein* is Professor of Literature and Director of the Women's Studies Program at American University in Washington, D.C. She is the author of *The Novelistic Vision of Doris Lessing: Breaking the Forms of Consciousness* (1979) and *Boundaries of the Self: Gender, Culture, Fiction* (1987). The latter book, a study of six contemporary women writers, includes a chapter on Margaret Atwood; she has also published articles on Atwood, Virginia Woolf, and Margaret Drabble.

*June Schlueter* is Associate Professor of English at Lafayette College, Easton, Pennsylvania. She is the author of *Metafictional Characters in Modern Drama* (Columbia University Press, 1979), *The Plays and Novels of Peter Handke* (University of Pittsburgh Press, 1981), and *Arthur Miller* (Frederick Ungar, 1987). She has coedited reference volumes on modern American literature and the British novel and is coeditor of *Shakespeare Bulletin.*

*Kathryn VanSpanckeren* is Associate Professor of English at the University of Tampa; she coedited *John Gardner: Critical Perspectives* (1982) and has edited the *Margaret Atwood Society Newsletter.* President-elect of the Atwood Society, she has published poetry and critical essays on contemporary authors including Atwood and is involved in international literary programs. Currently she is completing a short history of American literature for non-Americans.

*Kathleen Vogt* recently taught a senior seminar on Margaret Atwood at Wheaton College (Norton, Mass.), where she is Professor of English and Chair of the Department. Her interests include Irish literature (particularly Yeats), contemporary women writers, and writers about nature (particularly contemporary Cape Cod writers). An earlier version of the essay in this volume was presented at the special "Animal Rights" section of the MLA annual convention in 1980.

*Sharon R. Wilson* is Professor of English and Women's Studies at the University of Northern Colorado. Past copresident of the Margaret Atwood Society, she has published on romance, film, and modern literature, including a number of articles on Atwood. Currently she is working on fairy tales in Atwood's work; her articles on fairy tales in *The Edible Woman* and *The Handmaid's Tale* are forthcoming.

# Index


*Acta Victoriana,* 5–6
*Adam Bede* (Eliot), xxii, 12–13
Adams, Henry, 201
*Aeneid* (Virgil), 215
"After the Flood, We," 190
"Against Still Life," 132
Ainsley (*The Edible Woman*), 17, 18, 101
"All Bread," 177–78
*Alphabet,* 6
"America as the aging demon lover," 142, 143, 145–46
Amnesty International, xx, xxvi, 234, 237
Anansi Press, xxvii, 227–28
*Anatomy of Criticism* (Frye), 6
*Animal Farm* (Orwell), 106
Animals, xxi, 163–65, 180–82; and death, 171–75; human connection with, xxvi, 168–71; and metamorphosis, 175–78; victimization of, 165–68; in women's literature, 179–80
*Animals in That Country, The,* 132, 146, 161 n, 170–71, 207, 210; animals in, 166–67, 174–75, 180
Anna (*Surfacing*), 1–2, 39
*Anna's Pet,* xxi
Anorexia nervosa, xxii, 15, 18
"April, Radio, Planting, Easter," 177, 178
*Archetypal Patterns in Women's Fiction* (Pratt), 99
"Arctic Syndrome: dream fox," 170
Arthur (*Lady Oracle*), 58, 60
*Assembly of Ladies, The,* 50–51
Astrov, Margot, 187, 200
"At first I was given centuries," 124, 132
Athene (*The Odyssey*), 124, 134
Atwood, Margaret: on ambiguous endings, 220–21; on Canada, 223–24, 229–30; on Cuba, 235–38; as feminist, 9–10, 39; on her education, 215–16, 227–28, 234, 243; influences on, 24, 215–16, 227, 233; on language, 226–27; on media, 238–40; political involvement of, xx, xxvi–xxvii; on political writing, 102, 233–34, 241; and publishers, 220; on quest stories, 226; on research, 218; on the Writers' Union of Canada, 228–29; on writing about women's experience, 230–33; on writing as self-expression, 243; on zoos, 163, 181–82
"Atwoods as Birds," 212
"Atwood's Gorgon Touch" (Davey), 172
"Atwood Walking Backwards" (Davey), 3
Auerbach, Nina, 100 n
Austen, Jane, xiv, xxiii, 49–50, 56, 225
Avison, Margaret, 6
"Axiom," 132

Bachelard, Gaston, 203
*Badlands* (Kroetsch), 43
"Basic Victim Positions," 2, 9
Berger, John, 87
Berton, Pierre, 243
*Beyond Psychology* (Rank), 202
Bible, 216, 226
Bird imagery, 32, 39. *See also* Animals

Blais, Marie-Claire, 9
*Bluebeard's Egg,* xix, 42, 209
"Boarding House, The" (Joyce), 37
*Bodily Harm,* 85, 89–90, 94–95, 102, 221–22; ambiguity of, 86–87, 90–94; and Atwood's visual art, 206, 209, 212; Canadian nationalism in, 87–89; female text in, 89, 95–99; victimization of women in, xxiv, 87, 95–97, 103–4
Boleyn, Anne, 209, 210
"Book of Ancestors," 127, 135–37
Bosch, Hieronymus, 208
*Bostonians, The* (James), 43
Brewer, Chuck (*Lady Oracle*), 58
Brontë, Charlotte, xiv, 53–54, 203, 220–21
Brontë, Emily, xiv
Bruegel, Pieter, 208
Buckler, Ernest, 3
Buckley, Jerome H., 7
*Bush Garden* (Frye), 149
"Bus to Alliston, Ontario, The," 191

Campbell, Joseph, 184
Canada: Americanization of, 229; colonial mentality of, 1–2, 147–48; as Crone, 144, 146; as female, xxii, 96–97, 148, 150; humor of, 8; land of, 144–45; as neglected child, 148; as primitive society, 70; reading audience in, 227, 243; separatism in, 151–52, 155, 158–59, 223; shamanism in, 187–88; struggle literature of, 4–5; as victim, xxii, 2–4, 9, 11, 87–89, 96–97, 149–50. *See also* Canadian literature
"Canadian-American Relations: Surviving the Eighties," 11, 148
Canadian literature, xiii, 2–5, 6, 9–10, 100n, 148
"Canadian Monsters," 8, 192
Canlit. *See* Canadian literature
Cappon, Paul, 3
Carpenter, Edmund, 195
Carpenter, Mary Wilson, 118
Carrier, Roch, 3
"Carrion Spring" (Stegner), 3
Carter, Angela, 233
Castro, Fidel, 236
Catherine Morland (*Northanger Abbey*), 57
"Causes of Consciousness" (Jaynes), 153
Chatterjee, Gopal (*The Handmaid's Tale*), 118
Chris (*Life Before Man*), 66, 67, 68, 70, 71; and Elizabeth, 73, 74, 198; suicide of, 78, 198
Chuck Brewer (*Lady Oracle*), 58
Circe ("Circe/Mud Poems"), 133–34, 137–38; as victim and victimizer, 125, 126, 127, 128, 130–32
Circe (*The Odyssey*), xxv, 125
"Circe/Mud Poems," 122, 127, 130–32, 194–97. *See also* Circe; *Selected Poems*
*Circle Game, The,* xxv, 122, 139, 142–43, 146–50, 173–74, 206; shamanism in, 189–90, 192
Cixous, Hélène, 64, 96, 98
Clara (*The Edible Woman*), 16, 101
Coleman, Victor, 3
"Comic Books vs. History," 173
Commander (*The Handmaid's Tale*), 110–11, 116, 118
*Communities of Women* (Auerbach), 100n
*Consuelo* (Sand), 225
*Countess of Rudelstadt, The* (Sand), 225–26
Crescent Moon, Maryann (*The Handmaid's Tale*), 112, 118, 119
Cuba, 235, 238
"Curse of Eve—Or, What I Learned in School, The," 9

Daly, Mary, 213n
Daniel (*Bodily Harm*), 86–87, 93–94, 95, 198
Darnford (*Maria*), 55–56
Davey, Frank, 3, 83n
David (*Surfacing*), 1, 38, 40
Davidson, Arnold E., 84n
Davidson, Cathy, 115, 117
Davies, Robertson, 234
"Daybooks," 190
"Death as Bride," 208–9
de Beauvoir, Simone, xvi
*Deceived with Kindness* (Garnett), 43
de Courtivron, Isabelle, 98
Delacourt, Mrs. (*Lady Oracle*), 21–22, 102
Demeter, 36–38, 42, 43, 44, 45

*Les Demoiselles d'Avignon* (Picasso), 186
"Descent Through the Carpet," 189–90
Dewdney, Selwin, 224
Diamond, Stanley, 187
"Diary Down Under," 10
Dickens, Charles, 233
Dickinson, Emily, xiv
"Digging," 176
Dinah Morris (*Adam Bede*), 12–13
"Disneyland of the Soul, A," 35
Doctorow, E. L., 10, 234
Donne, John, 141 n
"Don't Expect the Bears to Dance," 163
*Double Persephone,* 46 n, 171–72, 189, 192, 206
"Double Voice, The," 172
Douglas, Mary, 70, 83–84 n
Drabble, Margaret, 233
"Dreams of the Animals," 167–68, 207
Duncan (*The Edible Woman*), 17, 18–20, 23
Du Plessis, Rachel Blau, 32, 36, 44

*Each Man's Son* (Wiseman), 3
Eating, 26–27, 33 n, 109–10, 206, 207; and self-image, 15, 16, 18
"Eating Fire," 139
*Edible Woman, The,* 13–14, 18–20, 23, 60, 101, 212, 217–18; eating in, xxii, 15, 16, 18, 207; marriage plot in, 14–18
"Eleven Years of *Alphabet,*" 6, 150
Eliade, Mircea, 184, 185, 186, 187, 194–95, 197, 202
Eliot, George, xiv, xxii, 12–13, 233
Eliot, T. S., 82
Elizabeth Schoenhof (*Life Before Man*). *See* Schoenhof, Elizabeth
Emily (*The Mysteries of Udolpho*), 52–53, 57
"Encounters with the Element Man," 146
"End to Audience?, An," 102
Engel, Marian, 234
Erishkigal, 192
"Euridice," 191, 192
Eurycleia (*The Odyssey*), 134
Eurydice, 192
Eve (*Paradise Lost*), 12
"Evening Train Station, Before Departure," 190
"Eventual Proteus," 190
Even-Zohar, Itamar, 123
"Explorers, The," 190, 192

"Fall and All," 161 n
Faulkner, William, xxvii, 233
Felicia (*Lady Oracle*), 59–60, 62
Feminist criticism, xi–xii, xx–xxi, 35, 36
"Feminist Criticism in the Wilderness" (Showalter), 36, 46 n
"Feminist *1984*, A" (Davidson), 115
Findley, Timothy, 10, 234
"First Neighbours," 128–29
"First Prayer," 193
"Fishing for Eel Totems," 174
"Fitcher's Feathered Bird" (Grimm), xxii, 24, 27, 32, 208–9
"Five Poems for Grandmothers," 190
Folklore, 24–25
Forché, Carolyn, 203, 241
Foster, Joan (*Lady Oracle*), 20–23, 49, 56, 61–64, 102, 197; victimization of, 57–61
Foster, John Wilson, 182 n
"Four Auguries," 126, 134
*Frankenstein* (Shelley), 210–11
Fred (*The Handmaid's Tale*). *See* Commander
Freud, Sigmund, 35, 93
Friedan, Betty, xvi
Friedrich, Paul, 37
Front de libération du Québec (FLQ), 152
Frye, Northrop, 6, 88, 91, 148, 149

Galt, George, 164
Garnett, Angelica, 43
Gaskell, Elizabeth, xiv
Gerstenberger, Donna, 182 n
*Gift, The* (Hyde), 242
Gilbert, Sandra M., 30, 54, 95, 203
Gilead. *See The Handmaid's Tale*
Ginsberg, Allen, xxv, 143
*Golden Notebook, The* (Lessing), 203
Gopal Chatterjee (*The Handmaid's Tale*), 118
Gordimer, Nadine, 10
Gothic novel, xxiii, awareness of death in, 184; chastity in, 50–52;

Gothic novel (*continued*)
fantasy in, 52–54; female victimization in, 48–49; "mixed Gothic" form of, 56–57, 61; naturalism in, 54–56
Grace, Sherrill E., 58, 63, 65, 81, 84 n, 122, 151, 223
Grant, George, 4
Grave, F. P., 3
Graves, Robert, xiv, 9, 185
Gray, Paul, xix
*Great Expectations* (Dickens), 221
*Great Gatsby, The* (Fitzgerald), 235
Greek mythology, 215, 216, 226. *See also* Homeric model; *Odyssey, The*
Green, Lesje (*Life Before Man*), 67, 69, 70, 74, 102; change in, 76–79, 82; and Nate, 77–78, 79, 80, 81; and process of time, 66, 68, 71
Gregg, Linda, 233
Grenada, 221–22
*Grimm's Fairy Tales,* 24
Grumbach, Doris, xix
Gubar, Susan, 54, 95, 100 n, 203
Guēdon, Marie-Françoise, 42, 183
*Gutenberg Galaxy, The* (McLuhan), 7

Hades, 37, 38
Haggard, H. Rider, 217
Hammond, Karla, 170
*Handmaid's Tale, The,* xix, xxiv, 101, 102, 103–5, 110–11, 113–14; and Atwood's visual art, 208, 212; chastity in, 51; food in, 109–10; history in, 114–16, 119–21; nature imagery in, 105–7, 111–12; odors in, 108–9; pollution in, 107–8; sexism in historical notes to, xxv, 112, 116
"Hanged Man," 211–12
Hardy, Thomas, xx
*Haunted Wilderness: The Gothic and Grotesque in Canadian Fiction, The* (Northey), 184
"Head Against White," 126, 134–35
Hecate, 37, 38
Heilbrun, Carolyn, 197
Helen (*The Odyssey*), 124, 125, 137
"Hesitation Outside the Door," 209
Hetty Sorrel (*Adam Bede*), 12
Hidgins, Jack, 100 n
Hillman, James, 201–2
Holland, Norman, 51
"Hollow Men, The" (Eliot), 82
Homans, Margaret, 13
Homer, 122
Homeric model: Circe and the Siren in, 127–32; female characters in, 125–26; fidelity in, 137–38; and gender politics, 122–23, 140; Penelope in, 132–37; polysystems of, 123–24; space and time in, 126–27, 139
*Howl* (Ginsberg), xxv, 143
Hutcheon, Linda, 81
Hyde, Lewis, 241

"Ice Women vs. Earth Mothers," 8–9
"Idea of Canada, The," 142, 143–45, 146
*Index on Censorship,* 238
*Indian Rock Paintings* (Dewdrey), 224
"Insect in Red Gown with Bouquet," 212
*Interlunar,* xix, 45, 46 n, 191–92, 206
International Margaret Atwood Society, xix
*Interpretation of Dreams, The* (Freud), 93
*Invention of the World, The* (Hodgins), 100 n
Irigaray, Luce, 13, 99
Irvine, Lorna, 45, 46 n
"Is Female to Male as Nature is to Culture?" (Ortner), 112 n
*Is It the Sun, Philibert?* (Carrier), 3
"Is/Not," 127, 134

Jacobson, Roman, 13
Jake (*Bodily Harm*), 86, 87, 91
James, Henry, 43
*Jane Eyre* (Brontë), 53–54, 203
Janine (*The Handmaid's Tale*), 108, 109
Jaynes, Julian, 151, 153, 154, 155, 156, 185
Jemima (*Maria*), 55
Jewett, Sarah Orne, 179
Joan Foster (*Lady Oracle*). *See* Foster, Joan
Jocasta ( Bodily Harm), 87
Joe (*Surfacing*), 29, 30, 39
James, D. G., 6
Jong, Erica, xx, 9
*Journals of Susanna Moodie, The,* 141 n, 145, 146, 160, 191, 206, 207; animals in, 166, 170, 172; loneliness

in, 128–29; shamanism in, 199–200; sources of, 216–17
"Journey to the Interior," 190
Joy (*The Handmaid's Tale*), 106
Joyce, James, 37, 179
Jung, Carl, 29, 202
"Juniper Tree, The" (Grimm), 24, 27

Kermode, Frank, 89–90
Kirby, Ernest Theodore, 185
Klein, A. M., 144, 148, 150
Knotly Wade (*The Handmaid's Tale*), 115–16
Kogawa, Joy, 38, 43
Kolodny, Annette, 121 n
Kroetsch, Robert, 43

LaBarre, Weston, 185
"Lady and Executioner with Axe," 210
"Lady and Sinister Figure," 209–10, 212
*Lady Oracle,* xxii, 5, 197, 207, 212, 220; as Gothic novel, xxiii, 49–50, 56–58, 61; mirror imagery in, 13–14, 20–23; motherhood in, 45, 102
"Late August," 126
"Laugh of the Medusa, The" (Cixous), 96
Laurence, Margaret, 3
Lawrence, D. H., xx
Layton, Irving, 3
Lee, Dennis, 151–52, 157
Lesje Green (*Life Before Man*). *See* Green, Lesje
Lessing, Doris, 45, 69, 71, 83 n, 203
"Letter from Persephone," 45, 191
Lévesque, René, 152
Lévi-Strauss, Claude, 185, 187
*Life Before Man,* xxiii–xxiv, 66–67, 102, 144, 164, 165, 198; hope in, 81–83; as realist fiction, 65–66; research for, 218, 243; time in, 67–72; transformations of characters in, 72–81
Limpkin, Wilfred (*The Handmaid's Tale*), 114, 118, 121
Lippard, Lucy, 187
"Literary Criticism of Margaret Atwood, The" (Steele), 3
Livesay, Dorothy, 3
"Looking In A Mirror," 141 n
Lora (*Bodily Harm*), xxiv, 87, 91, 92, 97, 197; and Rennie, 98, 198
Lou, Aunt (*Lady Oracle*), 22
Loup-garou motif, xxii–xxiii, 25–27, 30–31, 33
Lower, A. R. M., 148
Luke (*The Handmaid's Tale*), 109
Lydia, Aunt (*The Handmaid's Tale*), 104–5

MacAlpin, Marian (*The Edible Woman*), xxii, 15, 17–18, 60, 101; and Duncan, 18–20, 23; and mirror imagery, 14–17
McCarthy, Mary, xix
McCombs, Judith, 211
MacEwen, Gwendolyn, 3, 6
McGregor, Gaile, 100 n
MacLennan, Hugh, 152
McLuhan, Marshall, 6, 207
MacPherson, Jay, 220
*Madwoman in the Attic, The* (Gilbert and Gubar), 100 n
"Making of *Selected Poems,* the Process of Surfacing, The" (Wagner), 122
Mandel, Eli, 6
"Man Holding Woman's Body," 210–11
*Maria* (Wollstonecraft), xxiii, 54, 55–56, 60
Marian MacAlpin (*The Edible Woman*). *See* MacAlpin, Marian
Marks, Elaine, 98
"Marrying the Hangman," 210
"Marsh, Hawk," 178
Martha (*Life Before Man*), 68, 74, 82
*Martha Quest* (Lessing), 69, 83 n
Marvell, Andrew, 141 n
Maryann Crescent Moon (*The Handmaid's Tale*), 112, 118, 119
Mathews, Robin, 4, 9
"Mathews and Misrepresentation," 4–5
Matthews, J. P., 6
*Meaning of Aphrodite, The* (Friedrich), 37
*Mechanical Bride, The* (McLuhan), 207
Melville, Herman, 222, 234
*Memoirs of a Survivor* (Lessing), 71
Menelaus (*The Odyssey*), 137
"Message to Winnipeg" (Reaney), 143

*Metamorphoses* (Ovid), 215
*Middlemarch* (Eliot), 233
*Midnight Birds: Stories of Contemporary (American) Black Women Writers,* 10–11
"Migration: C. P. R., " 190
Millett, Kate, 9
Milton, John, xxii, 12
Minnow, Dr. (*Bodily Harm*), 88, 91, 197
Mirror imagery, 19–20, 30, 200; and female beauty, 12–13, 20–23; and loss of identity, 14–18; and woman as consumer item, 13–14
*Moby-Dick* (Melville), 222
Moers, Ellen, 32, 203
Moira (*The Handmaid's Tale*), 104, 109
Montoni (*The Mysteries of Udolpho*), 53
Moodie, Susanna, 216, 231–32
Moore, Brian, 148
"More and More," 180
Morland, Catherine (*Northanger Abbey*), 57
Morley, Patricia, 3
Morris, Dinah (*Adam Bede*), 12–13
*Mountain and the Valley, The* (Buckler), 3
"Mourners at Woman's Bier," 210, 211
*Mrs. Dalloway* (Woolf), 203
Munro, Alice, 234
*Murder in the Dark,* 206, 207
Muriel, Auntie (*Life Before Man*), 73–74, 75, 144
"My Poetic Principles," 143
*Mysteries of Udolpho, The* (Radcliffe), 49, 52–53

"Nasturtium," 190–91
Nate (*Life Before Man*), 66, 67, 68, 71, 73, 74; change in, 79–81, 82; determinism of, 69–70, 72; and Lesje, 77–78, 79, 80
"Nationalism, Limbo, and the Canadian Club," 6, 7–8
Nature imagery, 101, 105–7, 111–12. *See also* Animals
Nausicaa (*The Odyssey*), 137
"Newsreel: Man and Firing Squad," 192
Nichol, B. P., 3
Nick (*The Handmaid's Tale*), 108–9
"A Night in the Royal Ontario Museum," 174–75
"Night Poem," 191
*Northanger Abbey* (Austen), xxiii, 49, 56–58
Northey, Margot, 184
"Notes Towards a Poem That Can Never Be Written," 230

Oates, Joyce Carol, 7, 24
*Obasan* (Kogawa), 38, 43
Odysseus (*The Odyssey*), 125
Odysseus (*Selected Poems*), 124, 126, 129
*The Odyssey* (Homer), 122, 123–24, 125, 137. *See also* Greek mythology; Homeric model; *Selected Poems*
Offred (*The Handmaid's Tale*), xxv, 103, 104, 105, 106, 107–10; narrative of, 113, 114; uncertain fate of, 111, 116
"On Being a 'Woman Writer,'" 9, 220
*One Hundred Years of Solitude* (García Márquez), 222
"One Woman Leads to Another" (Irvine), 46 n
"One Writer's Use of Grimm," 33 n
*Origins of Consciousness in the Breakdown of the Bicameral Mind* (Jaynes), 151
"Orpheus," 191
Ortner, Sherry, 112 n
Orwell, George, 106
Ovid, 215
*Oxford Book of Canadian Short Stories, The,* xvi

Pachter, Charles, 146–47
*Paradise Lost* (Milton), xxii, 12
Paris (*The Odyssey*), 137
Paul (*Bodily Harm*), 87, 88, 91, 94, 197, 198
Paul (*Lady Oracle*), 58, 60
Penelope (*The Odyssey*), 124, 125, 126, 132–33
Penelope (*Selected Poems*), 125, 127, 133–35, 138; transformation of, 135–37
Percival, Mr. (*Surfacing*), 25, 33 n
Persephone, 36–38, 42, 43, 44, 45, 192
"Persephone Departing," 189
Peter Wollander (*The Edible Woman*), 14–19
Pieixoto, Professor (*The Handmaid's Tale*), 112, 116, 117, 118, 119, 120

Piercy, Marge, xx, 9
Plath, Sylvia, xvi, xx, 203
"Poetics of Duplicity, The," (Grace), 122
"Polysystem Theory" (Even-Zohar), 123
*Portrait of the Artist as a Young Man, A* (Joyce), 179–80
"Portrait of the Poet as Landscape" (Klein), 144
"Postcard," 90–91
*Power Politics,* 146, 156, 168–69, 180, 230; and Atwood's visual art, 205, 206, 207, 209, 211, 212
Pratt, Annis, 40, 41–42, 99, 179–80, 197
Prescott, Peter S., 116
*Pride and Prejudice* (Austen), 225
*Procedures for Underground,* 173, 174, 188–89, 192, 207
"Progressive Insanities of a Pioneer," 170–71
*Proper Marriage, A* (Lessing), 83n
"Psychological Journey: Mothers and Daughters in English-Canadian Fiction, A" (Irvine), 46n
"Puppet of the Wolf, The," 178
Purdy, Al, 6

Quest, Martha (*Martha Quest*), 69, 83n

Radcliffe, Ann, 49, 51, 52–53
Radway, Janice, 48, 50
Rasmussen, Knud, 187, 190, 193
Reaney, James, 6, 142, 143, 144, 145, 148, 150
Redmond (*Lady Oracle*), 59–60
"Red Shirt," 45
Rennie Wilford (*Bodily Harm*). *See* Wilford, Rennie
*Re-visioning Psychology* (Hillman), 207
"Rhetorics of Sexuality, The" (Homans), 13
Rhys, Jean, 54
Rich, Adrienne, 9, 203
Richler, Mordecai, 234
Rigney, Barbara Hill, 197
*Rite of Spring, The* (Stravinsky), 186
"Robber Bridegroom, The," 209
Rochester, Edward Fairfax (*Jane Eyre*), 53–54
Rosenberg, Jerome H., 151
Ross, W. W. E., 3
Rossetti, Christina, xii
Rothenberg, Jerome, 187
Roy, Gabrielle, 3
Royal Porcupine (*Lady Oracle*), 58, 60
"Royal Visit, The," (Reaney), 144
Rubinstein, Roberta, 71
Running Dog, Johnny (*The Handmaid's Tale*), 112

Sand, George, 225–26
Scarborough, Margaret, 32
Schoenhof, Elizabeth (*Life Before Man*), xxiii, 66, 67, 68, 70, 71–72, 102; change in, 75–76, 82; determinism of, 69, 72; and Lesje, 78–79; as shaman, 198
*Second Words,* xxi–xxii, 5–11, 230
"Secrets and Narrative Sequence" (Kermode), 90
*Selected Poems,* xxv, 15, 43, 122; as discourse on fidelity, 137–38; physical location of characters in, 126–27; polysystems of, 123–24; space and time in, 127, 138–39; transformation in, 132. *See also* Homeric model; *individual poems*
*Selected Poems II,* 151
"Settlers, The," 132, 190, 192
Sexton, Anne, xvi, 203
Shakespeare, William, xvi, 226–27
Shamanism, xxi, xxvi, 186–88, 198–200; and death, 192, 198; and descent theme, 188–92, 194–97; and feminism, 202–3; meaning of, 183–86, 201–3
*Shamanism: Archaic Techniques of Ecstasy* (Eliade), 187, 194–95
*She* (Haggard), 217–18
"She Considers Evading Him," 132
Shelley, Mary, xxiii, 210
Sherman, Leona, 51
Showalter, Elaine, 36, 46n
Siren (*The Odyssey*), 125
Siren (*Selected Poems*), 125–26, 127, 128, 129–30, 137
"Siren Song," 122, 127, 128, 176
Snitow, Ann, 52
"Snow" (Grove), 3

"Some Objects of Wood and Stone," 173–74
"Songs of the Hen's Head," 175
"Songs of the Transformed," 122, 169, 175–76, 193–94
Sorrel, Hetty (*Adam Bede*), 12
Spacks, Patricia Meyer, 53, 57
"Speeches for Doctor Frankenstein," 206, 210, 211
"Spring in the Igloo," 190
*Standard Dictionary of Folklore,* 25
Steele, James, 3, 4
Stegner, Wallace, 3
*Stone Angel, The* (Laurence), 3
Stowe, Harriet Beecher, xiv
Stuart, Mary, 209, 210
*Surfacing,* xxvi, 7, 11, 30, 41–42, 218–20, 224; animals in, 164, 181; Atwood on characters of, 219–20; Canada in, 1–2, 88, 159; as double-voiced discourse, 36, 38–39, 42–44; ending of, 222; female power in, 39–41; female victimization in, 60; and "Fitcher's Feathered Bird," 27–30; Indian myths in, 223–25; loss and silence themes of, 35–36, 38; as loup-garou story, xxii–xxiii, 25–27, 30–31; mother figure in, 44–45; procreation in, 101–2; as quest novel, 43–44; shamanism in, 189, 195, 197; visions in, 31–33, 41
"Survival, Affirmation, and Joy" (Morley), 3
*Survival: A Thematic Guide to Canadian Literature,* xxi, 10, 88, 144, 148, 158; animals in, 164, 165–66; Canada as victim in, xxii, 2, 9, 11; Canadian reaction to, 3–5, 242; colonial mentality in, 2, 147
Susannah Moodie, 216, 231
*Symposium of the Whole* (Rothenberg), 187

*Technicians of the Sacred* (Rothenberg), 187
"Termite Queen," 207, 212
"There Is Only One of Everything," 127, 135, 165
"They are hostile nations," 169
"Third Eye, The" (MacPherson), 220
"This Is a Photograph of Me," 138–39
*This Magazine,* 151, 152, 157
*This Sex* (Irigaray), 13
Thomas, Audrey, 9, 86
Thomas, Clara, 62
Thompson, John, 10
"Thoughts from Underground," 129
Tilney, General (*Northanger Abbey*), 57
Todorov, Tzvetan, 43
"To His Coy Mistress," 141n
"Towards a Sociology of English Canadian Literature" (Cappon), 3
*Tradition in Exile: A Comparative Study of Social Influences on the Development of Australian and Canadian Poetry in the Nineteenth Century* (Matthews), 6
"Travels Back," 8
"Tricks with Mirrors," 15, 20, 200
*Tristes Tropiques* (Lévi-Strauss), 187
Trudeau, Pierre Eliot, 152, 157, 159
*True Stories,* 89, 91, 96, 206, 213, 230
"Two-Headed Poems," 142, 143, 151–60; conclusion of, 159–60; disintegration in, 152–53, 154; Jaynesian stages of consciousness in, 154–55; structure of, 153; sun-spelling in, 156–57; two-headed monster in, 151–52; warnings in, 158–59
*Two-Headed Poems,* xxv, 42, 45, 46n, 177–79, 190–91; and Atwood's visual art, 206, 207, 210
"Two Miles Away," 190
Tzara, Tristan, 186

"Under Glass," 218
"Unearthing Suite," 42
United States: Atwood's views on, xx, 238–39, 240–41; cultural dominance of, 7, 229–30; as demon lover, 145–46, 160; disintegration of, 152, 154, 160; as dystopia, 113, 118; reading audience in, 228, 242; thinking in, 6; as victimizer, xxii, 1–2, 60, 146. *See also* Canada
Updike, John, xix
*Up in the Tree,* xxi
"Upper Canadian" (Reaney), 144

Valgardson, W. D., 10
"Variations on the Word 'Love,'" 213
*Villette* (Brontë), 220
*Violent Duality* (Grace), 46n
Virgil, 215

Visual art, 205–13, 217; annotations to watercolors, 208–12; and Atwood's literary art, 205–8, 213
von Franz, Marie, 203

*Wacousta Syndrome, The* (McGregor), 100 n
Wade, Knotly (*The Handmaid's Tale*), 115–16
Wagner, Linda W., 122
Walker, Alice, xx
Walpole, Horace, xxiii, 51
*Waste Land, The* (Eliot), 82
*Ways of Seeing* (Berger), 87
Weldon, Fay, 233
"The Wereman," 141 n
Werewolf. *See* Loup-garou
"What's So Funny? Notes on Canadian Humour," 8
"When you look at nothing," 124, 133–34
*Where Nests the Water Hen* (Roy), 3
*White Goddess, The,* xv, 8–9, 185
"White Heron, A" (Jewett), 179–80
Whitman, Walt, 234
*Wide Sargasso Sea* (Rhys), 54–55
Wilford, Rennie (*Bodily Harm*), xxiv, 85, 86, 90, 97, 197–98; as blank page, 95; and fertility, 102; incarceration of, 91–92; mastectomy of, 92–93; memories of, 86–87; naïvete of, 88; rebirth of, 97–98, 99; as victim of men, 60, 87; wandering thoughts of, 93–94; as writer, 89
William (*Life Before Man*), 70, 76, 77, 78
Wilson, F. O., 121 n
"Winnipeg" (Reaney), 148
Wiseman, Adele, 3
"Wish: Metamorphosis to Heraldic Emblem," 132
Wollander, Peter (*The Edible Woman*), 14–19
Wollstonecraft, Mary, xxiii, 54, 55–56, 60
"Women and Nature in Modern Fiction" (Pratt), 179–80
Wood, Gayle, 165
Woolf, Virginia, 67, 203
*Writing Beyond the Ending* (Du Plessis), 36
Writers' Union of Canada, xx, xxvii, 227–29

Yeats, W. B., 141 n
*Yellow Wallpaper, The* (Gilman), 54
*You Are Happy,* 122, 139, 169, 175–77, 192; shamanism in, 193–97, 199, 200

Zeus, 37, 38
Zwicky, Fay, 10